D1601289

3 0700 11178 9763

Staging Ireland

Ireland: Literature and History

Nicholas Allen & Eve Patten, series editors

STAGING IRELAND

Representations in Shakespeare and Renaissance Drama

Stephen O'Neill

FOUR COURTS PRESS

Set in 11.5 on 13.5 point Centaur for
FOUR COURTS PRESS
7 Malpas Street, Dublin 8, Ireland
e-mail: info@four-courts-press.ie
http://www.four-courts-press.ie
and in North America for
FOUR COURTS PRESS
c/o ISBS, 920 N.E. 58th Avenue, Suite 300, Portland, OR 97213.

A catalogue record for this title
is available from the British Library

ISBN (13-digit) 978–1–85182–989–7

Printed in England
by MPG Books, Bodmin, Cornwall.

Contents

Illustrations

Series editors' preface

The Four Courts Press series in *Irish Literature & History* publishes work by new and established Irish Studies scholars working in the modern period.

The series is peer reviewed and introduces some of the best current research and writing in the field. *Irish Literature & History* aims to contribute to evolving conversations between literature, culture and history, promoting clarity and rigour in intellectual engagement. The series begins with Stephen O'Neill's *Staging Ireland: representations in Shakespeare and Renaissance drama.*

NICHOLAS ALLEN & EVE PATTEN

Acknowledgments

I have incurred many debts in the completion of this book but particular thanks to Janet Clare, Padraig Kirwan, Carmel Nolan, Tadhg O'Dhuislaine, Margaret Robson and Moynagh Sullivan for their time and for their incisive comments on chapters. I also want to thank the series' editors at Four Courts Press for their critical insights and delineating clear directions at the early stages of the book. Also, John McGurk and Dave Edwards were kind enough to share aspects of their research. The book stems from my doctoral thesis, which was completed at University College Dublin in 2003 and I would like to renew my thanks to my supervisor Janet Clare and to my examiners John Gillies, Nicholas Grene and Anne Fogarty. The book was completed in the collegial environment of the Department of English, NUI Maynooth, where Brian Cosgrove, Margaret Kelleher, Joe Cleary, Colin Graham and Amanda Bent provided consistent encouragement and practical advice. Thanks also to the MA class of 2005–6 for taking my early modern seminar and for encouraging me to clarify and rethink arguments. Other debts of gratitude are less practical but no less important. Friends at home and abroad, including Wanda Balzano, Alan Kelly, Padraig Kirwan, Jeff Holdridge, Shuan Regan, Aoife Leahy, Gillian O'Brien, Justin Dolan, James Foster, David Bredin and Kerry Sinnan have implicitly shaped this book, as have former colleagues and teachers, in particular Anne Fogarty, Declan Kiberd, J.C.C. Mays, Ron Callan, Maria Stuart and Danielle Clarke. I would like to thank the National University of Ireland for the award of a Grant-in-aid of Publication and also the Dean of Research, NUI Maynooth for a grant towards publication. Past scholarships have been of both practical and academic benefit and I am pleased to acknowledge the support of the Government of Ireland IRCHSS doctoral scholarship and the UCD Open Postgraduate Award. My thanks also to the staff of the Special Collections library, UCD and the Early Printed Books Room, Trinity College Library. Finally, I would like to thank my family for their support throughout, especially my parents, Vera and Heuston; without their extraordinary generosity of spirit, this book simply could not have been completed.

Note on procedures

All references to Shakespeare, unless otherwise stated, are from *The Complete works*, ed. Stanley Wells and Gary Taylor (Oxford, 1988). References to the quarto editions of Shakespeare are from *Shakespeare's plays in quarto*, ed. Michael J. Allen and Kenneth Muir (Berkeley, 1981).

Dates given for plays are the performance date and, unless otherwise stated, follow Alfred Harbage and Samuel Schoenbaum, *Annals of English Drama 975–1700*, revd. Sylvia Stoler (3rd ed. London, 1989). When quoting from contemporary sources, I have retained original spelling and punctuation.

Abbreviations used in the notes:

DNB   *Oxford Dictionary of National Biography*, Oxford University Press (2004) www.oxforddnb.com

ELR   *English Literary Renaissance*

EMLS   *Early Modern Literary Studies www.shu.ac.uk/emls*

IHS   *Irish Historical Studies*

JEGP   *Journal of English and Germanic Philology*

MLN   *Modern Language Notes*

N&Q   *Notes and Queries*

OED   *Oxford English Dictionary*

PMLA   *Proceedings of the Modern Language Association*

SEL   *Studies in English Literature*

Introduction

Locating Ireland in Renaissance drama

MACKMORRICE   Of my nation? What ish my nation? Ish a
                villain, and a bastard, and a knave, and a rascal?
                What ish my nation? Who talks of my nation?
                                    Shakespeare, *Henry V*, III.ii.66–8

'Irishmen in England act as it were a part in a play, they are never themselves but in their own countrie', or so remarked Parr Lane, a captain serving in the Elizabethan army during the Nine Years War in Ireland. Lane, who was wounded in military action, also wrote of the 'malignity or mischief of that crazed country'.[1] Lane's words are only one example of numerous contemporaneous sources that demonstrate the ways in which Ireland entered Elizabethan consciousness, to constitute a significant text, subtext and context in the period. Here, the source that most concerns my argument is the drama of Shakespeare and his contemporaries in which can be found some of the most intriguing textual traces of the subject of early modern Ireland. For at precisely the moment when men like Lane were off fighting in Ireland, the stage Irishman – the cultural phenomenon that Lane's theatrical metaphor describes – became current on the Elizabethan stage. His comment is, then, entirely apposite to Shakespeare's only Irish character, Mackmorrice in *Henry V*, who broaches the subject of assigned identity when he asks of his nation. Refracted in Mackmorrice, as in Lane's observation, are the cultural issues of a specific historical moment, as efforts were underway to effect the conquest of Ireland. In both Lane and Mackmorrice, we encounter the Elizabethan image of the Irish as potential dissemblers, insidiously withholding their 'true' natures from English eyes, and of Ireland as England's Other. But there is also, perhaps unwittingly, recognition of the importance of place and a sense of belonging, as if to imply that 'the Irish' (as Lane characterizes them) have an identity to which they subscribe. In other words, we move beyond that all too familiar construction of Ireland as a reflective image against which concepts of Englishness were formed. More intriguing still, the theatrical metaphor, like

---

1 My thanks to John McGurk (emeritus professor of history, University of Liverpool) for kindly providing me with this reference. Similar views are conveyed in Lane's 'News from the Holy Ile' (1621) in Andrew Carpenter (ed.), *Verse in English from Tudor and Stuart Ireland* (Cork, 2003), pp 139–47.

Mackmorrice's loaded questions, suggests an implicit recognition of identity as performance, something friable and always in formation.

It is Mackmorrice and *Henry V* more generally, with its overt allusion to rebellion in Ireland in the fifth chorus, that most readily suggests the simultaneity of dramatic representation and Irish context. However, the privileging of these as isolated moments has obscured other plays from view. Indeed, there is a broad assumption that Ireland constituted something of a 'blind spot' or even absence in Renaissance drama, with critics referring to its absence as a 'significant silence' or 'one of the great and unexplained lacunae in the drama of the period'.² Andrew Hadfield partially redresses this narrow focus by looking for Ireland in Shakespeare's other plays but finds himself reduced to speculation; thus, *Othello*, among other plays by Shakespeare, is said to 'possess a (ghostly) Irish context'.³ Current understandings of how the drama was informed by and responded to the Irish wars have been refracted largely through the terms of Shakespearean drama and criticism. Critics have seemed reluctant to examine the representation of Ireland in plays outside an established canon.⁴ And it is by moving outside this frame, that this book demonstrates that Mackmorrice, like the stage Irishman more generally, is in fact just one example of the many interconnections between representations of Ireland in the drama and their synchronous Irish contexts. This book brings into particular focus late-Elizabethan plays such as *The Misfortunes of Arthur* (1588), *The Battle of Alcazar* (1589), *Captain Thomas Stukeley* (1596–7) and *Sir John Oldcastle* (1599), which engage with Ireland and yet have not been related to their Irish contexts, as well as more familiar plays like Marlowe's *Edward II* (1592) and Shakespeare's *2 Henry VI* (1590–1), *Richard II* (1595) and *Henry V* (1599). This list of Renaissance plays that contain an Irish character or allusion is by no means exhaustive. What these plays in particular suggest, however, is that the stage provided a fluid, though licensed, space where interest in Ireland and anxieties about Irish alterity could be negotiated and played out. Obviously, this raises the question of political censorship, specifically the question of how topical, and hence censorable, issues like Ireland

---

2 Peter Thomson, *Shakespeare's theatre* (London, 1983), p. 66; this claim was omitted from the second edition of Thomson's book. See Andrew Murphy, 'Shakespeare's Irish history', *Literature and History*, 5 (1996), 38–59 at 38; Michael Neill, 'Broken English and broken Irish: nation, language and the optic of power in Shakespeare's histories', *Shakespeare Quarterly*, 45 (1994), 1–32 at 11.   3 Andrew Hadfield, '"Hitherto she ne're could fancy him": Shakespeare's "British" plays and the exclusion of Ireland' in Mark Burnett and Ramona Wray (eds), *Shakespeare and Ireland* (London, 1997), pp 47–63.   4 Dramatic representations of Ireland have recently been integrated into the extended canon of English writing on Ireland in the early modern period. See Anne Fogarty, 'Literature in English, 1550–1690: from the Elizabethan settlement to the battle of the Boyne' in Margaret Kelleher and Philip O'Leary (eds), *Cambridge history of Irish literature*, 2 vols (Cambridge, 2006), i, pp 140–90. Another exception to the Shakespearean bias is Kathleen Rabl, 'Taming the "wild Irish" in English Renaissance drama' in Wolfgang Zach and Heinz Kosok (eds), *National images and stereotypes* (Tubingen, 1987), pp 47–59.

could be openly addressed or projected in a play.[5] Ireland was certainly a sensitive subject in the period, some would argue too sensitive to be discussed directly.[6] One possibility is that dramatists treated Irish affairs obliquely, deploying strategies of displacement and analogy so as to avoid the attention of the censor.[7] But this improbably presumes a uniformity of approach, as if to suggest that playwrights and the authorities were in agreement over how the situation in Ireland should be represented.[8] On the contrary, there is substantial textual evidence to indicate that the subject of Ireland was refracted in the drama both in dynamic and frequently overt ways.

Underpinning this argument is a broader concept of the ideology of the early modern theatre. Inflected by cultural materialism, it holds that while firmly rooted in the material realities and political constraints of its historical moment, the theatre was an enabling cultural site, where contemporary ideologies were confronted and, crucially, questioned.[9] By viewing the early modern theatre as a social organism where meaning is produced, representations of Ireland and the Irish in the drama can be attended to as a series of topical allusions that have multifarious ideological functions. Moreover, this approach importantly reorients the critical focus from playwrights to plays so that dramatic representations are regarded as part of a wider discourse about Ireland and less a matter of authorial engagement.[10] In other words, critical interest lies less in the biographical particularities and peculiarities of individual authors, as they are considered as part of wider social cultural production. Thus, the concerns of my book, reflected in the title, are not only with the figurative representation of Ireland and the Irish in Renaissance drama but are also about how the stage was itself a locus in early modern English culture where the range of issues that Ireland gave rise to were addressed.

To explore the potential resonances and implications of Ireland and the

---

5 Janet Clare, 'Art made tongue-tied by authority': Elizabethan and Jacobean dramatic censorship (2nd ed. Manchester, 1999), pp 60–3; pp 92–5. For an alternate view of the dramatic censor as a more benign agent of control, see Richard Dutton, *Mastering the revels: the regulation and censorship of English Renaissance drama* (Basingstoke, 1991). However, Dutton makes no mention of Ireland as a topical issue that was negotiated in the drama.   6 See Andrew Hadfield, 'Censoring Ireland in Elizabethan England, 1580–1600' in Andrew Hadfield (ed.), *Literature and censorship in Renaissance England* (London, 2001), pp 149–64; and 'Was Spenser's *View of the present state of Ireland* censored? A review of the evidence', *Notes and Queries* 41 (1994), 459–63.   7 Christopher Highley, *Shakespeare, Spenser and the crisis in Ireland* (Cambridge, 1997), pp 5–6. Highley draws on Annabel Patterson's contractual model of censorship, where authors and authorities implicitly decreed which issues required indirect forms of communication or a 'functional ambiguity'; see Annabel M. Patterson, *Censorship and interpretation: the conditions of writing and reading in early modern England* (Madison, WI, 1984), pp 17–18.   8 See Janet Clare, 'Censorship and negotiation' in Hadfield (ed.), *Literature and censorship*, p. 23.   9 Influential works here are Jean E. Howard, *The stage and social struggle in early modern England* (London, 1994); and Jonathan Dollimore, *Radical tragedy: religion, ideology and power in the drama of Shakespeare and his contemporaries* (Brighton, 1984).   10 The assumption of authorial engagement with Ireland runs through James Shapiro's *1599: a year in the life of Shakespeare* (London, 2005); and is also claimed more subtly in Highley, *Shakespeare, Spenser* (pp 8–9, 66; 87).

Irish in the drama is to move between the corpus of Renaissance drama and the terrain of early modern Ireland itself. This book privileges the late Elizabethan period and the Nine Years War as a key point in a long history of English settlement, colonization and conquest in Ireland. As a primary context for the drama, the Nine Years War is virtually self-selecting. Modern accounts have described the war as a crisis point of an Elizabethan fin de siècle and with some justification.[11] For whereas in the earlier part of the reign, English settlement and governance in Ireland had been met by local, intermittent rebellions, by the late 1590s frustration with the altered balance of power manifested itself in a broadly national confederacy of Gaelic chieftains led by Hugh O'Neill, earl of Tyrone. The literature of this period 'bears the strain of a period of conflict that threatened to topple English rule in Ireland'.[12] Of those involved in the Irish wars, the figure of O'Neill constitutes a recurrent point of reference in the ensuing analyses. This is not just because he was a crucial agent in the changing power relations between the Elizabethan state and its Irish subjects but also because he appears to represent the complexities and contradictions associated with the English image of the Irish. The political realities of O'Neill's career belie depictions of him as the 'arch-Rebell' or, in Thomas Gainsford's post-conquest assessment, one who disguised his seemingly sinister nature beneath a 'foxes skin'.[13] O'Neill's relations with the crown oscillated between mutual co-operation and direct conflict, making his intentions and objectives difficult to gauge.[14] O'Neill was 'the Janus-face of Ireland' who simultaneously imagined himself as earl of Tyrone and Gaelic chieftain.[15] His ambivalence cuts across both preconceived concepts of Irish and English identity in the period.[16]

My focus on the 1590s produces a micro-history of the period, while also paying attention to its broader contours. The crisis decade, though significant and one that conferred on Ireland a heightened visibility, must be seen in the

11 John McGurk, *The Elizabethan conquest of Ireland: the 1590s crisis* (Manchester, 1997); Highley, *Shakespeare, Spenser*, pp 1–2; John Guy, 'Introduction: the second reign of Elizabeth I?' in John Guy (ed.), *The reign of Elizabeth: court and culture in the last decade* (Cambridge, 1995), pp 1–19.   12 Fogarty, 'Literature in English, 1550–1690' in Kelleher and O'Leary (eds), *Cambridge history of Irish literature*, p. 155.   13 The term was a recurrent synonym for O'Neill: see, for example, Edmund Spenser, *A view of the state of Ireland*, ed. Andrew Hadfield and Willy Maley (London, 1997), p. 108; *Calendar of state papers, Ireland, 1599–1600*, ed. Ernest George Atkinson (London, 1899), p. 152. Thomas Gainsford, *The true, exemplary, and remarkable history of the earle of Tirone* (London, 1619), p. 34.   14 For an incisive assessment of O'Neill, see Hiram Morgan, *Tyrone's rebellion: the outbreak of the Nine Years war in Tudor Ireland* (Woodbridge, 1993). See also Nicholas Canny, 'Taking sides in early modern Ireland: the case of Hugh O'Neill, earl of Tyrone' in Vincent Carey and Ute Lotz-Heumann (eds), *Taking sides? Colonial and confessional mentalities in early modern Ireland* (Dublin, 2003), pp 94–115.   15 Roy Foster, *Modern Ireland, 1600–1972* (London, 1989), p. 4.   16 See Andrew Murphy, *But the Irish sea betwixt us: Ireland, colonialism and Renaissance literature* (Lexington, KY, 1999), pp 100–8. On O'Neill as a crucial site for postcolonial interpretations of narratives of Irish history, see Anne Fogarty, 'The romance of history: renegotiating the past in Thomas Kilroy's *The O'Neill* and Brian Friel's *Making History*', *IUR*, 32 (2002), 18–32.

context of a longer history of relations between Ireland and Britain. Indeed, this history dated back to the Anglo-Norman conquest in the late twelfth century; its legacy was keenly felt in the Elizabethan period in the form of the descendants of the original settlers, the old English. Suggesting their supposed degenerative status, the epithet was used by the new English – those settlers in Ireland from the mid-sixteenth century – to differentiate themselves from the original settlers, whose cross-cultural contact with the Gaelic Irish was viewed with extreme suspicion and unease. The political, social and cultural tensions that characterize Ireland in the period, tensions refracted in the literature and drama, were a consequence of the interrelations between these three communities. The problem or crisis in the Elizabethan 'the land of Ire' was also bound up with Ireland's dual constitutional position as a kingdom (from 1541) and also a colony.[17] This meant that, in legal terms, the native Irish population, the 'mere Irish' in official eyes, possessed the status and rights of subjects of the crown.[18] However, as the anathema to the English politically and religiously, they were 'constructed as enemies in their native land'.[19] Arguably, Ireland's anomalous status was reflected in the governance of the country and also in debates about the form that governance took. For the most part, official policy was characterized by the gradual introduction and implementation of English administrative and judicial structures, although there are numerous examples from the period to indicate that this pattern of reform was punctuated by the use of force.[20] Policy towards Ireland 'was characterized by a judicious blend of conciliation and coercion' but in practice such a combination indicated a fundamental lack of a coherent, consistent policy rather than a premeditated, dual-strategy for governance.[21]

There has been considerable debate about the reasons behind the ambivalence at the root of official policy and its implications. Of crucial importance is to what extent such ambivalence related to attitudes towards the native Irish in the period. Historians have disagreed over the ideology of English attitudes to the native population and at what point, if at all, a shift occurred. It has been argued that with the arrival of new English settlers in Ireland from the 1560s, there emerged a colonialist mentality towards the Gaelic Irish.[22] At issue

---

17 Quoted in D.B. Quinn, *The Elizabethans and the Irish* (Ithaca, 1966), p. 135. 18 Karl Bottigheimer, 'Kingdom and colony: Ireland in the westward enterprise, 1536–1660' in K.R Andrews, N.P. Canny and K.E.H. Hair (eds), *The westward enterprise: English activities in Ireland, the Atlantic and America, 1480–1650* (Liverpool, 1978), pp 45–64; Ciaran Brady and Raymond Gillespie (eds), *Natives and newcomers: essays on the making of Irish colonial society, 1534–1641* (Dublin, 1986), pp 11–21. 19 Clare Carroll, *Circe's cup: cultural transformations in early modern Ireland*, Field Day Essays (Cork, 2001), p. 25. 20 On the prevalence of the use of force in Ireland by the state, see David Edwards, 'Beyond reform: martial law and the Tudor reconquest of Ireland', *History Ireland*, 5 (1997), 16–21. 21 Ciaran Brady, *The chief governors: the rise and fall of reform government in Tudor Ireland, 1536–1588* (Cambridge, 1994), p. 246. 22 Nicholas Canny, *The Elizabethan conquest of Ireland: a pattern established, 1565–76* (Hassocks, Sussex, 1976), p. 131.

here are important questions about understandings of the interrelations between the different groupings in Ireland and their wider contexts. In determining these questions, the recent debate about early modern Ireland seems to demand that we adopt one of two possible interpretative frameworks. Privileging alternate contexts and ideologies, these have significantly informed understandings of cross-cultural relations in the period. Broadly speaking, the first regards Ireland as a colony and situates English settlement there within a wider context of emergent English colonialism in the new world. In this Atlantic perspective, English attitudes to and perceptions of the Gaelic Irish from the mid-Tudor period are understood as signalling a new ethnography and are interpreted as analogous to and informed by perceptions of the indigenous peoples of the new world.[23] Conversely, the second position foregrounds Ireland's geographic proximity to and prior history of contact with Britain; settlement and colonization is seen in terms of internal expansion within the British Isles and attitudes to the Gaelic Irish are understood as operating along lines of cultural rather than racial difference.[24] The Atlantic and British approach have for too long been regarded as mutually exclusive, their oppositional positions producing totalizing accounts of early modern Ireland and its representations. If we are to attend to the realities and nuances of historical and cultural interrelations in early modern Ireland, what is required is not just a greater awareness of how Ireland accommodates a number of contexts — colonial, archipelagic, European — but also an adjustment of our methodologies to accommodate its particularity.[25]

It is with this is mind, that I frame Elizabethan attitudes to and images of the Irish. As with cultural encounters more generally, these attitudes and their textual and visual figurations, were conditioned by a set of unconscious or 'implicit understandings' about indigenous society and culture and also by direct experience of that culture.[26] In the case of Ireland, these could be traced

23 David B. Quinn, 'Ireland and sixteenth-century European expansion' in T.D. Williams (ed.), *Historical Studies* (London, 1958), pp 20–32; Nicholas Canny, 'The ideology of English colonization: from Ireland to America', *William and Mary Quarterly*, 30 (1973), 575–98; Paul Brown, '"This thing of darkness I acknowledge mine": *The Tempest* and the discourse of colonialism' in Jonathan Dollimore and Alan Sinfield (eds), *Political Shakespeare: essays in cultural materialism* (2nd ed. Manchester, 1994), pp 48–71. 24 See Steven G. Ellis, 'Writing Irish history: revisionism, colonialism and the British Isles', *Irish Review* 19 (1996), 1–21. The seminal essay on a British approach to the history and culture of the period is J.G.A. Pocock, 'A British history: a plea for a new subject', *Journal of Modern History*, 47 (1975), 601–28; see also David Cannadine, 'British history as a "new subject": politics, perspectives and prospects' in Alexander Grant and Keith Stringer (eds), *Uniting the kingdom: the making of British history* (London, 1995), pp 12–28. For a slightly sceptical, and occasionally critical, overview of the British approach to literature, see Jane Ohlmeyer, 'Literature and the new British and Irish histories' in David Baker and Willy Maley (eds), *British identities and English Renaissance literature* (Cambridge, 2002), pp 245–55. 25 See Andrew Murphy, 'Revising criticism: Ireland and the British model' in Baker and Maley (eds), *British identities and English Renaissance literature*, pp 24–33. 26 On the concept of implicit ethnography, see Stuart B. Schwartz (ed.), *Implicit understandings: observing, reporting, and reflecting on the encounters between Europeans and other peoples in the early modern era* (Cambridge, 1994), pp 1–19.

back to the Anglo-Norman conquest and, specifically, to Gerald of Wales, whose writings on the strange customs and practices of the native Irish provided a blueprint for Elizabethan images.[27] But, as Steve Garner has noted, the Elizabethan period constitutes 'a crucial phase' in the 'racialization of populations in Ireland', as concepts of Irish barbarity were extended to the land itself, producing a conjunction between uncivilized people and uncivilized space.[28] New English texts such as Derricke's *Image of Irelande* (1581) and Spenser's *View of the State of Ireland* (1596), though informed by an earlier medieval tradition, also mark a significant departure from it.[29] As reflected in these texts, this emergent discourse of Irish barbarism positions the native Irish and also the old English as 'absolute' rather than 'proximate' Others, whose innate natures could only be reformed by force.[30] The distinction is an important one. As Hooker writes of the Irish in his contribution to Holinshed's *Chronicles*: 'such is their stubbornesse and pride, that with a continuall feare it must be bridled; and such is the hardnesse of their hearts, that with the rod it must be still chastised and subdued'.[31] In light of similar, if less sustained, textual traces of such logic, these compositions would appear to be representative of more pervasive concepts of Irish alterity in the period. Yet, the nature of implicit ethnography implies that these concepts overlaid rather than entirely displaced pre-existing views of the indigenous inhabitants; thus, the Irish could be both absolute and also proximate Others, just as policies of coercion operated alongside those of conciliation.

Of concern throughout this book is what bearing emergent ideologies had on figurations of the Irish in the drama. This raises a wider question, explored by Ania Loomba, about connections between representations of alterity and their particular historical circumstance. Loomba notes how 'representations of various "Others" in Renaissance theatre, travelogues and other writings are derived from specific histories of contact, but these texts also blur these histories and posit stereotypes that amalgamate suppositions about diverse peoples'. The consequence of this blurring of the representational spectrum is that 'the

---

27 The texts in question are the *Topographia Hiberniae* (1187) and the *Expugnatio Hibernica* (1189). The *Expugnatio Hibernica* or *Conquest of Ireland* was translated by Hooker and included in the Irish section of the second edition of Holinshed's *Chronicles*. On the correspondence between Gerald's attitudes towards the native Irish and those in the Elizabethan period, see Andrew Hadfield, *Edmund Spenser's Irish experience: wilde fruit and savage soyl* (Oxford, 1997), p. 93; and John Gillingham, 'The English invasion of Ireland' in Brendan Bradshaw, Andrew Hadfield and Willy Maley (eds), *Representing Ireland: literature and the origins of conflict, 1534–1660* (Cambridge, 1993), pp 24–42. 28 Steve Garner, *Racism and the Irish experience* (London, 2004), pp 69–90 (p. 73). 29 Carroll, *Circe's cup*, pp 11–27. 30 On the 'absolute Otherness' of the Irish, see Ann Rosalind Jones and Peter Stallybrass, 'Dismantling Irena: the sexualizing of Ireland in early modern England' in Andrew Parker et al., *Nationalism and sexualities* (London, 1992), p. 158. For a convincing case for the proximate or imperfect alterity of the Irish in English writings, see Andrew Murphy, *But the Irish sea*, pp 1–32. 31 Hooker, 'Supplie of the Irish Chronicles extended to this present year of Our Lord 1586' in *Holinshed's chronicles of England, Scotland, and Ireland*, ed. Henry Ellis, 6 vols (London, 1807–8), vi, p. 369.

Irish, Jews, "Moors", the Welsh, Turks, "Savages", Africans, "Indians" (from India as well as from the Americas) are shown as distinct from one another, and yet as sharing characteristic differences from the English'.[32] This brings to mind the moment in Webster's *White Devil* (1612), where Francisco tells Zanche the moor that he has dreamt of covering her naked body with an 'Irish mantle'.[33] In this erotic fantasy, blackness is temporarily displaced by the fetishized Irish cloak, an equally potent signifier of alterity and, to the English imagination, a symbol of Gaelic male wildness and female promiscuity. Loomba's observation suggests the need for close attention to historical difference within cultural difference but also a critical responsibility to analyse representations with a view to the 'specific histories' that underpin them. Accordingly, plays are conjoined here with a range of contemporary materials on Ireland, from state papers, poems and travelogues to texts such as the *Image of Irelande* and Spenser's *A View*. It is only through the contextualization of the dramatic text that we can arrive at a sense of the contemporary resonances of its representations of Ireland and the Irish and explore the various ideological forces shaping those representations. However, it is also important to attend to the potential force of such representations and, drawing on Walter Mignolo's argument that representations are in fact enactments, consider how they are not merely reflective of ideologies of the Irish in the period but also engage with them.[34] From the earliest extant representation of the stage Irishman in the *Misfortunes of Arthur* to the Irish servant Mack Chane in *Sir John Oldcastle*, it is evident that the drama was informed by 'implicit understandings' and contributed to their perpetuation. This can be understood in terms of Homi Bhabha's description of colonial stereotyping as a series of already loaded signifiers 'that must be anxiously repeated'. The stereotype, he notes, 'requires, for its successful signification, a continual and repetitive chain of other stereotypes'.[35] Arguably, what emerges here is 'nothing but the same old story' of the wild Irishman.[36] Yet in the drama, as in the period more generally, the resonance of a stereotype was subject to change, being determined not just by its prior meaning but also by the context in which it was produced and received. For instance, the description of Irish rebels in *Captain Thomas Stukeley* as 'naked savages' relies on a well-established tradition of the wild man, the early modern image of the indigenous peoples of the new world and also an Elizabethan discourse of Irish barbarism.[37] A similar ethnographic layering is evident in *Oldcastle*, where

32 Ania Loomba and Martin Orkin, 'Introduction: Shakespeare and the post-colonial question' in Ania Loomba and Martin Orkin (eds), *Post-colonial Shakespeares* (London, 1998), p. 13.   33 John Webster, *The White Devil*, ed. Christina Luckyj (London, 1996), V.iii.234.   34 Walter D. Mignolo, *The darker side of the Renaissance: literacy, territoriality and colonization* (Ann Arbor, 1995), pp 332–4.   35 Homi K. Bhabha, *The location of culture* (London, 1994), p. 66; p. 77.   36 Liz Curtis, *Nothing but the same old story: the roots of anti-Irish racism* (Belfast, 1996); the phrase is from Paul Brady's song 'Hard station'.   37 *The famous history of Captain Thomas Stukeley*, ed. Judith C. Levinson

the trope of cannibalism is applied to the Irish character. Such images are informed by an implicit or older ethnography but they are charged with a distinctly contemporary ideology of Irish alterity. Representations of Irishness in the drama are thus implicated in and conditioned by the early modern discourse about Ireland.

However, while complicit in the construction of Irish alterity, representations in Renaissance drama and theatre could potentially delimit an audience's sense of presumed difference. The language of the stage could dissolve the alien identities that it enabled. In *Oldcastle*, for instance, the Irish character is at once the threatening Other who occupies the hinterland of the play and also, along with an English servant, the other half of a comic scene of ethnic cross-dressing in which seemingly fixed categories of racial and cultural difference are destabilised. On the stage, then, assigned identity, far from inhering in the individual, is shown to be a malleable cultural construct. This has broader implications for the stage as a site of identity formation, namely that representations of alterity do not automatically occupy a fixed position in a hierarchical dyad of self and Other through which Englishness is fashioned.[38] With reference to representations of Irish alterity in the theatre, it suggests the need to modify understandings of the stage Irishman as less an inventory of static colonialist stereotypes than a complex, self-reflexive layering of signifiers of Irish difference.

If the mimesis of Irish alterity opens it up as a construct, a role embodied by an actor, then the theatre discloses the fact that there are no 'authentic "Others" – raced or gendered – of any kind, only their representations'.[39] There is an obvious dichotomy between representations of Irish difference and real social identities, such as the Gaelic Irish or old English, in the period.[40] Invariably, viewing representations of the Irish through the prism of Renaissance drama and also through English language texts runs the risk of replicating the elision that occurs in contemporary texts, where the Irish language and native reactions are silenced.[41] However, while attention to Irish language texts furnishes different insights into the period, a monolingual focus need not reproduce the ideology of the discourse it assays.[42] Throughout the

(Oxford, 1975), line 1179.   **38** For the argument that Englishness was defined precisely in terms of its instability in the face of Irishness, see Mary Floyd-Wilson, *English ethnicity and race in early modern drama* (Cambridge, 2003), pp 56–60.   **39** Dympna Callaghan, '"Othello was a white man": properties of race on Shakespeare's stage' in Terence Hawkes (ed.), *Alternative Shakespeares*, vol. 2 (London, 1996), p. 193.   **40** I draw here on Dympna Callaghan's discussion of alterity in *Shakespeare without women: representing gender and race on the Renaissance stage* (London, 2000), pp 9–11.   **41** See Patricia Palmer, *Language and conquest in early modern Ireland: English Renaissance literature and Elizabethan imperial expansion* (Cambridge, 2001), pp 40–73; pp 173–211. On the elision of pre-conquest and native history from Holinshed, see Richard A. McCabe, 'Making history: Holinshed's Irish *Chronicles*, 1577 and 1587' in Baker and Maley (eds), *British identities and English Renaissance literature*, pp 51–67.   **42** Clare Carroll has called for a comparative approach to early modern texts on Ireland and gives an impressive demonstration of such an book, I have sought to convey a sense of the enigmatic social identities that lurk beyond their representations and also retain an awareness of the 'imbalance of speech' by examining the use of Gaelic in *Stukeley* and its residual traces in other plays.[43]

In interpreting Ireland in Renaissance drama, this book adopts a historicist analysis, with particular focus on topical meanings as they unfold in a play, where my emphasis is on the dynamic interplay between the dramatic text and its contemporary moment. Thus, the Irish war and the discourse about Ireland are interpreted as a fluid, ideologically indeterminate context to the plays and history more generally as a set of 'unforeclosed processes'.[44] As Leah Marcus has argued, a topical reading involves the localization of the text. As an interpretative paradigm, localization can take the form of 'thick description', to employ Clifford Geertz's phrase, although it differs from new historicism in its use of Geertz's technique.[45] Where new historicism tended to take one aspect of early modern culture as emblematic of the culture more generally, localization is attentive to the unstable dialectic between the immediately topical and its wider cultural and historical resonances.[46] Through an excavation of historical details, it is possible to move between a play's contemporary meanings, insofar as that can be accessed, towards its general cultural contexts, without losing sight of the specific historical point of reference within the text from which those larger cultural issues are addressed.

As deployed here, this localization or contextual reading is about a conscious prioritising of the point in the dramatic text that contains an Irish character or allusion to Ireland. These points in the text are interpreted as contextual mnemonics, which reveal in conscious form the unconscious shaping influence of its contemporary moment. What emerges is an insight into how the text bears the impact or burden of its context, both in terms of the immediacy and urgency of the wars in Ireland but also general anxieties about Irish alterity in the period. By reading plays through a mnemonics of context – from 'the swarms of Irish kerns [...] uncontroll'd within the English pale' in Marlowe's *Edward II* to Mackmorrice in *Henry V* – it is possible to

approach in *Circe's cup*, pp 61–8; 91–123. On the response of Gaelic writers to colonization, see Marc Caball, 'Faith, culture and sovereignty: Irish nationality and its development, 1558–1625' in Brendan Bradshaw and Peter Roberts (eds), *British consciousness and identity: the making of Britain, 1533–1707* (Cambridge, 1998), pp 112–39. On the varieties of drama in Gaelic Irish culture in the period, see Alan J. Fletcher, *Drama, performance and polity in pre-Cromwellian Ireland* (Toronto, 2000) pp 9–60.   43 Ania Loomba, 'Shakespeare and cultural difference' in Hawkes (ed.), *Alternative Shakespeare*, ii, p. 173.   44 I am indebted to Anne Fogarty for this phrase and indeed for engaging conversations about early modern Ireland.   45 Clifford Geertz, *The interpretation of cultures* (New York, 1973), pp 3–30; Leah Marcus, *Puzzling Shakespeare: local reading and its discontents* (Berkeley, 1988), pp 32–40.   46 For a cogent discussion of historicist criticism 'post' new historicism and cultural materialism, see David Scott Kastan, *Shakespeare after theory* (New York, 1999), pp 23–55.

interpret images of Ireland or the stage Irishman as heterogeneous but related figurations that are historically contingent and culturally determined.[47] This is not to suggest that representations have an ideological cohesiveness; rather, it is about analyzing the specificity of an individual play's representation in relation to its broader contexts. Moreover, contextual traces are understood as carrying and eliciting meanings beyond those suggested by the contemporary materials brought to bear on them here. For it is important to be aware of potential discrepancies between the meanings of a play to contemporaries and our attempts to recover that meaning. As Catherine Belsey puts it, 'we *make* a relation [...] out of *our* reading practices and *their* documents'.[48] Thus, the concept of contextual mnemonics is intended to register recovery as an active process located in and conditioned by the present.

A contextual analysis can neither claim absolute authenticity for the results of its probing into a text's contemporary resonances nor political innocence. Instead, it 'should be a process of continual negotiation between our own place, to the extent that we are able to identify it, and the local places of the texts we read'.[49] Thus, my focus on the Irish dimension to and context of Renaissance drama may partially stem from a sense of historical and cultural place, from reading the literature and drama of the period from and in Ireland. This is not to say there is an 'Irish reading' of the material; such a position would presuppose the existence of homogeneous categories, perpetuate a politics of marginality and, ultimately, produce as exclusionary a viewpoint as earlier Anglocentric readings of the drama. But it is to acknowledge an emphasis that, it is hoped, affords a different slant on representations of Ireland and Irish alterity in the drama.

The following chapters approach plays in broadly chronological order and within an unfolding narrative of the Irish wars to reveal the evolving nature of dramatic figurations of Ireland. Chapter one explores Ireland as the source of political, cultural and religious anxieties in two overlooked plays from the late 1580s: *The Misfortunes of Arthur* by Thomas Hughes and others, and *The Battle of Alcazar* by George Peele. Locating these topically charged plays within contemporaneous debates about reforming the Irish, with particular reference to Derricke's *Image of Irelande*, this chapter argues that, much earlier than has been previously allowed, the public stage provided an important space upon which the subject of Ireland could be addressed.

Chapter two is similarly concerned with the correlation between the Irish crisis and the representation of Ireland, although the perspective here is slightly different. My interest in this chapter is on figurations of Irish space in

47 Christopher Marlowe, *Edward II*, ed. Charles Forker (Manchester, 1994), II.ii.164–5. **48** Catherine Belsey, *Shakespeare and the loss of Eden* (London, 2001), p. 12. **49** Marcus, *Puzzling Shakespeare*, p. 36.

Shakespeare's *2 Henry VI, Richard II* and Marlowe's *Edward II.* The chapter situates the plays' representation of Ireland as a dramatic and figurative space in relation to contemporary assumptions about native and topographical intractability as evidenced in a range of materials, including Spenser's *View.* Through an analysis of *2 Henry VI* and *Edward II*, I examine how figurations of Ireland as offstage and geographically distant intimate that it is dangerously beyond political control. The ideological function of representations of Irish space is also addressed in *Richard II*, where Ireland is of both dramatic and also topical significance. The preoccupation with unregulated, distant and threatening Irish space in these plays reveals profound disquiet not only about the security of English power over the natives but also the security of English identity itself.

The focus of chapter three is *Captain Thomas Stukeley*, the most extensive and direct treatment of Ireland on the Elizabethan stage. In the play, a character cautions: 'go not to Ireland: The countries rude | and full of tumult and rebellious strife, | Rather make choice of Italy or France' (lines 538–40). An Elizabethan audience may have shared this impression of Ireland and appreciated the travel advice but it goes unheeded in the play. Whereas in the earlier plays, Ireland is figured offstage, in *Stukeley* it is a significant location of the dramatic action. The play's dramatization of recent history – the siege of Dundalk by Shane O'Neill in 1562 – is evocative of contemporary anxieties about Hugh O'Neill, earl of Tyrone, and the situation in Ireland. More intriguing still, the Irish characters utter Gaelic words and phrases along with their broken English; this play enables its audience to hear, if only fleetingly, the Gaelic language that elsewhere in the drama was translated or erased. The recognition and incorporation of the 'rebell tonge' in *Stukeley* is considered alongside perceptions of the language in the period and in contrast to its silent translation into a laughable phonetic English in plays like Dekker's *Honest Whore, part 2* (1605). I explore to what extent the play's efforts to effect spatial control over Ireland and linguistic control over the Irish discharge anxieties about Irish recalcitrance.

Chapter four centres on a key historical and cultural moment of the Elizabethan period, 1599, when the outcome of the Irish wars hung in the balance. Shakespeare's *Henry V* and the collaborative venture *Sir John Oldcastle* bear significant traces of this moment, not least in their incorporation of Irish characters. The chapter explores the interaction between these plays and the context of the wars. In relation to *Henry V*, the indeterminate Irish crisis gave rise to textual indeterminacy and ideological equivocation: the play does not march in step with Elizabeth's army in Ireland. *Oldcastle* is also marked by its immediate context but engages with that context in a different way. The relationship of Irish servant to English master serves to focus tensions within Anglo-Irish relations and figuratively expresses relations between the queen and her Irish subjects, in particular perceptions of Hugh O'Neill as supplicant turned rebel. What is especially intriguing about the two 1599 plays is those scenes that address the larger cultural issues underpinning the crisis in Ireland: as with Mackmorrice in *Henry V*, the scene of mistaken identities in *Oldcastle* broaches the interrelated issues of degeneration, language, hybridity and national identity. Contextualizing these scenes, which address the recognition and classification of cultural Others, I consider how both plays reveal the limits of national identity. It is argued that these plays ultimately fail to re-shape the anxieties about the Irish wars by which they are largely shaped.

The drama of Shakespeare and his contemporaries, though geographically located in London, was figuratively engaged in Ireland and inflected by the ambiguities and multifaceted realities of English colonization there. The plays considered in this book attest to Ireland as a malleable presence, which did not have a singular or overriding ideological function: plays did not necessarily effect the containment of the Irish problem nor did representations of Irish difference bolster English identity. Exploring the dynamic Irish contexts and resonances of Renaissance drama, this book reveals the cultural power of the early modern theatre and signals new directions for the debate about Ireland in the period.

CHAPTER ONE

Topical plots

Drama and the reform of Ireland in the 1580s

In 1588 at the Great Hall, Greenwich Palace, Elizabeth and her court were entertained by *The Misfortunes of Arthur*, a play composed and produced by a group of students (among them one Francis Bacon) from the Inns of Court.[1] The play, which presents the story of King Arthur in the form of a Senecan tragedy and topical allegory, contains the earliest extant instance of what would later become a commonplace in English drama, the stage Irishman.[2] In the play's second dumb show, the royal spectator is confronted with an 'Irishman' with 'long black shagged hair down to his shoulders, apparelled with an Irish jacket and shirt, having an Irish dagger by his side, and a dart in his hand'.[3] Just two years later, this time in the public theatre, another Irish character appeared: in George Peele's *Battle of Alcazar* (1589), an Irish bishop is heard defending his faith and nation before being rendered risible. What is the significance of these representations of the Irish on the Elizabethan stage in the 1580s, some ten years before Captain Mackmorrice in *Henry V* and the wars in Ireland that shaped Shakespeare's play? What are the ideological implications of bringing Ireland and Irishness onto the stage? There are notable generic and thematic differences between *The Misfortunes of Arthur* and *The Battle of Alcazar*. As a play about an event from recent history (the battle occurred in 1578) involving the English adventurer Tom Stukeley, *The Battle of Alcazar* is clearly different to *The Misfortunes of Arthur* where the remote past facilitates an opaque form of topical allegory. But it is possible to interpret the plays' Irish characters and references as an instance of intertextuality in the Elizabethan theatre, whereby playwrights engaged in both conscious and unconscious borrowing and allusion. More intriguingly, when read historically, the figuration of Ireland and the Irish in these plays can be seen as a form of contextual mnemonics, revealing the shaping influence of a common discursive Irish context.

1 The other contributors were Thomas Hughes, Christopher Yelverton, and John Lancaster. See *The Misfortunes of Arthur: a critical old-spelling edition*, ed. Brian Jay Corrigan (New York, 1992), pp 3–4.   2 On the earliest, though unfortunately now lost, examples of the stage Irishman, see J.O. Bartley, *Teague, Shenkin and Sawney: being an historical study of the earliest Irish, Welsh, and Scottish characters in English plays* (Cork, 1954), pp 9–10; and Charles William Wallace, *The evolution of the English drama up to Shakespeare* (Berlin, 1912), pp 73–4. There is a record of a performance of a play called *Cutwell, or The Irish knight* by the earl of Warwick's men in 1577. See E.K. Chambers, *The Elizabethan stage*, 4 vols (Oxford, 1923), iv, p. 152.   3 *The Misfortunes of Arthur*, in *A select collection of old English plays*, ed. Robert Dodsley, 12 vols (4th ed. London, 1874), iv, p. 279. All quotations are from this edition.

Ireland in the 1580s was not the problem that it would become during the 1590s, when rebellion and later war gave it a prominence and even notoriety in official circles and arguably Elizabethan culture more generally. Other matters of state, such as the Mary Stuart crisis and the threat from Spain, were of far greater concern in the 1580s. Open hostilities with Spain from 1585 onwards meant that the privy council did not have time to concern itself with Irish matters.[4] Ireland did seem relatively peaceful: William Cecil, the lord treasurer, received reports of 'the universal quiet state of this Her Highness' Realm.'[5] This impression of a static state of affairs should not, however, obscure the underlying anxieties that persisted concerning both the reform of the native Irish and the possibility of foreign intervention in Ireland. Precedence fuelled anxieties about the latter. In 1579, the rebellion of James Fitzmaurice Fitzgerald, who had become the 'focus for all disaffected elements in Munster', took on a broader dimension.[6] Influenced by the ideology of the counter-reformation, Fitzmaurice had approached Philip of Spain and Pope Gregory XIII for assistance; he had even suggested that Philip's nephew become king of Ireland, promising the loyalty of the Irish in return.[7] While help from Spain was not forthcoming, the pope did grant Fitzmaurice a small force under the command of Tom Stukeley. He proved a poor choice and a significant number of the papal force ended up fighting with Sebastian of Portugal in the battle of Alcazar. The entire episode is dramatized in *The Battle of Alcazar*, suggesting intriguing resonances with political and religious anxieties about Ireland. A small papal force did land at Smerwick in support of Fitzmaurice and his followers, who included the English Jesuit Nicholas Sanders, but the holy war they proclaimed against Elizabeth failed to secure local support. Fitzmaurice's cause was re-ignited in 1580 by the rebellion of James Eustace in Leinster and also the landing at Smerwick of another foreign expeditionary force. However, in what proved a controversial display of state power, the mainly Italian forces were killed by the then lord deputy Arthur Grey. Perhaps the extremity of the response was a consequence of anxiety levels about foreign intervention in Ireland, the prospect of which remained. For before the Spanish armada of 1588 and indeed after it, rumours circulated about the Spanish landing in Ireland. The Irish council told the privy council in London that 'the Irishry make great joy at any rumours blown hither', adding that 'one came lately out of England, that gave it out that King Philip would invade there and here before May-day next'.[8] Sir John Perrot, lord deputy of Ireland from 1584 to

4 Steven G. Ellis, *Ireland in the age of the Tudors, 1447–1603: English expansion and the end of Gaelic rule* (Harlow, 1998), p. 319. 5 *Calendar of state papers, Ireland, 1586–1588*, ed. Hans Claude Hamilton (London, 1877), p. 207. 6 Colm Lennon, *Sixteenth century Ireland: the incomplete conquest* (Dublin, 1994), p. 222. 7 Lennon, *Sixteenth century Ireland*, pp 223–7; Richard Bagwell, *Ireland under the Tudors*, 3 vols (London, 1890), iii, pp 51–8. 8 *Cal. S.P.Ire., 1586–1588*, p. 5.

1588, was particularly perturbed about such reports. Writing about the 'doubtful state of things here, the causes, both foreign and domestical', Perrot urged the privy councillors in London to 'cast your eyes more carefully this way', a plea that suggested their neglect of Irish matters.[9] Here, Perrot identifies how Ireland was bound up with the broader or, as he termed it, 'foreign' threat that Spain, the papacy and the counter-reformation in general presented to England. From the 1580s, then, rebellions in Ireland 'consistently brought with them the spectre of foreign intervention' and, consequently, 'assumed more significance than they had previously'.[10] Moreover, Ireland's strategic location as a potential entryway into England meant that the appearance of a Spanish armada could pose a direct threat to Elizabeth's sovereignty.

Political anxieties of this nature were compounded by anxieties about reforming the indigenous population. These stemmed from deep suspicions about the cultural and ethnic difference of the Gaelic Irish as well as the perceived degeneration of the old English. The archbishop of Dublin, Adam Loftus, warned Sir Francis Walsingham, Elizabeth's principal secretary, that given the 'weakness of Her Majestie's garrison, [...] and the doubtfulness of the Irish, even in these civil parts [...] the whole kingdom shall be in danger upon the sudden to be lost'.[11] Alarmist in tone, Loftus' observation nonetheless provides insight into the debate in the 1580s about whether or not the Gaelic Irish could be translated into civil subjects of the crown. The debate centred on the alternate positions of coercion and conciliation and the radically different concepts of native difference underpinning them. As this chapter demonstrates, the interconnecting issues of native recalcitrance and of a pan-Catholic alliance intervening in Ireland are registered in *The Misfortunes of Arthur* and *The Battle of Alcazar*. What I want to consider is how these dramatic texts are conditioned by and indeed react to the contemporaneous debate about the state of Ireland. Particular attention is given to the plays' Irish characters, which though peripheral, evince a topical and ideologically conscious drama.

'SEVERITY UPHOLDS BOTH REALM AND RULE':
REFORMING THE IRISH IN *THE MISFORTUNES OF ARTHUR*

That representations of the past had a direct application to the present was a commonplace of Renaissance historiography.[12] In *The Book Named the Governor* (1531), for instance, Thomas Elyot advocated that English princes read 'the

---

9 Ibid., *1586–1588*, p. 17.   10 William Palmer, *The problem of Ireland in Tudor foreign policy: 1485–1603* (Woodbridge, 1994), p. 143.   11 *Cal. S.P.Ire., 1586–1588*, p. 164.   12 Phyllis Rackin, *Stages of history: Shakespeare's English chronicles* (London, 1990), pp 11–12.

commentaries Julius Cesar' because 'thereof may be taken necessary instructions concernynge the warres agayne Irisshe men or Scottes: who be of the same rudness and wilde disposition that the Suises and Britons were in the time of Casear'.[13] A similar concept of history is apparent in *The Misfortunes of Arthur*, where the story of King Arthur's struggle to balance public responsibilities with personal loyalties provides 'necessary instructions' for the Elizabethan present. The issues of usurpation and civil war feature prominently in the play but the primary concern is to draw parallels between Arthur's leniency towards his disloyal nephew Mordred – which results in the loss of Arthur's kingdom and the deaths of both men – and Elizabeth's dealings with her half-sister Mary Stuart. Arthur is 'a vehicle to carry a political message of contemporary relevance'.[14] Critics have generally interpreted the play as a compliment to Elizabeth for not succumbing to the leniency that is Arthur's downfall, thus justifying her decision to execute Mary Stuart the previous year.[15] The play offers 'a nightmare fantasy of what might have been' had Elizabeth, like Arthur, been soft on her enemies.[16] However, it is salutary to recall David Bevington's conception of the topical in Renaissance drama 'in terms of ideas and platforms rather than personalities'. As Bevington points out, warnings about the 'dangers of indulgent lenity' in *The Misfortunes of Arthur* need not specify Mary alone and Mordred need not represent just one threat.[17] The very fact that Elizabeth is offered a reminder about the dangers of over indulgence and indecision over a year after the Stuart affair, indicates that the play is neither entirely celebratory nor retrospective in tone.

From the outset, the dramatists establish clear parameters to address the queen on topical matters. Adopting a deferential tone, the induction initiates a poetics of praise:

> How suits a tragedy for such a time?
> Thus- for that since your sacred Majesty
> In gracious hands the regal sceptre held,
> All tragedies are fled from State to stage. (lines 77–80)

---

13 Thomas Elyot, *The book named the Governor* (Menston, West Yorks., 1970), p. 40.   14 Christopher Dean, *Arthur of England: English attitudes to king Arthur and the knights of the round table in the middle ages and the Renaissance* (Toronto, 1987), p. 119.   15 On the play as a complimentary allegory, see Evangelia H. Waller, 'A possible interpretation of *The Misfortunes of Arthur*', *JEGP*, 24 (1925), 219–45; and Gertrude Reese, 'Political import of *The Misfortunes of Arthur*', *Review of English Studies*, 21 (1945), 81–91. See also Christopher J Crosbie, 'Sexuality, corruption and the body politic: the paradoxical tribute of *The Misfortunes of Arthur* to Elizabeth I', *Arthuriana*, 9 (1999), 68–90.   16 Corrigan, (ed.), *The Misfortunes of Arthur*, p. 49.   17 David Bevington, *Tudor drama and politics: a critical approach to topical meaning* (Cambridge, MA, 1968), p. 154; p. 25.

Royal spectator and the play itself are imbued with considerable power: Elizabeth is figured as an effective ruler while the stage is envisaged as a safety valve that absorbs and contains potential threats. The play constructs a relationship of dependency with the monarch as her presence is crucial to the disclosure of its topical allegories.[19] What is interesting here is how the play tries to disavow its topicality, while simultaneously declaring it. Yet, the fiction of separating past and present is soon abandoned in act one, where the reign of Elizabeth is compared to Arthur's general misfortunes:

> Forsee what present plagues do threat this isle,
> Prevent not this my wreak. For you there rests
> A happier age, a thousand years to come;
> An age for peace, religion, wealth and ease,
> When all the world shall wonder at your bliss
> That, that is yours!   (I.i.61–5)

Opening itself to the gaze of the monarch, the play operates as a mirror and invites the queen to compare her reign favourably with the one presented on stage. It is a comparison Elizabeth and her court would have been familiar with and most likely interpreted as a form of panegyric. Arthur was not only a figure of history and romance who featured prominently in texts such as Geoffrey of Monmouth's *History of the Kings of Britain*, Malory's *Morte Arthur* and Spenser's *Faerie Queene* but also an important tool in Tudor ideology. As in the above speech, Elizabeth could be portrayed as Arthur's ancestor and also as the fulfilment of prophecies that envisaged a new Arthur who would bring peace to the kingdom.[20] The Arthur legend could also be used to serve Elizabethan imperialist ambitions, since 'Arthurian imagery perennially included imperial conquest and the geographical expansion of the realm'.[21] In Geoffrey of Monmouth's *History* – the primary source text for the play – Elizabethan writers such as John Dee found stories of conquest that could be appropriated to support English claims over territories in the new world.[22] As Andrew Hadfield has shown, Dee was not alone in his view that the 'Tudors were restoring an Arthurian empire rather than establishing a new one'.[23] Spenser

19 On the politics of court entertainment, see Steven Orgel, 'Spectacles of state' in *The Authentic Shakespeare* (London, 2002), pp 70–88.   20 For the different meanings of Arthur, see *The Spenser encyclopaedia*, ed. A.C. Hamilton (Toronto, 1990), pp 66–9. On the Tudor myth during Elizabeth's reign, see Frances A. Yates, *Astraea: the imperial theme* (London, 1975).   21 Derrick Spradlin, 'Imperial anxiety in Thomas Hughes's *The Misfortunes of Arthur*', *EMLS* 10.3 (2005), www.shu.ac.uk/emls, accessed January 2005.   22 Andrew Hadfield, 'Briton and Scythian: Tudor representations of Irish origins', *IHS*, 28 (1993), 390–408 at 391; *Spenser Encyclopaedia*, p. 66. 23 Hadfield, 'Briton and Scythian', p. 391.

recognized the ideological currency of the Arthurian legend to English claims to Ireland: in *A view of the state of Ireland*, Irenaeus notes: 'It appeareth by good record yet extant, that King Arthur [...] had all that iland under [his] alleagiance and subjection'.²⁴ *The Misfortunes of Arthur* exploits the powerful symbolism associated with the Arthur legend, delivering instructive parallels that are, ostensibly, complimentary. Elizabeth 'becomes the focal point of an extended drama – a power play – in which she is simultaneously flattered and coerced to follow the advice which the on-stage play presents'.²⁵ It is possible to go further and argue that the playwrights are cleverly negotiating the politics of praise, offering an encomium but qualifying it. In this play, praise is a preface to advice, counsel and, occasionally, admonition. The celebration of Elizabeth's 'happier age' thus becomes a warning about how that age is to be preserved; the problems on stage, the play makes it abundantly clear, are also the present problems of the state.

The sense in which the Arthurian subject matter provides a camouflage for advice and criticism is evident in the play's treatment of Ireland. In the source material, Geoffrey narrates how Arthur sailed to Ireland 'determined to subject [the island] to his own authority'.²⁶ He defeats the Irish king, Gilmaurius, whose army is 'cut to pieces where it stood and ran away'. The other princes of the country, 'thunderstruck by what had happened,' follow Gilmaurius' example and surrender to Arthur. 'The whole of Ireland was thus conquered,' concludes Geoffrey.²⁷ It might be expected that, as in the example from Spenser's *View*, the play would appropriate this aspect of its source to contemporary ends to underwrite Elizabeth's claim to and control over Ireland. As Spenser and others recognized, the idea of prior conquest was especially useful in dismissing arguments that England's claim over Ireland rested on the papal bull, *Laudabilitier*, which had been granted to King Henry II by Pope Adrian IV.²⁸ Recourse to papal legitimation for English sovereignty over Ireland did not sit well after the Reformation and became even less appealing following Elizabeth's excommunication in 1576. *The Misfortunes of Arthur* playwrights do not, however, follow their contemporaries in playing up the Arthurian conquest of Ireland as precedence. In contrast to the source text, they foreground Arthur's reluctance to use force against a blood relative and also the negative aspect of his relations with the Irish. Geoffrey briefly mentions that Mordred 'had brought the Scots, Picts and Irish into his alliance, with anyone

24 Spenser, *A view*, p. 52.   25 Giles Y. Gamble, 'Power play: Elizabeth I and *The Misfortunes of Arthur*', *Quondum et Futurus*, 1: 2 (1991), 59–69 at 60.   26 Geoffrey of Monmouth, *The history of the kings of Britain*, ed. Lewis Thorpe (London, 1966), p. 221. On the use of Geoffrey's *History* in the play, see Crosbie, 'Sexuality, corruption and the body politic', pp 69–71.   27 *History of the kings of Britain*, p. 222.   28 Hadfield, 'Briton and Scythian', pp 393–5.

else whom he knew to be filled with hatred' for Arthur.[29] It is this moment that the playwrights take as starting point for their engagement with Ireland. As David Bevington notes of the play more generally, 'only in the handling of their sources do Thomas Hughes and his fellow authors reveal topical intent'.[30] The fact that they chose to emphasize Mordred's alliance with the Irish rather than Arthur's successful conquest is highly significant, for in focusing on the former, the playwrights were signalling to their courtly audience that Ireland was a cause for present concern.

One of the strategies available to a playwright to condition the audience into interpreting events or action in a particular way is through the use of framing devices such as a chorus or dumb show. Ophelia's rather innocent observation of that most famous dumb show in *Hamlet*, 'belike this show imports the argument of the play,' belies its more pointed objective that its author knows only too well (III.ii.148). As a selective mimetic foreshadowing of the action the audience is about to see, the dumb show reveals something of the playwright's purpose, providing further insight into a play's topical meaning. Dumb shows were required not only to impress a play's deeper significance upon the minds of the audience, but also to relieve the 'strict form of rhetorical tragedies' like *The Misfortunes of Arthur*.[31] In the play, each act is preceded by a dumb show that is of allegorical significance not just within the context of the play, but also beyond it. In the second dumb show, an 'Irishman' appears. As the stage directions are detailed and crucial to the play's engagement with Ireland, I quote them in full:

> Whiles the music sounded, there came out of Mordred's house a man stately attired, representing a king who, walking once about the stage, then out of the house appointed for Arthur there came three Nymphs apparelled accordingly, the first holding a Cornucopia in her hand, the second a golden branch of olive, the third a sheaf of corn. These orderly, one after another, offered these presents to the king, who scornfully refused: a second after which there came a man bareheaded, with *long black shagged hair* down to his shoulders, apparelled with an *Irish jacket and shirt*, having an *Irish dagger* by his side, and a *dart* in his hand. Who first with a threatening countenance looking about, and then spying the king did furiously chase and drive him into Mordred's house. The king represented Mordred; the three Nymphs with their proffers of the treaty of peace, for the which Arthur sent Gawain with an herald unto Mordred, who rejected it: the *Irishman signified Revenge and*

29 *History of the kings of Britain*, p. 258.   30 Bevington, *Tudor drama*, p. 153.   31 Dieter Mehl, *The Elizabethan dumb show: the history of a dramatic convention* (London, 1965), p. 169.

> *Fury*, which Mordred conceived after his foil on the shores, whereunto
> Mordred headlong yieldeth himself. [emphasis added]

How is the royal spectator supposed to react to this representation of the
Irishman, that not only positions him as an enemy of Arthur but also the
driving force behind the usurper, Mordred? It has been argued that such character types would have confirmed the audience's sense of superiority, defusing
'the ongoing political conflict of which his nationality is a reminder.'[32] But the
argument that the stage Irishman works to mollify tensions between nations is
compromised by his very presence in the play, which simultaneously brings
those tensions to the fore. What is required here is closer attention to the
dramatic context within which the Irishman appears and also the range of
potential resonances he gives rise to.

The primary indication of the figure's Irishness is the 'long black shagged
hair', a reference to the ubiquitous Irish glib or long fringe. Surviving records
about an earlier though now lost masque suggests how this was represented on
stage. In 1551, Edward VI saw a masque of Irishmen on Twelfth Night and
Irishwomen on Shrovetide; among the props listed in the Revels' accounts was
a wig of black flax to represent the glib.[33] While such visual signs of Irishness
are obviously necessary in *The Misfortunes of Arthur* dumb show, in the later
drama there appears to have been an increasing reliance on stage Irish dialect,
although it seems reasonable to assume that this was supplemented by the use
of props and costume.[34] The glib is a potent signifier of Irishness in the dumb
show. To the Elizabethans, the glib denoted the wildness and deceptiveness of
the Gaelic Irish. In Spenser's *View*, Irenius notes that the glibs are 'as fit maskes
as a mantle is for a thiefe' because whenever the rebel

> run himselfe into that perill of law, that he will not be knowne, he
> either cutteth of his glibbe quite, by which he becommeth nothing like
> himselfe, or pulleth it so low downe over his eyes, that it is very hard
> to discern his theevish countenance.[35]

Providing the rebel with a natural disguise, the glib permits him literally to
transform himself, hide his true intent, which to Spenser is inevitably invid-
ious, and to escape capture. 'English order is baffled: not to be able to identify
the enemy is to be at his mercy.'[36] The anxieties about the glib are thus deep

32 Leerssen, *Mere Irish and fior Ghael: studies in the idea of Irish nationality, its development and literary expression prior to the nineteenth century*, Field Day essays and monographs (2nd ed. Cork, 1996), p. 79. 33 Bartley, *Teague, Shenkin and Sawney*, p. 9. 34 On the use of Irish stage dialects in the drama, see Paula Blank, *Broken English: dialects and the politics of language in Renaissance writings* (London, 1996), pp 127–50. 35 Spenser, *A view*, p. 59. 36 Jones and

rooted. The rebel becomes impossible to identify, categorize and control. Chameleon like, his body occludes the controlling optic of English law and power.

Another new English description of the native Irish, John Derricke's *Image of Irelande* (1581), provides an interesting parallel with the figuration of the Irishman in the play and suggests the likely resonances it would have had for a contemporary audience. An eclectic combination of narrative, verse and illustration, the text is a vitriolic description of the kern or Irish foot soldier.[37] While the kern frequently functioned in the period as a metonym for the Gaelic Irish, they were also perceived as embodying the most savage, detestable and feared aspects of the natives and of native custom. 'My harte abhorreth their dealynges', writes Derricke, 'and my soule dooeth detest their wilde shamrocke manners' and, throughout the narrative and accompanying wood-cuts, the author strives to persuade the reader as to the truth of his personal convictions.[38] The text's focus is on the mien of the kern:

> With writhed glibbes like wicked sprits,
> with visage rough and stearne
> [...]
> With speares in hand and swordes by sides,
> to bear of after clappes.
> With jackets long and large, which shroude simplicitie
> though spitful dartes which thei doe beare
> Importe iniquitie
> [...]
> Their shirtes be verie strange,
> not reachyng past the thie.[39]

As in the play, the description moves downward, with attention being drawn to the apparel and weaponry. The appearance of the kern is detailed because, as Derricke's text sets out to show, each aspect of appearance is an indication of their innate state. A marginal note to the text reinforces this point: 'the sowe returnes to the mire, and the dog to his vomit', with the biblical allusion reminding readers that, savage and satanic in form, the kern are also savage and satanic in nature.[40] The *Image*, as implied by its title, persuades its readers by repeatedly placing emphasis on the visual, exhibiting the kern in such a way

Stallybrass 'Dismantling Irena', p. 165. 37 John Derricke, *The Image of Irelande, with a discourse of woodkarne*, ed. John Small (Edinburgh, 1883), p. 1. 38 Derricke, *Image of Irelande*, p. 8. 39 Ibid., pp 49–51. 40 Ibid., p. 42.

that readers 'may perfectly see, as in a glasse'.[41] By invoking associations with the kern, *The Misfortunes of Arthur* also presents its audience with ocular proof of Irish alterity.

The various connotations of kern, glib and Irish dress, which are invoked in the presentation of the play's Irish figure, all serve to enhance his symbolic role as an ally of Mordred. He not only looks threatening, his actions confirm that he is, because the moment Mordred rejects peace – represented in the dumb show by the three nymphs – the Irishman appears. He is the antithesis of peace for, instead of the Cornucopia, olive branch and sheaf of corn (which the nymphs hold), kern-like he has a dagger, dart and a threatening countenance. In performance, the juxtaposition of the 'Irishman' and 'Peace' could have been underlined through the division of the stage space, with one side representing Arthur's house and the other Mordred's; the Irishman probably would have entered from Mordred's side. Moreover, the text of the dumb show reveals that the Irishman does not just represent the Irish assistance Mordred has procured but is in fact the catalyst for his actions: 'the Irishman signified Revenge and Fury'. National traits are combined with allegorical types in order to align the Irish directly and closely with Mordred and his decision to reject peace. As Mordred himself says, full of revenge and fury, 'now my sword is flesh'd | And taught to gore and bathe in hottest blood | Then think not, Arthur, that the crown is won!'(II.ii.6–8). The dumb show has already characterized such bloody sentiments as Irish, thus establishing the Irish as central to Mordred's determination to resist Arthur and reclaim power.

With the Irishman functioning as a signifier loaded with meanings, the audience is being asked to recognize him as emblematic of Mordred's treachery against Arthur and also the embodiment of Irish alterity. While the two meanings are closely connected, it is the latter, extra-dramatic meaning of the Irish figure, which is especially interesting. That extra-dramatic meaning is suggested by the emphasis on the figure's apparel and appearance, which although essential in denoting Irishness on stage, also points towards the queen's relationship with her Irish subjects. Native dress and customs were not only regarded with abhorrence by the English but also outlawed in sumptuary legislation. In 1571, the then lord president of Munster, Sir John Perrot, issued an ordinance in an attempt to curb indigenous cultural habits within his jurisdiction. 'The inhabitants of cities and corporate towns,' the ordinance stated, 'shall wear no mantles [...] Irish coats, or great shirts, nor suffer their hair to grow to glib, but to wear [...] some civil garments.'[42] The purpose of such controls can be seen from a similar, though earlier, proclamation. Published in 1537, it called

41 Ibid., p. 83. 42 'Ordinances proclaimed at Limerick by Sir John Perrot' (1571), quoted in Constantia Maxwell (ed.), *Irish history from contemporary sources* (London, 1923), p. 167.

for conformity of language, apparel and behaviour throughout Ireland so that the 'English tongue, habit and order may be henceforth continually … used by all men that will acknowledge themselves … to be his Highness's true and faithfull subjects'.[43] By abandoning the Gaelic language and indigenous dress, the monarch's Irish subjects could demonstrate their allegiance. Linguistic and sartorial conformity becomes an outward sign of obedience and, crucially, a visible indication of a successful conquest. As Stanyhurst explains in the Irish section of Holinshed's *Chronicles*:

> For where the countrie is subdued, there the inhabitants ought to be ruled by the same law that the conqueror is governed, to weare the same fashion of attyre, wherewith the victour is vested, and to speake the same language, that the vanquisher parleth and if any of these three lacke, doubtlesse the conquest limpeth.[44]

With this in mind, we can see that in presenting Elizabeth with a figure who bears the forbidden Irish characteristics adumbrated in the two proclamations, *The Misfortunes of Arthur* indirectly addresses its audience about the pace of English reform in Ireland. The sartorial difference of the Irish figure does not just represent a rejection of English style but a defiance of English authority. In representing Irish difference, therefore, the play reminds its royal spectator that the conquest of Ireland 'limpeth'. It is a reminder that, as we shall see, the play reiterates.

If the Irishman evokes Elizabethan frustrations with the situation in Ireland, frustrations that may very well have been directed toward the queen and her council, equally he has the potential to elicit a sense of curiosity. Once again, Derricke's *Image* provides an analogy, for beneath the concern to anatomize the kern is an interest and curiosity about them that the text envisages its readers will share. The title page offers the text for the 'pleasure and delight of the well disposed reader', a standard dedication perhaps, but significant in a text that anatomizes the kern and emphasizes their aberrant nature. While, throughout, the text highlights the villainies of the kern, there is also an element of fascination with their alterity: 'Like as their weedes be strange, | and monstrous to beholde: | So doe their manners far surpasse, | them all a thousand folde'.[45] A similar level of curiosity is evident in Gervase Markham's poem 'The Newe Metapmorphosis', where the kern are compared to 'brutish Indians'.[46] Like the wild Irishman in the play, these texts can be regarded as

43 'An act for the English order, habit and language' (1537) in *Irish history from contemporary sources*, p. 113.
44 Stanyhurst, 'Historie of Ireland' in *Holinshed's Irish chronicle*, ed. Liam Miller and Eileen Power (Dublin, 1979), p. 16.   45 Derricke, *Image of Irelande*, p.1; p. 51.   46 Quoted in Carpenter (ed.), *Verse in English from Tudor and Stuart*

instances of what Steven Mullaney has described as the 'pleasures of the strange', or the early modern phenomenon of interest in and curiosity about cultural "Others". Taking many forms, from the wonder-cabinet to the public theatre, the exhibition and representation of the customs and even individuals of marginal, though not necessarily new world, cultures constitutes a 'rehearsal of cultures'.[47] This 'cultural practice', Mullaney notes, 'allows, invites, and even demands full and potentially self-consuming review of unfamiliar things.'[48] Invariably, the processing of the exotic always seems to express the concerns of the dominant culture, amounting to its desire to achieve a level of control over the other culture, which it marginalizes as strange, alien. 'Learning strange tongues or collecting strange things, rehearsing the words and ways of marginal or alien cultures' are, Mullaney explains, 'the activities of a culture in the process of extending its boundaries and reformulating itself.'[49] Elizabeth's England was undergoing this very process, expanding its boundaries politically, culturally and spatially, perhaps most notably in Ireland.

To the extent, then, that the 'rehearsal of cultures' assumes the privileged vantage point of the dominant culture, it could be said to describe the audience's reaction to the presentation of the Irishman in *The Misfortunes of Arthur*. Seeing the Irish figure on stage in the Great Hall at Greenwich, we might imagine that Elizabeth's response was one of assured curiosity. This may also have been her reaction to a different, though equally staged, display of Irish wildness: the visit of Shane O'Neill to court in 1562.[50] Before the commencement of negotiations between himself and the queen, Shane made a ceremonial submission before Elizabeth, the council and foreign ambassadors at Whitehall on Twelfth Day.[51] Accompanied by a bodyguard of Gaelic soldiers, Shane played the role of obedient subject with irony by appearing before the monarch in his native clothing and addressing her in Irish. Camden's description gives some sense of the spectacle that Elizabeth witnessed:

> And now Shane O'Neill came from Ireland [...] with an escort of gallowglasses, armed with battle-axes, bare headed, with flowing curls, yellow shirts dyed with saffron [...] large sleeves, short tunics and rough cloaks, whom the English followed with as much wonderment as if they had come from China or America. O'Neill was received with all kindness, and throwing himself at the queen's feet he owned with lamentation his crime of rebellion and begged for pardon.[52]

Ireland, p. 109.   **47** Steven Mullaney, *The place of the stage: license, play and power in Renaissance England* (Chicago, 1988), p. 63.   **48** Mullaney, *Place of the stage*, p. 71.   **49** Ibid., p. 82.   **50** Alternatively, as noted by D.B. Quinn, Shane's visit may have suggested the Irish figure in the play. See *The Elizabethans and the Irish*, pp 153–4. Quinn also notes that ballads about Shane's visit circulated in London, but they no longer survive.   **51** Seamus Pender, 'Shane O'Neill comes to the court of Elizabeth' in *Feilscríbhinn Torna* (Cork, 1947), p. 166.   **52** William Camden, *Annales rerum Anglicarum et Hibernicarum Regnante Elizabetha, ad Annum Salutis, 1589*, quoted in *Irish history from contemporary sources,*

Although Camden records Shane's symbolically submissive position at the feet of Elizabeth, the narrative of this carefully choreographed demonstration of royal power over troublesome subjects unwittingly reveals Shane's daring assertion of difference. Indeed, Shane is portrayed as such an extravagant figure in Camden's description that the Irish rebel almost upstages the queen. The example of Shane O'Neill suggests that while the rehearsal of an alien culture may produce a seductive blend of pleasure and control, there is always the possibility that it will give that culture a presence. Since the pleasure experienced is dependent precisely upon the alterity of the culture being rehearsed, the difference of that culture, simultaneously alluring and threatening, is also registered. The 'pleasure of the strange' brings with it anxieties about difference. Accordingly, just as Shane's presence challenges monarchical authority (or at least its symbolism), so the rehearsal of Irish difference in *The Misfortunes of Arthur* has the potential to unsettle its audience.

There had been a more recent, if somewhat less dramatic, visit by Hugh O'Neill, the young earl of Tyrone, in spring 1587. Educated in the Pale, Hugh could speak English and did not provide the same show of Irish difference that Shane so consciously exhibited before the court in 1562. It is tempting to speculate about the proximity of this court visit to the performance of *The Misfortunes of Arthur*. At the start of the year, three prominent government officials in Ireland advised the privy council in advance of O'Neill's visit that it was his 'ambition to be supreme in Ulster'.[53] Perhaps *The Misfortunes of Arthur* is similarly proleptic but it seems more likely that its allegorical Irishman figures Irish political recalcitrance along more general lines. It was only from the mid-1590s that O'Neill became the focus of official anxieties about Ireland and, accordingly, a subtext in the drama.

The dramatization of the dumb show corroborates the argument that the play's treatment of topical matters is in general, rather than specific, terms. In the dumb show, Mordred has been firmly established as an unstoppable usurper and this impression is reinforced throughout the second act. Through the rhetorical device of stichomythia or rapid verbal crossfire between characters, one of several Senecan influences on the play, Mordred is portrayed as resolute, rejecting attempts by Conan and Gawain to reason with him.[54] For instance, Gawain speaks of the 'doubtful state of wars' (II.3.90) and the fickleness of Mars, who occasionally allows the weaker side to prevail, occasionally the stronger, but Mordred boasts that 'The smallest axe may fell the largest tree' (II.3.107), a comment charged with topical resonance. In preparation for

p. 172.   53 Quoted in Morgan, *Tyrone's rebellion*, p. 51.   54 On use of Senecan conventions, see William A. Armstrong, 'Elizabethan themes in *The Misfortunes of Arthur*', *Review of English Studies*, 27 (1956), 238–49.

war, Mordred forges an alliance with the Irish, as prefigured in the dumb show, and also the Picts and the Saxons. This alignment of the ancestors of the English (the ancient Britons and Saxons) with the Irish, those 'others' to the English, is an example of the faultlines generated by the re-writing of history for a contemporary moment. Each leader is greeted individually by Morded in order of dramatic importance, with the emphasis being on Gillamor, the Irish king, who is first to reply:

> MORDRED   For your great help and valiant Irish force,
> If I obtain the conquest in these wars,
> Whereas my father claims a tribute due
> Out of your realm; I here renounce it quite:
> And if assistance need in doubtful times,
> I will not fail to aid you with the like.
>
> GILLAMOR   It doth suffice me to discharge my realm,
> Or at the least to wreak me on my foes.
> I rather like to live your friend and peer,
> Than rest in Arthur's homage and disgrace.
>
> (II.iv.7–16)

Mordred's offer to relieve the Irish king of his fealty to Arthur is the only allusion to the Arthurian conquest of Ireland. In the mouth of the usurper, that conquest is emptied of its Elizabethan meaning as a convenient precedence for English sovereignty over Ireland. Moreover, any such claim is further undermined as Gillamor repudiates Arthur's authority and asserts his right to govern his own kingdom. From the exchange, it is evident that Mordred's overtures to Gillamor are motivated by self-interest and that the Irish king is too easily persuaded by him. Gillamor is given 'individualized reasons' for supporting Mordred that 'transcend the necessities of the plot'.[55] Here, narrative and characterization are determined by the dramatists' concern to project topical matters into the play.

Gillamor is shown to be as equally fickle, disloyal and traitorous as his new found sponsor, a characterization that carries a potentially pointed application to the queen about the loyalty of her Irish subjects. His willingness to become Mordred's 'friend and peer' rather than remain loyal to Arthur mirrors the efforts in 1579 of Sir James Fitzmaurice Fitzgerald and his supporters to solicit the Spanish monarchy to accept them as loyal subjects, thus rejecting

---

55 Corrigan (ed.), *The Misfortunes of Arthur*, p. 24.

Elizabethan sovereignty over Ireland. Fitzmaurice instructed his papal envoy to approach King Philip with a view to the king's nephew being 'proclaimed our king'; in return, the Irish would become Philip's 'most faithful subjects and vassals'.[56] Catholic Spain was just one aspect of Fitzmaurice's plans for, as noted earlier, he had also secured a small papal force and, in the language of the counter-reformation, proclaimed a holy war against Elizabeth and absolved her Irish subjects of their allegiance.[57] While Fitzmaurice's efforts were frustrated by a number of factors, the threat of foreign assistance that they represented continued to be a possibility. In the spring of 1586, Sir John Perrot informed Walsingham of 'secret and certain intelligences of a Spanish preparation' for Ireland; Perrot went on to state that 'the Irishry here do hearken greedily for the coming over of foreign forces'.[58] One year later, a report to the privy council on the same subject cautioned that 'many of this country birth [. . .] are not to be trusted'.[59]

Similar views and anxieties are evident in *The Misfortunes of Arthur*, where the subjects of Catholic plotting and Irish rebellion form an active subtext to this play and, as we shall see later, Peele's *Battle of Alcazar*. Hughes and his fellow playwrights not only evoke fears of a Catholic league but, by moulding audience response in an overt, almost self-reflexive way, they also work to advise Elizabeth on the best course of action for this urgent, contemporary problem. As a negative example for Elizabeth, Arthur is the medium through which the playwrights offer warning and advice. In particular, Arthur's defeatist reaction to Mordred's alliance and readiness for war becomes a drama of counsel, where the dramatists converse with the queen. Crucial to this process is the character of Cador, whose role as advisor to Arthur takes on a metadramatic force, reflecting the playwrights' own self-appointed role as advisers to Elizabeth. Arthur's lament for the altered balance of power – full of self-pity, he tells himself 'Thy kingdoms gone' (III.i.17) – is countered by Cador who urges him 'to pursue your foes with present force' (III.i.31). This call for decisive action is underscored as Arthur is urged to adopt a more kingly resolve: 'No worse a vice than lenity in kings: | Remiss indulgence soon undoes a realm' (III.i.62–3). Equally, the play implies, leniency is a vice in queens. Cador continues in his attempt to advise and persuade by reminding Arthur of Mordred's crimes. Anyone who violates the law, he argues, should be punished by it: 'So let it fare with all that dare the like: | Let sword, let fire, let torments be their end. | Severity upholds both realm and rule' (III.i.81–3).

What are the student-lawyers doing here in defending their future profession but also insisting on the necessity of force? Is 'severity' only to be reserved

56 Quoted in Cyril Falls, *Elizabeth's Irish wars* (London, 1950), p. 140.   57 Bagwell, *Ireland under the Tudors*, iii, pp 51–8.   58 *Cal. S.P.Ire., 1586–1588*, p. 26.   59 Ibid., p. 419.

for isolated cases? As if conscious of what they might be suggesting, the playwrights have Arthur reply 'Ah too severe!' (III.1.84). Ultimately, Arthur resolves
to go to war, a resolution that seems an endorsement of the kind of rough
justice proposed by Cador. As they gather for battle, one of Arthur's men,
Howell, remarks: 'We most mislike that your too mild a mood | Hath thus
withheld our hands and swords from strokes' (III.iii.68–9). Arthur now begins
to act like the king his advisers want him to be; in tune with the play's advo-
cacy of force, he rallies his forces together with a prophecy of victory over
Mordred's 'market-mates, so highly hir'd' (III.iii.33):

> The better cause gives us the greater hope
> Of prosperous wars; wherein, if once I hap
> To spy the wonted signs, that never fail'd
> Their guide —your threatening looks, your fiery eyes,
> And bustling bodies prest to present spoil,
> The field is won! Even then, methinks, I see
> The wonted wastes and scattered heads of foes,
> The Irish carcass kick'd, and Picts oppress'd,
> And Saxons slain to swim in streams of blood.
> I quake with hope.   (III.iii.118–30)

Arthur is proving adept at political symbolism. The vision of the battlefield is
wish-fulfilment on a grand scale, not just for Arthur himself, but Elizabeth
too. Having pointed to the Irish problem, as well as the more general problem
of a Catholic alliance, the play now allows its audience to imagine the 'Irish
carcass kick'd'. This is an extremely evocative phrase, the deeper function of
which can be understood in relation to a contemporary pictorial analogue. In
Derricke's *Image*, one of the woodcuts depicts English soldiers returning
triumphant from battle carrying the heads of kern. Another shows the lord
deputy, Sir Henry Sidney, and two of his officials leaving Dublin castle, with
three heads impaled on stakes over the castle gate (see fig. 1). The picture's
symmetrical arrangement, three representatives of state in the foreground and
three enemies of state in the background, creates a pageant of state power that
seems to juxtapose English mastery with Irish rebelliousness. The inscription
above the etching reads: 'These trunckles heddes do playnly showe, each rebeles
fatall end, | And what a haynous crime it is, the queene for to offend'.[60] The
inference is that the 'showe' of the punished body may be as important as the

---

60 Derricke, *Image of Irelande*, plate vi.

These trunckles heddes do playnly showe, eache rebeles fatall end,
And what a haynous crime it is , the Queene for to offend.

Although the theeues are plagued thus, by princes trusty frendes,   6   For he that gouernes Jrishe soyle , presenting there her grace,
And brought for their innoumpties, to sondry wretched endes: whose fame made rebelles often flye , the presence of his face:
Yet may not that a warning be , to those they leaue behinde,   He he I saw , he goeth forth , with Marsis noble trayne,
But needes their treasons must appeare , long kept in festred mynde.   To iustifie his Princes cause , but their demeanures bayne:
whereby the matter groweth at length , into a bloudy fielde,   Thus Queene he will haue honored , in middest of all her foes,
Euen to the rebells ouerthrow , except the traytours yelde.   And knowne to be a royall Prince , euen in despight of those.

1 John Derricke, The Image of Irelande, ed. John Small (Edinburgh, 1883), plate vi.

punishment itself. In its visual re-creation of broken and punished Irish bodies, the text conveys the full effect of the play's image: Irish bodies are inscribed with royal power. Both are instances of what Foucault calls 'punishment-as-spectacle'.[61] As Foucault argues, punishment and torture are important manifestations of power, but their effectiveness lies in the exposure of the condemned body. Torture, he writes,

> must mark the victim; it is intended either by the scar it leaves on the body, or by the spectacle that accompanies it, to brand the victim with infamy [...] it traces around or, rather, on the very body of the condemned man signs that must not be effaced.[62]

Body is reduced to sign. Like the decapitated head of the rebel in the woodcut, allusion to the 'Irish carcass' in *The Misfortunes of Arthur* symbolizes the strength of the monarch 'beating down upon the body of the adversary and mastering it'.[63] Elizabeth is reassured of the state's capacity to control subversive elements and, simultaneously, reminded about the necessity and efficacy of force.

While it is necessary to distinguish between figurations of bodily violence and violence as it was experienced on the ground in Ireland, there is a sense in which such images convey changing attitudes towards the native Irish. From the 1570s onwards, the question of how best to reform the queen's Irish subjects became increasingly fractious. Sir William Fitzwilliam maintained that 'till the sword have thoroughly and universally tamed [the native Irish] in vain is law brought amongst them'.[64] But others, not least the queen herself, believed that as subjects of the crown, the native population could (and should) be reformed without recourse to policies of deliberate aggression. Elizabeth, for instance, instructed her officers in Ireland that potential rebels were to be offered 'our gracious general pardon' and 'received to grace'.[65] The ideal of the benevolent and lenient monarch Elizabeth fashions here is of course precisely the style of monarch *The Misfortunes of Arthur* subjects to much discussion and critique. In placing equal emphasis upon on the dangers of leniency and the need for force, the play itself intervenes in the contemporary debate about the reformation of Ireland. In fact, the playwrights, somewhat controversially, may even be registering frustration with official policy on Ireland, which in oscillating between conciliation and coercion, lacked both direction and consistency. This can partly be attributed to fiscal considerations

61 Michel Foucault, *Discipline and punish: the birth of the prison*, trans. Alan Sheridan (London, 1977), p. 9. 62 Ibid., p. 34. 63 Ibid., p. 49. 64 Quoted in Canny, *Elizabethan conquest*, p. 128. 65 David Edwards, 'Ideology and experience: Spenser's *View* and martial law in Ireland' in Hiram Morgan (ed.), *Political ideology in Ireland, 1541–1641* (Dublin, 1999), p. 137.

since the Elizabethan state could not afford to implement a policy of total conquest and, in any case, the notoriously frugal queen probably would not have countenanced it. By the mid-1580s, the failure of Elizabethan policy 'was painfully becoming obvious' as Gaelic lords appeared 'more rebellious and more resistant to law than ever before.'[66]

Unsurprisingly, the government line was frequently 'at variance with what many captains and commanders in the field thought best.'[67] This discrepancy between the queen's ideas about how Ireland should be governed and the actions of the provincial governors and new English colonists is highlighted by the increase in the use of martial law to stamp out local unrest. Arguing for its necessity, Captain Thomas Lee wrote: 'it ought to be granted to all governors of remote and savage places where your Majesty's laws are not received … until such time as the people shall become civil, and embrace the laws, and peaceable living'.[68] Lee's emphasis on the civilizing potential of martial law belies harsh realities. As David Edwards has argued, the various commissions of martial law permitted English governors to enact 'strategies of brutal repression' against the indigenous population; the more widespread its use became, 'the more the level of violence escalated drastically.'[69] One of the most infamous incidents associated with martial law occurred in 1578 when, as part of a prolonged disagreement between the Laois-Offaly planters and local Gaelic clans, Francis Cosby and Robert Hartpole murdered a large group of the O'Mores at Mullaghmast in Kildare.[70] Describing the massacre as a 'horrible and abominable act of treachery,' the Annals of the Four Masters, a collection of contemporary Gaelic sources, explained how the O'Mores

> were all summoned to show themselves with greatest number they could be able to bring with them, at the great rath of Mullagh-Maisteam; and on their arrival at that place, they were surrounded on every side by four lines of soldiers and cavalry, who proceeded to shoot and slaughter without mercy, so that not a single individual escaped.[71]

The incident at Mullaghmast, which is justified in Derricke's *Image*, may indicate that attitudes towards the Gaelic Irish were becoming 'increasingly racialist and supremacist', even within government circles.[72] Certainly, the murder of members of the O'More clan was neither isolated nor accidental, having been

66 Brady, *The chief governors: the rise and fall of reform government in Tudor Ireland, 1536–1588* (Cambridge, 1994), p. 247; p. 246.   67 McGurk, *Elizabethan conquest*, p. 19.   68 Quoted in Canny, *Elizabethan conquest*, p. 118. 69 Edwards, 'Beyond reform', p. 17.   70 Vincent Carey, 'John Derricke's *Image of Irelande*, Sir Henry Sidney and the massacre at Mullaghmast, 1578', *IHS*, 31 (1999), 305–27 at 319–20.   71 Quoted in *Irish history from contemporary sources*, p. 236.   72 Edwards, 'Beyond reform', p. 18.

performed in accordance with a commission of martial law signed by the then lord deputy, Sir Henry Sidney. But it is important to remember that, as with official policy towards Ireland, attitudes towards the native population were not static, making it difficult to determine how embedded and widespread these extreme attitudes were. Policies of extremity like martial law were criticized: Sir James Croft denounced that 'basterd and unnaturall lawe,' for ruining the prospect of 'good government in Ireland' and in 1586, the privy council instructed the lord deputy Perrot to curb its use.[73]

As I have been suggesting, *The Misfortunes of Arthur* reacts against reservations about state-sanctioned violence and the use of force more generally. In the battle between Arthur and Mordred, which is reported by the messenger Nuntius, the play foregrounds the adverse consequences of inaction and indecision. It is Mordred's ally Gillamor who, ominously, wins the first victory in battle: 'The Irish king whirl'd out a poisoned dart | That lighting pierced deep in Howell's brains | A peerless prince and near of Arthur's blood' (IV.ii.100–2). The impact of the moment, and of the battle scenes in general, may be somewhat lessened because it is reported rather than represented on stage but the allusion to the dart nonetheless underscores the impression of the Irish as wild and threatening. Gillamor is subsequently killed by Arthur: Nuntius describes how Arthur 'spied the Irish king, | Whose life he took as price of broken truce' (IV.ii.60–1). This is a just punishment as Gillamor has been disloyal; of course, such detail seems inconsequential as the play has previously insinuated that Irishness itself is sufficient justification for the use of force. Once again, the limitations of the play's narrative method do not compromise its politics. While the queen may only hear about the defeated Irishman, the symbolic meaning is abundantly clear: Elizabeth is being asked to recognize that when it comes to the recalcitrant Irish, the sword is the best option.

The moment of victory and of control over the Irish is overshadowed by Arthur's fight with Mordred; in this final battle, the culmination of the plot, Arthur kills his son but is fatally wounded. The observation that all is 'topsy-turvy turn'd' (IV.ii.136) sets the tone for the ensuing scenes. With Arthur's defeat and imminent death, it seems as if the natural order of things has been subverted. Gildas laments the outcome of the battle:

> What nations erst the former age subdu'd
> With hourly toils to Britain's yoke this day
> Hath set at large, and backwards turn's the fates
> Henceforth the Kerns may safely tread their bogs.
>
> (IV.iii.10–13)

---

73 Quoted in Edwards, 'Ideology and experience', p. 137.

While these reversals are the immediate consequences of defeat, the inference is that Arthur himself is to blame. Functioning as a cautionary coda to Elizabeth about the dangers of leniency and indecision, the image of the kern at large in Ireland, traversing the bogs that gave them a tactical advantage over the English, confronts the queen with a possible reality where conquest is suspended or, at worst, reversed.

Intriguingly, later in the play, there is a temporary move away from the emphasis on Arthur's weakness and the 'topsy-turvy' state to which it has reduced the kingdom towards a reassurance that all has not been lost. Listing his achievements, the dying king attempts to lessen the impact of his ignoble defeat: 'Yet go we not inglorious to the ground: | Set wish apart, we have perform'd enough | The Irish king and nation wild we tam'd' (V.i.155–7). That this is the first of Arthur's boasts makes it a clear exercise in damage control. Through Arthur's act of revisionism, Elizabeth is offered the reassuring image of the Irish controlled, civilized and reformed, or an alternative, more favourable, reality in Ireland should she act decisively. However, Arthur's victory myth is shattered in the final chorus, which judges his reign harshly: 'The many wars and conquests which he gain'd | Are dash'd at once' (V. Chorus, 5–6). David Spradlin argues that in such moments, the play registers the drawbacks of conquest abroad. 'Arthur's imperialist-mindedness', he writes, 'overlooks his duty to prohibit domestic unrest and instability'.[74] Yet, the play is also insistent on the need to tackle problems that accrue from empire building directly and resolutely. The chorus's reinscription of history over myth, where the reality of defeat displaces Arthur's past conquests, is, therefore, entirely appropriate to a play that has repeatedly advised its royal spectator about how not to govern the kingdom at home and away. The play tempers its admonitory tone by engaging in its own myth making: the deaths of Arthur and Mordred pave the way for 'the glorious star' (V.ii.14) that 'Shall of all wars compound eternal peace' (V.ii.22–3), bringing about a 'rule that else no realm shall ever find' (V.ii.27). Of course, this imagined Elizabethan future is dependent upon the queen's recognition that, as with other enemies of the state, the Irish may not be easily tamed.

CATHOLIC AND IRISH PLOTS IN PEELE'S *BATTLE OF ALCAZAR*

Hughes and his fellow playwrights come extraordinarily close to criticizing Elizabeth over her response to the Irish problem but in a play written specifi-

---

74 Spradlin, 'Imperial anxiety in Thomas Hughes's *The Misfortunes of Arthur*', p. 17.

cally for the monarch's entertainment and with her presence in mind, it is inevitable that they should also incline towards some degree of flattery. The play's occasional 'complimentary effusions' about Elizabeth are not exclusive, however, to drama designed for the court, finding their parallel in plays performed on the public stage, where the victory over the Armada in 1588 produced a popular blend of jingoism and praise for the monarch.[75] First performed in 1589 and possibly revived between 1598 and 1599, George Peele's *Battle of Alcazar* contains an extended eulogy to the queen, which emphasizes the impenetrability of her kingdom from foreign attack.[76] This is to be expected from a post-Armada play and *The Battle of Alcazar* certainly lacks the sense of foreboding evident in the subtext of *The Misfortunes of Arthur*. But as with the court entertainment, such moments of confidence do not always operate in a straightforward manner. Crucially, for instance, the paean to Elizabeth comes immediately after the audience has heard that a papal force intends to conquer her other kingdom, Ireland. The topical jingoism exhibited in Peele's play does not, therefore, presuppose a definitive ideological position. While capturing the sense of assurance that victory over the Armada temporarily gave to Elizabethan culture and exploiting anti-Spanish feeling that was undoubtedly running high at the time, the play also registers anxieties about Elizabethan sovereignty and the stability of national identity, anxieties that Ireland brings to the fore.

In dramatizing an event from recent history, Peele abandons the safety of historical distance that so many of his contemporaries relied upon when it came to topical matters. The play focuses on how King Sebastian of Portugal becomes embroiled in a succession dispute between two members of the Moroccan royal family, Abdilmelec and his usurping nephew Muly Mahamet. The induction establishes the terms in which Sebastian's story is to be understood: the 'honourable and couragious king' is drawn into war by his own fatal ambition and the pleas of Muly Mahamet, characterized as 'black in his looke, and bloudie in his deeds'.[77] This perspective can be explained with reference to contemporary politics. As A.R. Braunmuller notes, 'while politics and war in northern Africa might have only an exotic rather than nationalistic interest for Elizabethans, Portuguese affairs were a very different matter'.[78] The death of

---

75 Bevington, *Tudor drama and politics*, p. 168.   76 The title page of the 1594 quarto says *Alcazar* 'was sundrie times plaid by the Lord high Admirall his servants', firmly placing it before 1591, when the Admiral's men left London. The reference to the play in Peele's own 'Farewell to Norris and Drake' (entered into the Stationer's Register in April 1589) has led critics to fix the original performances to 1589. See *The Battle of Alcazar*, ed. John Yoklavich in *The dramatic works of George Peele*, ed. Charles Tyler Prouty, 3 vols (New Haven, 1961), ii, pp 221–6; and Harold M. Dowling, 'The date and order of Peele's plays', *N&Q*, 164 (1933), 164–8.   77 *The Battle of Alcazar*, ed. W.W. Greg (Oxford, 1963), line 7; line 19. All quotations are from this edition.   78 A.R. Braunmuller, *George Peele* (Boston, 1983), p. 66.

the heirless Sebastian at Alcazar in 1578 was of special relevance to England. While Elizabeth had backed the claim of Sebastian's illegitimate nephew, Don Antonio, her old enemy Philip II of Spain had asserted his right to the throne. The entire Alcazar episode thus raised English anxieties about the expansion of Spain. In this regard, the Presenter's description of the story as 'a modern matter' (line 64) is particularly apposite.

The play localizes the broad subject of international power politics through the character of Thomas Stukeley, who in the play abandons his leadership of a papal force destined for Ireland in order to fight alongside Sebastian. Stukeley was an English adventurer turned pirate, whose travels took him from London to Ireland, Spain and, finally, Portugal.[79] His life intersected with Ireland in significant ways and, as with other Englishmen in the period, it was there that he sought social advancement. Sir Henry Sidney employed him to negotiate with Shane O'Neill, whom Stukeley had befriended during the rebel's court visit of 1562. Stukeley also attempted to purchase various administrative and military posts in Ireland. Despite the fact that Elizabeth refused to sanction these appointments, he adopted the self-styled title of 'Marquis of Ireland'. In 1569, Stukeley was imprisoned for dealings with Irish rebels but escaped to Spain where he continued his treasonous activities by scheming for the invasion of England and Ireland. His plan was to 'reduce the realm of Ireland to the service and devotion of his Majesty [Philip of Spain] and defend it against all his enemies'.[80] The former ally of the Elizabethan state was now proving its enemy. However, it was Stukeley's association with James Fitzmaurice Fitzgerald and his papal sponsored force for Ireland that gained him notoriety in official circles. In May 1578, for instance, the privy council informed the lord president of Munster, William Drury, that it had 'suspicions of Stucley attempting to invade Ireland' and recommended that the 'havens of Waterford, Cork and Kinsale be fortified to hinder any landing of the enemy'.[81] Charged with an expeditionary force of 1,000 men, Stukeley did set sail for Ireland to meet with Fitzmaurice but was detained at Lisbon because, as Anthony Munday noted in *The English Romaine Life*, 'thinges went not forwarde according as they should have done'.[82]

The treatment of Stukeley in *The Battle of Alcazar*, which begins with the adventurer's stay at Lisbon, is the earliest extant stage representation of his life and also an early example of 'biographical drama'.[83] The life appears to have

79 The most detailed discussion of the literary tradition surrounding Stukeley's life is Yoklavich (ed.), *Battle of Alcazar*, pp 249–73. For a recent assessment, see Charles Edelman (ed.), *The Stukeley plays* (Manchester, 2005), pp 1–10.   80 Quoted in Daniel A. Binchy, 'An Irish ambassador at the Spanish court, 1569–1574', *Studies*, 14 (1925), 102–19 at 110.   81 *Calendar of state papers, domestic, 1581–1590*, ed. Robert Lemon (London, 1865), p. 134.   82 Quoted in Yoklavich (ed.), *The Battle of Alcazar*, p. 266.   83 See Irving Ribner, *The English history play in the age of Shakespeare* (London, 1965), pp 194–5; Joseph Candido, 'Captain Thomas Stukeley: the man, the theatrical record

entered popular consciousness in the period, featuring in a later play *Captain Thomas Stukeley* (1596/7), discussed in chapter three, as well as in ballads and prose fictions. Peele clearly assumes audience familiarity with Stukeley, with the Governor of Lisbon introducing him as 'noble *Stukeley* famous by thy name' (line 428). In addition, Stukeley's name is flagged on the title page of the 1594 Quarto; clearly, it was perceived as an additional selling point for the play.[84] Stukeley's biography does make for an effective and dynamic subplot. 'The colourful details of his life', as Joseph Candido observes, 'read like a perpetual gyration in the wheel of fortune'.[85] More particularly, as Claire Jowitt has pointed out, Stukeley's competing political affiliations 'allowed him to be represented, sometimes simultaneously, as both patriot and traitor to the English nation and its queen'.[86] In this sense, the figure of Stukeley afforded a playwright like Peele considerable dramatic scope while also being open to ideological appropriation. Accordingly, while it might be argued that Ireland only features in the play because of its connection with Stukeley (certainly the Irish scheme is of secondary dramatic importance), the life also functions as a filter through which current and sensitive issues such as Ireland are broached in the play.

The extent to which the engagement with Ireland is on a conscious level is suggested by the play's relationship with its primary source text, John Polemon's *Second Part of the Booke of Battailes*.[87] Polemon gives 'only the slightest hint for the story of Stukeley's role' in the battle of Alcazar.[88] The text briefly refers to '600 Italians, with whom the Pope had furnished the Counte of Ireland, who being arrived at Lisbon, offered his service to the king' [Sebastian] and mentions the 'Marques of Ireland' as being among the casualties of the battle.[89] Moreover, the source does not provide for Peele's character of the Irish bishop. In a play that in other key respects closely follows its source text, such moments are significant, revealing less a concern with historical accuracy than the promotion of topical matter. Thus, the delineation of Stukeley's Irish exploits in the play can be understood as a consequence of an emerging consciousness about Ireland in the period.

The Stukeley scene opens with an expository tone as the Governor of Lisbon warmly welcomes the English adventurer, the Irish bishop and their

---

and the origins of Tudor "biographical" drama', *Anglia*, 105, (1987), 50–68 at 55. **84** The title page reads: 'THE BATTELL OF ALCAZAR, FOUGHT in Barbarie, betweene Sebastian king of Portugall, and Abdelmelec king of Marocco. With the death of Captaine *Stukeley*.' I have retained the title page spelling throughout, although the name is also spelt 'Stukley' within the play. **85** Candido, 'Captain Thomas Stukeley', p. 52. **86** Claire Jowitt, *Voyage drama and gender politics, 1589–1642* (Manchester, 2003), p. 66. **87** For a full discussion of Peele's use of this and other source texts, see David Bradley, *From text to performance in the Elizabethan theatre: preparing the play for the stage* (Cambridge, 1992), pp 130–6. See also Warner G. Rice, 'A principal source of *The Battle of Alcazar*', *MLN*, 58 (1943), 428–31. **88** Yoklavich (ed.), *The Battle of Alcazar*, p. 236. **89** John Polemon, *The second part of the booke of battailes, fought in our age* (London, 1587), p. 72; p. 81.

companions as 'valiant Catholikes' (line 425), thus disclosing his own religious loyalties. The Irish bishop is greeted as the 'most reverend primate of the Irish church' (line 424) but he is never named in the play.[90] The delineation of his character and nationality is at best minimal but then presumably within the context of the religious ideologies of the period, the figure of a Catholic bishop was an already loaded signifier. However, in performance, it is likely that his cultural difference would also have been suggested; certainly, his involvement in the plot to invade Ireland would call for a nationalized portrait. From the outset, the bishop is firmly associated with the papal invasion scheme:

> These welcomes worthie governor of Lisborne,
> Argue an honorable minde in thee,
> But treate of our misfortune therewithall,
> To Ireland by pope Gregories command,
> Were we all bound, and therefore thus imbarkt,
> To land our forces there at unawares,
> Conquering the land for his holynesse,
> And to restore it to the Romane faith,
> This was the cause of our expedition,
> And Ireland long ere this had bin subdude,
> Had not foule weather brought us to this bay.   (lines 433–44)

The implications of what the bishop says here are immediately discernible: although the seditious plan for the invasion of Ireland might be construed as Catholic wish-fulfilment, it nonetheless amounts to a denial of Elizabethan sovereignty. The speech is topically allusive and overtly so, pointing less to memories of the defeated Armada than to fears of yet another invading force. What is striking here is the use of a direct mode of representation, an indication that the topical issue of Ireland was played out on the Renaissance stage. The directness of the report could be attributed to the fact that the papal plan is being discussed in retrospect but the reference to an invasion force does evoke fears of Catholic intrigue and, more pointedly, foreign assistance for Irish rebels. As noted earlier, the prospect of foreign intervention in Ireland, and the related possibility that it would be used as a staging post for a Catholic plot against England, was a concern throughout the last decade of Elizabeth's reign. Stukeley's plan was just one of several schemes, both real and rumoured.

---

90 G.C. Duggan, *The stage Irishman* (London, 1937), p. 233. On possible historical counterparts for the character, see Edelman (ed.), *The Stukeley plays*, pp 233–5.

Rather than providing a convenient precedent to dispel anxieties surrounding these fears, however, the play has the Irish bishop speak a language of conquest (as evidenced by 'subdude' and 'conquering') to suggest that Stukeley's force might easily overrun and transform Elizabeth's Ireland. The implied inversion of power relations – 'Ireland long ere this had bin subdude' – recalls the image of reversed conquest in *The Misfortunes of Arthur*. Like that play, *The Battle of Alcazar* seems to offer a warning about the need for greater vigilance of enemies of the state in the future.

Mention of the papal plan leads to a series of exchanges between the characters about faith and national allegiance, exchanges that reveal something of the scene's politics. Significantly, for instance, the Governor responds to the bishop in a tone that exceeds the demands of his dramatic role.

> Under correction, are ye not all Englishmen,
> And longs not Ireland to that kingdome Lords?
> Then may I speak my conscience in the cause,
> Sance scandall to the holy sea of Rome,
> Unhonorable is this expedition,
> And misbeseeming yoo to meddle in.   (lines 445–50)

While it is possible to interpret this question as a polite enquiry, the scene's subject matter suggests otherwise. By having the seemingly impartial outsider raise such an evocative question, the play attempts to silence Irish and Catholic rebellion. The expedition is deemed 'unhonorable', the participants condemned for their involvement. Speaking authoritatively, the Governor also speaks with metadramatic force. Simon Shepherd reminds us that 'we know that the Presenter doubled the Governor of Lisbon in *Alcazar*, which gives more weight to the Governor's "correct" censuring of Stukeley's expedition to win Ireland from the English'.[91] His moral condemnation of the plan is predicated on two interdependent assumptions; firstly, that the visitors are English and should not be involved in an enterprise that undermines their country's interests; and, secondly, that Ireland already 'longs' to England. It is at this point that an ideological position becomes evident in *The Battle of Alcazar*, whereby the Stukeley story serves as a counterpoint to a politically urgent and contentious issue, namely seditious activity in Ireland. In this instance, the play's intervention in contemporary politics appears to reflect the interests of the state: the audience is not only reminded of the fact of English sovereignty over Ireland but the troubling category of Irishness itself is also effaced. This is the political unconscious of the Governor's question, 'Are ye not all Englishmen?'

91 Simon Shepherd, *Marlowe and the politics of the Elizabethan theatre* (Brighton, 1986), p. 66.

It is Stukeley who responds to the Governor first but there is no pragmatic defence of the Irish cause; that is left to the bishop. Instead, Stukeley boasts:

> As we are Englishmen, so we are men,
> And I am Stukley so resolude in all,
> To follow rule, honor, and Emperie,
> Not to be bent so strictly to the place,
> Wherein at first I blew the fire of life,
> But that I may at libertie make choice,
> Of all the continents that bounds the world.   (lines 452–8)

Stukeley's flexible notion of identity formation and sense of a geographic expanse that can accommodate his ambition makes him sound like Tamburlaine, the self-made hero of Marlowe's popular play. For Stukeley, it seems that involvement in the papal scheme is of as much value as being an 'Englishman'. What we are seeing here is how the characterization of Stukeley as would-be-hero intersects with and indeed complicates the play's treatment of contemporary issues. Stukeley's expedient sense of personal loyalty and national allegiance has a dramatic function, preparing the audience for his later, and rather sudden, abandonment of the Irish scheme and decision to join Sebastian. Equally, however, Stukeley's self-interest effects a distancing of him from too close an association with either Catholicism or Ireland. At this point in the play, Stukeley is cast as an imperfect English patriot but certainly not a rebel.

If Stukeley's opportunism reveals the limits of national allegiance, however, it is not left unchecked, with the Irish bishop interjecting:

> Yet captaine give me leave to speake,
> We must affect our countrie as our parents,
> And if at anie time we alianate
> Our love and industrie from doing it honor,
> It must respect the effects and touch the soule,
> Matter of conscience and religion,
> And not desire of rule or benefite.   (lines 466–72)

What is at stake in the Irish bishop's explicit defence of his nation and his faith? Joep Leerssen notes that 'the question of national allegiance is raised (as a moral one), and the ambiguity of the Irish position (whether loyal to England or Catholicism) is hinted at – but nothing more'.[92] However the

---

92 Leerssen, *Mere Irish and fior Ghael* , p. 82.

suggestion of a reluctance to pursue these issues is shortsighted, for when one recalls the context in which the bishop speaks, his defence is surprisingly unequivocal and credible. In contradistinction to Stukeley's selfish opportunism, here characterized as 'desire of rule or benefite', the Irish bishop affirms his belief in a stable sense of identity based on place. There is a pointed irony here that cannot have been lost on the audience: as Claire Jowitt notes, the prelate's 'articulation of orthodox values of national allegiance sits uncomfortably with his Catholic rebelliousness against England's Protestant control of Ireland'.[93] But this contradiction is not left open: although the bishop expresses a sense of loyalty to his nation and faith that is at odds with the political and religious sympathies of the play, it is only momentary; Stukeley's reaction quickly dispels any possibility of the bishop's "cause" being recognized. The English adventurer 'finds in the bishop's arguments only a subject for ribald jest' and mocks him accordingly: 'Well said Bishop, spoken like your selfe | The reverent lordly bishop of saint Asses' (473–4).[94] Considering the bishop's criticism of Stukeley and also the broader implication of that criticism for concepts of national identity, Stukeley's response is unsurprising. Its function is to ridicule the bishop and deflect attention from the seriousness of his objection to Stukeley. One of Stukeley's men, Hercules, participates in making the Irish bishop appear risible:

> The bishop talkes according to his coate,
> And takes not measure of it by his minde,
> You see he hath it made thus large and wide,
> Because he may convert it as he list,
> To anie form may fit the fashion best.　　　　　(lines 475–9)

Here, the play is concerned with discrediting the Irish bishop, with the coat signifying his perceived hypocrisy. In view of the scene's focus on the elision of religious and political recalcitrance, the metaphor of the coat may also be racially allusive, indirectly evoking the Irish mantle. To the English imagination, the mantle was a potent signifier of native Irish alterity and rebellion. In Spenser's *View*, for example, Irenius includes the mantle among the native customs that he believes should be eradicated, noting 'is a fit house for an outlaw, a meet bed for a rebel, and an apt cloke for a theife'.[95] As Spenser's text suggests, the mantle was synonymous with Gaelic deceptiveness and transgression because it appeared to enable the natives to hide themselves, and their

---

93 Jowitt, *Voyage drama*, 76.　94 Duggan, *The stage Irishman*, p. 233. The pun appears to be on 'Saint Asaph' in Wales.　95 Spenser, *A view*, p. 57.

seemingly mischievous deeds, from the English. If the mantle is implied here
– and the emphasis on conversion and transformation bears out this reading
– then this is the only point in the play where the bishop is racialized. While
it is possible that in performance his Irishness would have been registered,
what is especially interesting about this moment is how an Irish stereotype is
combined with an anti-Catholic subtext to single out the bishop as doubly
threatening. The bishop is afforded the right to reply, protesting: 'Captaine you
do me wrong to descant thus, | Upon my coate or double conscience' (lines
480–1). But not even the Governor's 'Tis but in jest' (line 483) can obscure the
fact that it is the bishop who is the primary object of laughter.

Clearly, the dynamic between the characters only partially accounts for this
ridiculing of the Irish bishop in the scene. A further consideration of the
potential connotations this character might have had for a contemporary audience provides insight why the play represents him in a comic mode. As an
Irishman, a Catholic and an advocate of the invasion of Elizabethan Ireland
by a papal force, the Irish prelate gives rise to fears concerning militant
Catholicism that emerged in Ireland during the 1570s. Influenced by the
counter-reformation, rebellions in Ireland increasingly took on a religious
fervour while Irish clerics were closely involved in efforts to secure foreign
backing for such revolts. The Elizabethan state was aware of covert diplomatic
initiatives by Irish clerics to obtain such assistance. Writing to the earl of
Leicester in 1584, Geoffrey Fenton, lord president of Connacht, described the
arrival of 'two Romish priests of this country birth who deliver to the people
seditious rumours of a preparation in Spain for a force of men and shipping
to be sent to Ireland'.[96] The state made efforts to curtail the flow of information within this Catholic subculture; in 1593, for example, it prohibited the
importation of Catholic ballads into Ireland.[97] But there is also evidence that
the state reacted more directly to the manifestation of militant Catholicism.
In 1583, for example, the archbishop of Cashel, Dermot O'Hurley, was found
'bringing letters from Rome'. Walsingham recommended the use of 'torture or
any other severe manner to gain his knowledge of all foreign practices against
Her Majesty'.[98] The bishop's feet were roasted in hot boots, 'a horrible spectacle for the bystanders', as the Irish writer Philip O'Sullivan Beare later wrote.
O'Hurley was subsequently executed in Dublin 'before the people were up', for
fear that they would 'raise a disturbance and rescue their pastor from death'.[99]
There was a similar concern about Archbishop Richard Creagh of Armagh

96 *Calendar of Carew Manuscripts, 1575–1588*, ed. J.S. Brewer and W. Bullen, 2 vols (London, 1868), ii, p. 375.
97 Raymond Gillespie, *Reading Ireland: print, reading and social change in early modern Ireland* (Manchester, 2005), p. 113.
98 Bagwell, *Ireland under the Tudors*, p. 115.   99 Philip O'Sullivan Beare, *Catholic history of Ireland* (1621), quoted in
Irish history from contemporary sources, p.142.

who, on charges of conspiracy with Shane O'Neill, was imprisoned in the Tower from 1567 until 1586, when he was poisoned. The privy council was told Creagh was a 'dangerous man to be among the Irish for the reverence that is by that nation borne unto him and therefore fit to be continued in prison'.[1] The perception of Irish clerics as catalysts of sedition was not specific to the world of government officials and informants. In *The Image of Irelande*, for instance, Derricke perceives a direct relationship between priests and native Irish recalcitrance: 'Friers are the cause | The fountaine and the spring | Of hurleburles in this lande | Of eche unhappy thyng thei cause them to rebell | Against their sovereigne Quene'.[2] As with the case of Creagh, Derricke's text affords a glimpse of the atmosphere of suspicion and fear surrounding Catholicism, an atmosphere that lurks behind the comic jibes at the Irish bishop in the *Battle of Alcazar*. Derricke's text reveals the crux of the matter: Catholic clerics constitute an affront to Elizabeth's sovereignty and authority. Catholic plots and rumours of Spanish intentions were to remain a part of the political landscape of Elizabethan Ireland. At the height of rebellion in Ireland in the late 1590s, the northern chieftains relied on clerics such as Archbishop James O'Hely of Tuam to negotiate with Philip II on their behalf. The long-term outcome of such overtures was the arrival of a Spanish armada at Kinsale in 1601 in support of the national rebellion led by Hugh O'Neill.[3]

Through the character of the Irish bishop, then, Peele mediates a contemporary problem to his audience and works to alleviate the anxieties that it generates. Although clearly different to the punitive tools deployed by the state, the play's comic presentation of the prelate, which is designed to sublimate the connotations of treason that he evokes, is ideologically motivated. On the Elizabethan stage, the Irish bishop who reveals a scheme to conquer Ireland must become the 'bishop of saint Asses'. If Stukeley's joke has the effect of making the prelate appear an ass, it is because he brings to mind a problem as urgent in late 1598 when *The Battle of Alcazar* enjoyed a revival as it had been in 1589 when it was first performed.

With the scheming Irish bishop the object of ribaldry, it seems that audience laughter serves the interests of the play's politics. Revealingly, however, the last laugh is not at the bishop but Stukeley himself who, like a new-Tamburlaine, now elaborates on his desire for greatness:

STUKELEY   There shall no action pase my hand or sword,
            That cannot make a step to gaine a crowne,
            [...]

1 Quoted in Colm Lennon, *An Irish prisoner of conscience of the Tudor era: Archbishop Richard Creagh of Armagh, 1523–1586* (Dublin, 2000), p. 108.   2 Derricke, *Image of Irelande*, p. 59.   3 See McGurk, *Elizabethan conquest*, pp 21–3; Lennon, *Sixteenth century Ireland*, pp 322–4.

No thought have being in my lordly brest,
That workes not everie waie to win a crowne,
Deeds, wordes and thoughts shall all be as kings,
My chiefest companie shall be with kings,
And my deserts shall counterpoise a kings,
Why should not I then looke to be a king?
I am the marques now of Ireland made,
And will be shortly king of Ireland,
King of a mole-hill had I rather be,
Than the richest subiect of a monarchie,
Have it brave minde, and never cease t'aspire,
Before thou raigne sole king of thy desire.   (lines 494–509)

Peele makes comic capital of Stukeley's ambitions and monarchic aspirations, which were a well-established aspect of the Stukeley story. The queen herself had objected to Stukeley's efforts to obtain office in Ireland. 'We find it strange', she wrote, 'that Thomas Stukely should be used in any service in such credit as we perceive he is, considering the general discredit wherein he remaineth, not only in our own realm, but also in other countries.'[4] Furthermore, in a letter to Walsingham, Elizabeth referred to Stukeley's activities in Spain, where she noted that he was pretending to 'be a person of some quality and estimation, and able to do some great things in Ireland, whereas indeed he hath not the value of a marmaduc in land or livelihood'.[5] Like Elizabeth's 'marmaduc', Peele's dramatic incarnation of Stukeley renders him a comic aspirer. Nevertheless, for an audience that has just heard of a plot to invade Ireland, his comical egotism has an undercurrent of sedition. It had been reported in the 1570s that Stukeley would 'divide the land of Ireland' with Fitzmaurice, a rumour that anticipates the accusation levelled at Robert Devereux, second earl of Essex, of collusion with Hugh O'Neill.[6] The play wants its audience to remember Stukeley as merely a would-be-king among kings but, in the process, it allows them to imagine a king of Ireland rather than a queen. As with the later example of Essex, Stukeley's idea of a king of Ireland rather than a queen taps into contemporary fears that Ireland could provide an alternative source of power or even be an alternate court.[7] The related danger of a royal deputy present in Ireland, where the monarch was

4 Cited in Daniel A. Binchy, 'An Irish ambassador at the Spanish court, 1569–1574', *Studies*, 11 (1922), 199–214 at 202.   5 Quoted in Daniel A. Binchy, 'An Irish ambassador at the Spanish court, 1569–1574', *Studies*, 14 (1925), 102–19 at 105.   6 *Cal. Carew MSS, 1575–1588*, p. 308.   7 See Willy Maley, *Salvaging Spenser: colonialism, culture and identity* (London, 1997), p. 99.

conspicuous by her absence, is addressed more fully in Shakespeare's *2 Henry VI* and Marlowe's *Edward II.*

If Stukeley's pretensions generate laughter, laughter that inappropriately reverberates on the queen, it is quickly counterbalanced by the adoption of a more serious tone in the scene at the court of Sebastian. The king tries to persuade Stukeley to 'follow us to fruitful Barbarie' (line 711) and fight with Muly Mahamet in his internecine struggle against Abdilmelec but Stukeley declines: 'with pardon understand, | My selfe and these, whom weather hath inforst, | To lie at roade upon thy gracious coast, | Did bend our coarse and made amaine for Ireland' (lines 718–21). Although inconsistent with the attitude exhibited by him in the previous scene, this newly discovered sense of commitment provides for the introduction of Sebastian's lengthy eulogy to Elizabeth, which is intended to dissuade Stukeley from proceeding with the invasion. As the eulogy foregrounds a number of issues that I have been discussing, I quote it in full:

> For Ireland Stukley, thou mistakst me wonderous much,
> With seven shippes, two pinnaces, and sixe thousand men,
> I tell thee Stukley, they are farre too weake,
> To violate the Queene of Irelands right,
> For Irelands Queene commandeth Englands force,
> Were everie ship ten thousand on the seas,
> Mand with the strength of all the Easterne kings,
> Convaying all the monarchs of the world,
> To invade the Iland where her highnes raignes,
> Twere all in vaine, for heavens and destinies
> Attend and wait upon her Maiestie,
> Sacred, imperiall, and holy is her seate,
> Shining with wisedome, love and mightiness.
> Nature that everie thing imperfect made,
> Fortune that never yet was constant found,
> Time that defaceth everie golden shew,
> Dare not decay, remoue, or be impure,
> Both nature, time and fortune, all agree,
> To bless and serve her roiall maiestie,
> The wallowing Ocean hems her round about,
> Whose raging flouds do swallow up her foes,
> And on the rockes their ships in peeces split,
> And even in Spaine where all the traitors dance,
> And plaie themselves upon a funny daie,

Securely gard the west part of her Isle,
The South the narrow Britaine sea begirts,
Where [N]eptune sits in triumph, to direct
Their course to hell that aime at her disgrace,
The Germaine seas alongst the East to run,
Where [V]enus banquets all her water Nymphs,
That with her beautie glansing on the waves,
Disdaines the checke of faire Proserpina,
Advise thee then proud Stukley ere thou passe,
To wrong the wonder of the highest God,
Sith danger, death and hell doth follow thee,
Thee and them all that seek to danger her.
If honor be the marke wherat thou aimst,
Then follow me in holy christian warres,
And leave to seeke thy Countries overthrow.   (lines 723–62)

As a conventional eulogy to Elizabeth, an exercise in nation building, a post-Armada celebration and a warning against sedition, this set piece works on various levels, for it is the most obviously topical and ideological aspect of the play.[8] The speech serves a more specific purpose, namely to redress the uncertainties surrounding sovereignty over Ireland raised in the previous scene. Where that scene had alluded to the invasion of Ireland and Stukeley's kingly ambitions, this speech consistently strives to reassert Elizabeth's authority over her Irish kingdom. In other words, the play works to control the reception of its topical elements. The weakness of Stukeley's force is juxtaposed with the might of Elizabeth's in order to illustrate the futility of his expedition in the face of her divinely anointed sovereignty and innate strength. Through the tautological phrasing – 'Queene of Ireland', 'Irelands Queene' – Elizabeth's sovereignty over Ireland, which had been unsettled in the earlier scene, is now re-inscribed, while the paralleling of 'Irelands queen' with 'Englands force' shows that her sovereignty is bolstered by military might. Both audiences, that is Stukeley himself and the theatre audience, are reminded precisely what is at stake in claims about a 'king of Ireland'.

Elizabeth's power is further conveyed when Sebastian refers to the inability of foreign kings to 'invade the Iland where her highness raignes', a contention that acts as a riposte to the Irish bishop's assertion that the papal force could easily have conquered Ireland. Revealingly, it is unclear whether 'Iland' refers to

8 There are echoes of this speech in Peele's *Anglorum Feriae, England's Holidays* (1595). See *Works of George Peele*, ed. A.H. Bullen (London, 1888), pp 339–55.

Ireland or England. Perhaps the use of the geographic term to denote the two kingdoms is meant to illustrate how schemes for the invasion of Ireland were perceived as a threat to England too. Alternatively, it might be intended to elide the differences between Ireland and England. As the encomium proceeds, it becomes apparent that the latter is the case. The queen's body functions as a synecdoche for geographic boundaries, which in turn signify the nation. By imagining Elizabeth as an impenetrable geographical space protected from her enemies by the various elements, the distance between Ireland and England is effaced. They become 'the Iland' or 'her Isle'. The elision has the effect of undermining the political and geographic separateness of Ireland that the Irish bishop had gestured towards earlier. The idea of Elizabeth's kingdom as a cohesive, national entity is sustained by the image of foreign ships wrecked on rocks which, in recalling the recent failure of the Armada, persuades the audience to believe Sebastian's boasts concerning Elizabethan inviolability. The Armada allusion functions here as a convenient and comforting precedent, a reassurance that attempts like Stukeley's will meet a similar fate. Thus, one Catholic plot is used to suggest the failure of another. In the peroration, the direct advice to Stukeley, which echoes the Governor's condemnation of the plan in the earlier scene, becomes a general warning to recalcitrant subjects.

Sebastian's speech is, according to Braunmuller, indicative of Peele's stylistic tendency to allow 'stiff formality and heavily ritualized scenes substitute for conflict among characters'. As Braunmuller points out, 'most debates or hints of debate' in the play 'quickly become occasions for exhortation'.[9] Certainly, the speech seems to function as a powerful counterbalance to the subversive arguments of the earlier scene, with the conflicting and dissenting voices of the Irish bishop and Stukeley replaced by a single authoritative voice. However, the fact that the voice of authority is Sebastian's is problematic because the king who eulogizes Elizabeth and mocks the Spanish is also an ally of the Moor, and a potential ally of Elizabeth's old rival, Philip of Spain. As Simon Shepherd observes of Sebastian, 'the language of Christian honour is made ambivalent by his actions: the eulogist of Elizabeth is the same fictional character who makes mistaken alliances'.[10] The play's hyperbolic paean may well attest to Elizabeth's absolute control over Ireland but the dubious loyalties of the eulogist partially undermine its credibility and force; not even the play's most obviously ideologically determined moment is without its contradictions or ambiguities.

Apart from the difficulty with the eulogist, the eulogy itself is ineffectual, as evidenced by Stukeley's disregard for Sebastian's admonitions and entreaties:

9 Braunmuller, *George Peele*, p. 82.   10 Shepherd, *Marlowe*, p. 146.

'Rather my Lord, let me admire these wordes, | Than answere to your firme objections' (763–4). In quintessential fashion, Stukeley proves untroubled by 'firm objections' concerning allegiance to crown and country, being more concerned with achieving personal honour. Stukeley does, however, display some sense of duty, albeit short-lived, to his co-conspirators and the papal scheme, telling Sebastian that his participation is contingent on their approval (lines 765–9). The treatment of Stukeley's decision to pursue an African adventure has been regarded as unconvincing. John Yoklavich writes that 'there is little dramatic motivation for Sebastian's "command" or for Stukley's rather abrupt acceptance'.[11] But Peele has drawn Stukeley in such a way as to make his sudden defection from the Irish scheme seem characteristic; the audience always anticipated that the ambitious English adventurer would change sides abruptly. Moreover, in the scene between Sebastian and Stukeley, Peele does draw attention to the consequences of Stukeley's decision by incorporating the marginal voices of Stukeley's associates – Jonas, Hercules and the Irish bishop, who now makes his last appearance:

SEBASTIAN	Tell me Lord Bishop, Captaines tell me all, Are you content to leave this enterprise, Against your countrie and your countrie men, To aide Mahamet king of Barbarie?
BISHOP	To aide Mahamet king of Barbarie, Tis gainst our vowes great king of Portugall.
SEBASTIAN	Then Captaines what saie you?
JONAS	I saie my Lord as the Bishop said, We may not turne from conquering Ireland.
HERCULES	Our countrie and our country-men will condemne Us worthie of death, if we neglect our vowes.

(lines 770–81)

In an exchange indicating that Sebastian's set piece fails in its extra-dramatic ideological objective of containing the Irish problem, the men display a firm resolve to continue with the invasion scheme. Neither Sebastian's glorification of Elizabeth nor the catalogue of her defences has been an effective deterrent for them.[12] Their refusal to re-direct the papal force from 'conquering Ireland'

---

11 Yoklavich (ed.), *Battle of Alcazar*, p. 268.   12 For the argument that this scene evokes a code of honour based on a masculine system of values that highlights the limits of queenly, see Jowitt, *Voyage drama and gender politics*, pp 75–9.

reactivates the challenge to Elizabethan sovereignty over Ireland. Sebastian reminds the men that because they have accidentally landed at Lisbon, they are 'captives to our roiall will' (line 785), a point Jonas is prepared to concede. But Jonas also reiterates their commitment to the plan: 'But if you make us voluntarie men | Our course is then direct for Ireland' (lines 790–1). It is at this point that Sebastian asserts his authority over the others: 'That course will we direct for Barbary' (line 790). Where the eulogy attempted to imaginatively remove the threat of invasion, here it is quite literally removed. The banishment of the Irish problem is underscored by Stukeley, who takes the opportunity to clarify where his loyalties lie: 'Saint George for England, and Ireland nowe adue, | For here Tom Stukley shapes his course anue' (lines 793–4). The forced redirection of Stukeley and his cohorts not only concludes one phase of his career but also marks the play's effort to finally conclude discussion of Ireland, with the rhyming couplet conveying a sense of finality. The sense of closure is compounded by the recuperation of Stukeley as a specifically English adventurer, as suggested by his invocation of England's patron saint and the sudden outburst of national pride that it implies. This 'Englishing' of Stukeley has the effect of distancing him from any previous association with Irish and Catholic transgression. His decision to take a new course might be said, therefore, to function metadramatically, reflecting the play's own change of direction away from the subject of Ireland. So just as the character of Stukeley introduces Ireland, he now brings that subject to a close.

The account of Stukeley in *The Battle of Alcazar* is just one version of the popular hero's life. For instance, an earlier account, a pamphlet on Stukeley published in 1579, provides a different assessment of his intentions than the play's. While the text resembles the play in noting that Stukeley joined Sebastian, it adds: 'hopinge by these meanes, the more easyer to bring to passe his aforesaude pretended enterprise and purpose in Ireland'. This comment intimates that for Stukeley, Alcazar did not mean the end of the Irish scheme, as the play would have it, but a step towards its realization.[13] The claim in the 1579 pamphlet appears to have formed part of the tradition surrounding Stukeley's life. One contemporary noted 'it seems that the said Marquis chews, as the saying goes, with two pairs of jaws, and is minded to serve his Majesty in this enterprise and afterwards to make the other'.[14] Another remarked that Stukeley 'took his African in order to [aid] his Irish design; such [was] his

---

1 3 *Newe news contayning a shorte rehersall of the late enterprise of certain fugytiue rebelles: fyrst pretended by Captaine Stukeley*, cited in Prouty (ed.), *Dramatic works of George Peele*, pp 267–8.   **14** *Calendar of state papers, Rome, 1572–1578*, ed. J.M. Rigg (London, 1926), p. 430.

confidence of conquest, that his break-fast on the Turks would the better enable him to dine on the English in Ireland'.[15] Corroborating these reports is a letter in May 1578 from Philip Sega, the bishop of Ripa (in Italy) to Cardinal Ptolemo Galli of Como, revealing how Sebastian had promised Stukeley 'all the aid that he could lend him, to despatch him on his Irish campaign' in return for the Englishman's participation in the war.[16] If this version of Stukeley's role in the battle of Alcazar was available to Peele – and, considering the detailed portrayal of the life, it seems likely that it was – then its omission is rather curious. Clearly, a degree of caution is always necessary when attributing intention to a playwright. But with this play, where Stukeley's life is dramatized in accordance with the demands of topical politics and Elizabethan ideology, it is tempting to speculate about intended meaning. Thus, the play's containment of the Irish problem requires the suppression of the more subversive and insidious aspects of Stukeley's plans.

The play's presentation of the circumstances surrounding Stukeley's death certainly supports this reading. In the penultimate scene, Hercules and Jonas, two of his co-conspirators in the papal scheme, take revenge on Stukeley for abandoning the Irish expedition:

> Stand traitor, stand ambitious English-man
> Proud Stukley stand, and stirre not ere thou die,
> Thy forwardnes to follow wrongfull armes,
> And leave our famous expedition earst,
> Intended by his holynes for Ireland,
> Fouly hath here betraide, and tide us all
> To ruthlesse furie of our heathen foe,
> For which as we are sure to die,
> Tho shalt paie satisfaction with thy bloud.   (lines 1430–9)

Although the historical Stukeley died in this manner, the reference to the murder is not out of concern for verisimilitude. The subtext of the character's articulation of revenge is the play's silent re-writing of history. The play makes its audience believe that the death of Stukeley and his disgruntled followers among 'heathen foe' means the end of Catholic plotting, thus side-stepping the fact that some of the papal force succeeded in their original objective, landing in Ireland in 1579 as part of the Fitzmaurice rebellion. The worrying precedent of foreign invasion is effaced in order to assuage present and, indeed,

15 Quoted in *Dramatic and poetical works of Robert Greene and George Peele*, ed. Alexander Dyce (London, 1861), p. 418.
16 Cited in Dyce (ed.), *Dramatic and poetical works of Robert Greene and George Peele*, p. 427.

future anxieties. Moreover, while the play creates the impression that the papal scheme ended in failure, a revealing slip occurs later in the text. In Stukeley's final soliloquy, a rehearsal of his adventures delivered just before he dies, he mentions: 'Then was I made Leiftennant Generall | Of those small forces that for Ireland went' (line 1484–5). The allusion to Ireland within Stukeley's autobiographical narrative is suggestive of the play's engagement with the topical subject of Ireland more generally. Through Stukeley, the play raises the spectre of a foreign invasion of Elizabeth's kingdom and then attempts to provide ways of imagining this threat as either an inevitable failure or simply impossible. But in order to allay anxieties and contain the Irish problem, it must re-introduce and hence remind the audience of the plan, thus foregrounding and making present what had previously been made to appear distant and in the past. This circular pattern, whereby the play's efforts to disengage with the subject of Ireland prove counter-productive, registers the difficulty of resolving the Irish problem. On a symbolic level, then, the so-called 'Stukeley subplot' might be more accurately thought of as the Irish subplot, revealing how *The Battle of Alcazar* struggles to control its contemporary moment.[17]

There are important theatrical, dramatic and ideological differences between *The Misfortunes of Arthur* and *The Battle of Alcazar* but, as I have demonstrated, the plays are shaped by a common historical and cultural moment and, when analysed in terms of their representation of Ireland, reveal some suggestive similarities. Reading contextually, it is apparent that although Ireland may be somewhat marginal to the general thematic concerns of the plays, it nonetheless constitutes a significant presence. What is striking about both plays is their direct and active response to the Irish problem: even the remote Arthurian past of *The Misfortunes of Arthur* produces a direct topical allegory and, like Peele's play, firmly establishes Ireland as part of the much wider threat posed by Catholicism. Simultaneously both a local problem and, as the potential location and objective of Catholic plots, also a more general problem, Ireland is positioned as doubly threatening in the plays. It is with Ireland, both plays insinuate, that Elizabethan sovereignty comes undone. In view of the growing anxieties about the state of Ireland in the 1580s, anxieties exacerbated by the possibility of foreign intervention there, this dimension of the plays should not be underestimated. Of course, both plays work to allay such topical anxieties, employing strategies of containment that, as we have seen, occasionally suggest an ideological position in the text. But *The Misfortunes of Arthur* and *The Battle of Alcazar* do not simply replicate the interests of the

17 Yoklavich (ed.), *The Battle of Alcazar*, p. 247.

Elizabethan state; in both texts, there are moments of potential indeterminacy that preclude a coherent political stance on the Irish problem. In broad terms then, the plays remind us of the complex relationship between the drama and ideology. More specifically, as discursive interventions in the heterogeneous debate about Ireland, they reveal how in the late 1580s Ireland did constitute a subject and subtext in the drama. Much earlier than has been previously thought, therefore, the stage provided an important space where the Elizabethan matter of Ireland could be addressed.

CHAPTER TWO

'Wand'ring with the Antipodes'

Spatial anxieties, the Irish wars and Elizabethan drama

English representations of Ireland in the early modern period frequently centred on the figure of the wild Irishman, that most enduring of stereotypes. Yet, throughout the period, perceptions of Ireland also reveal a concern with landscape and space. One could even go so far as to suggest that perceptions of Ireland were spatially focused. For contemporaries there was a close correlation between the topographical characteristics of the Irish landscape and native intractability. To the Elizabethan mind in particular, Ireland was a place full of wild, hidden and dangerous spaces, a treacherous terrain that seemed as difficult to traverse and control as it did to travel to. In one sense, it was the very antithesis of the ordered space of the English garden-state, the garden being a common image, as in Shakespeare's *Richard II*, for an idyllic English nation. Despite Ireland's geographical proximity to England, it was viewed as inaccessible and distant, the imagined physical distance registering perceived cultural and ethnic difference. Writing in the early 1600s, Fynes Moryson noted the dangers of travelling to Ireland because the coast was covered in mists whereas the English coast was 'commonly clear'.[1] The comparison of the two coastlines can be considered an example of what John Gillies has described as 'poetic geography'; that is 'any geography, which differentiates between an us and a them'.[2] This is less a geographic knowledge than a conception of identity based on a spatial awareness implicitly informed by the classical geographic relationship of the 'oikumene' (meaning house or world) to what lies beyond it or outside it, a relationship of 'divorce and difference'.[3] The implicit, conceptual opposition between civil, inhabited spaces and a wilderness or wasteland that Gillies refers to, underpins figurations of Irish space in a range of texts from the period, including plays performed on the public stage. Accordingly, references to bogs, the Pale being overrun, travel across the Irish sea, or the representation of Ireland as an offstage space, all of which occur in plays by Shakespeare and his contemporaries, begin to take on a much greater significance. Geraldo de Sousa's description of concepts of

---

1 Fynes Moryson, 'A description of Ireland' in *Ireland under Elizabeth and James I*, ed. Henry Morley (London, 1890), p. 419. Moryson was secretary to Lord Mountjoy (who succeeded Essex as lord deputy of Ireland in 1600) and had eyewitness experience of the Irish wars. 2 John Gillies, *Shakespeare and the geography of difference* (Cambridge, 1994), pp 6–7. 3 Gillies, *Shakespeare and the geography*, p. 8.

space in Shakespeare's plays is especially useful here. He notes how 'the environment becomes allegorical, functioning as a place of projections for the culture's fears, prejudices, desires, and textual and sexual fantasies'.[4] With De Sousa's observation in mind, I argue that spatial representations of Ireland in the drama not only have deep cultural resonances but also function ideologically. This chapter analyses the representation of Ireland as a dramatic and figurative space in three history plays from the 1590s that reveal the shaping influence of their Irish contexts: Shakespeare's *2 Henry VI* (1590–1) and *Richard II* (1595) and Marlowe's *Edward II* (1592). In each of these plays, Ireland's status as an offstage world confers a distance on Irish space that makes it appear especially threatening precisely because it seems beyond control. Approaching the plays in chronological order, the emphasis here is on the interconnections between their figuration of Irish space, English identity and contemporary events in Ireland.

In order to consider how Irish space can be said to function ideologically in the drama, it is first necessary to consider some of the implicit assumptions about Irish space and landscape that were current in the period. A good illustration of how widespread assumptions about Irish space were is the well known scene from Shakespeare's *Comedy of Errors* (1591) in which Dromio and Antipholus of Syracuse imagine Nell's body as a globe and allocate countries to its various parts. It is with Ireland that they begin their geographic anatomy:

DROMIO   She is spherical, like a globe. I could find out countries in
                her.

ANTIPHOLUS   In what part of her body stands Ireland?

DROMIO   Marry, sir, in her buttocks. I found it out by the bogs.
                                                                    (III.ii.116–21)

The episode concludes with the Netherlands – 'O, Sir, I did not look so low' (III.ii.144) – but in order to arrive at this punning climax, a series of ethnographic assumptions and associations about Ireland are made. Shakespeare is relying on his audience associating Ireland with bogs, an association that must have been almost proverbial, given its presence in other plays that make no other mention of Ireland. In Jonson's *Every Man out of his Humor* (1599), for instance, Carlo Buffone remarks 'These be our nimble-spirited Catso's, that ha' their evasions at pleasure, will run over a bog like your wild Irish: no sooner started, but they'le leape from one thing to another, like a squirrel'.[5] Similarly, in the anonymous *Blurt Master Constable* (1601), Hippolito says to Lazarillo, a

4 Geraldo U. de Sousa, *Shakespeare's cross-cultural encounters* (London, 1999), p. 3.   5 *Ben Jonson*, ed. C.H. Hereford and Evelyn Simpson, 11 vols (Oxford, 1927), iii, p. 460, II.i.20–2.

Spaniard, 'There be many of your countrymen in Ireland Signior, travaile to them' to which he replies, 'No, I will fall no more into bogges'.[6] The association of Ireland with bogs had become naturalized in the minds of Elizabethans.

Although only marginal to the plays, such allusions would have resonated with a contemporary audience in ways that modern editorial glosses are unable adequately to convey. It is possible, however, to achieve a sense of that contemporary resonance by situating these references alongside a topographical description of Ireland, such as that contained in Thomas Gainsford's *Glory of England*. As a soldier serving with lord deputy Mountjoy at the height of the Nine Years War, Gainsford inevitably wrote from a military perspective, but his focus on the bogs as strategic space also reveals their deeper meaning:

> The country and kingdome of Ireland is generallly for naturall aire, and commoditie of blessings, sufficient to satisfie a covetous, or curious appetite: but withall divided into such fastnes of mountaine, bogg, and wood, that it hath emboldened the inhabitants to presume an hereditary securitie, as if disobedience had a protection. For the mountaines denie any cariages, but by great industry and strength of men (so have we drawne the canon over the deepest boggs, and stoniest hills) and the passages are every way dangerous both for unfirmnes of ground, and the lurking rebell, who will plashe downe whole trees over the paces and so intricately winde them, or laye them, that they shall be a strong barracado, and then lurke in ambush amongst the standing wood, playing upon all commers, as they intend to goe along. On the bogg they likewise presume with a naked celeritie to come as neere our foote and horse, as is possible, and then flie off againe, knowing we cannot, or indeed dare not follow them: and thus they serve us in the narrow entrances into their glins, and stony paths, or if you will dangerous quagmires of their mountaines, where a 100 shot shall rebate the hasty approach of 500; and a few muskets [...] well placed, will stagger a pretty Armie, not aquainted with the terror, or unpreventing mischeefe.[7]

Outlining the tactical advantage possessed by the native Irish, Gainsford imagines Irish space – or, more precisely, what Bernhard Klein describes as 'space signified as Irish' – as providing natural cover for their sinister activities, and

6 *Blurt Master Constable, or, The Spaniards night-walke* (London, 1602), line 1492.   7 Thomas Gainsford, *The glory of England* (1618) cited in Andrew Hadfield and John McVeagh (eds), *Strangers to that land: British perceptions of Ireland from the Reformation to the Famine* (Gerrards Cross, 1994), pp 69–70.

as something that can be carefully contrived by the Irish to confuse and entrap the English.[8] Gainsford's insistence on Elizabethan military strength (the English canon has been brought over the seemingly intractable landscape) does little to offset the anxiety about the dangers involved in straying into Irish space. This space is imagined as doubly threatening, as both a hostile terrain that poses several logistical difficulties for the English, and a natural environment for the 'lurking rebell', the place where Irish resistance is encountered. The wonderfully suggestive phrase hints at the implied meaning or undertone of the bog imagery noted earlier in the plays. Consequently, what initially appeared to be little more than superficial references to bogs intended for comic effect can in fact be seen to participate in a broader conception of Irish space. To Dromio and Antipholus, equating Ireland with bodily functions, Irish space is dark and impure; to Carlo it is synonymous with the mobility of the wild Irish; and to Lazarillo, it is a potential trap.

The natural affinity that the indigenous population appears to possess with the Irish landscape is also addressed in Spenser's *View*, when Eudoxus' characteristically naïve inquiry as to why the Irish rebel is not pursued, elicits a lengthy response from Irenius:

> It is well known that he is a flying enemie, hiding himselfe in woodes and bogges, from whence he will not draw forth, but into some straight passage or perillous foord, where he knowes the army must needes passe, there will he lye in waite, and, if hee find advantage fit, will dangerously hazard the troubled souldiour. Therefore to seeke him out that still flitteth, and follow him that can hardly bee found, were vain and bootlesse, but I would devide my men in garrison upon his countrey, in such places as I should think might most annoy him.[9]

Spenser's text attaches great importance to the mobility Irish space affords the rebels, and despite Irenius' assurance that garrisons will be established – part of his plan for the conquest of Ireland – he is clearly troubled by the alien landscape. As Bruce McLeod notes of *A View*, 'particular attention has to be paid by the colonizer to the geographical points that have strategic value (outside the Pale) or are removed from immediate colonization; space such as woods, bogs, hills, river crossings and "blind" routes that discount English army tactics and knowledge are of greatest danger'.[10] The concern expressed here, however, exceeds that of military strategy: the spatial phrase 'follow him

that can hardly bee found' hints at the elusiveness of the Irish and the inability
of the English to negotiate and control Irish space.

Describing a landscape that seems physically hostile, Gainsford and
Spenser register anxieties about the perceived cultural threat it poses. This is a
crucial point for, as McLeod argues, 'to be in a foreign landscape and see no
sign of danger is to misread that space. An unfamiliar landscape is by definition threatening. It should bear the marks of the erasure of difference'.[11] Both
Gainsford and Spenser read Irish space closely and, in the process, attempt to
erase the difference that Irish landscape stubbornly refuses to give up.
Similarly, in Derricke's *Image of Irelande*, the author invites the vilified kern 'who
haunt the wood' to exchange their nomadic existence for the queen's mercy and
become good subjects, a process which involves a spatial reconfiguration: 'In
stead of woodes, then houses you maie use | In stead of bogges, the Cities at
your will'.[12] Spenser shares Derricke's belief that the alteration of native space
is a prerequisite to reform. Thus, included among Irenius' measures to effect
change is the clearing of 'waste wild places':

> And first I wish that order were taken for the cutting and opening of
> all places through the woods, so that a wide way of the space of 100.
> yards might be layde open in every of them for the safety of travellers,
> which use often in such perillous places to be robbed, and sometimes
> murdered [...] Also that in all straights and narrow passages, as
> between 2 boggs, or through any deepe foord, or under mountaine
> side, there should be some little fortilage, or wooden castle set, which
> should keepe and command that straight, wherby any rebells that
> should come into the country might be stopped that way, or passe
> with great perill.[13]

These plans illustrate how anxieties about Irish space were matched by a desire
to disclose hidden spaces, then enclose them; to survey, and then map; in
short, to claim possession of the land. The clearing of the woods and bogs is,
then, simultaneously literal and metaphorical: 'layde open' to an English view,
Ireland will be transformed into an ordered space resembling England itself.
Re-drawn in this way, Irish space could be imagined as a fertile, abundant and
readily available extension of England. Sir Thomas Smith's proposal for a
plantation in Co. Down, for instance, extols the benefits of settlement in
Ireland, highlighting the natural resources afforded by the topography of
Ireland. Addressing potential planters, the tract declares: 'Let us therefore, use
the persuasions which Moses used to Israel, [...] and tell them that they shall

11 McLeod, *Geography of empire*, p. 57.   12 Derricke, *Image of Irelande*, p. 90.   13 Spenser, *A view*, p. 156.

go to possess a land that floweth with milk and honey'.[14] Through Smith's colonial venture, here presented as a Christianising mission involving the elect, the 'waste wild places' of Ireland will be cultivated and turned to profit. A similar reconstitution of Irish space is envisaged in *A View*, where Irenius advocates the construction of bridges and gatehouses at river crossings and fences at highways. As Hooper writes, Spenser saw such plans as 'offering the best protection from the native Irish, both in militaristic and miscegenistic terms'.[15] This point can be extended to perceptions of Irish space more generally. For if, as Bruce McLeod argues, the 'way space is regulated and reproduced is central to a hegemonic and expansionist culture', allowing that culture to gain 'control over opposition real or imagined', then control over Irish space becomes a question of control over Ireland and its indigenous inhabitants.[16] To transform the landscape was to reform the country.

As this brief overview of early modern constructions of the Irish landscape suggests, such representations were not merely topographical but also conceptual and ideological. There is a risk of reinforcing a rigid colonial binary whereby Ireland is positioned as the Other against which Englishness is defined and asserted. Clearly, there is always some sense in which Ireland is a defining space and that representations of it are always in some sense about English identity. Declan Kiberd's provocative contention that 'if Ireland had never existed, the English would have invented it' is therefore relevant in this context.[17] But the spaces that Spenser and his contemporaries describe might be more accurately regarded as examples of what Mary Louise Pratt calls 'contact zones'; that is, 'social spaces where disparate cultures meet, clash, and grapple with each other, often in highly asymmetrical relations of domination and subordination'.[18] Pratt's emphasis on the unstable relations of power within encounters between cultures reminds us how the recurring references to unregulated spaces and broken borders in early modern representations of Ireland constitute moments of tension and reversal, where English hegemony proves vulnerable. I use the term 'spatial anxieties' here to encapsulate these moments in texts, moments when reference to Irish space crystallizes contemporary English fears about Gaelic Irish society and, more fundamentally, corresponding insecurities about English identity.[19]

---

14 Sir Thomas Smith, 'Tract on the colonisation of the Ards in the County of Down' (1572) quoted in *Irish history from contemporary sources*, p. 255. For a similar view of Ireland as a potential land of abundance and opportunity, see Robert Payne, 'A brief description of Ireland' (1590) in *Tracts relating to Ireland*, ed. Aguilia Smith, 2 vols (Dublin, 1841), i, pp 1–165. Payne notes, for example, that while the Irish woods serve as 'a covert unto rebelles and theeves' they also have a commercial value, supplying the requirements of ship and house building (p. 160). 15 Glenn Hooper, 'Writing and landscape in early modern Ireland', *Literature and History*, 5 (1996), 1–18 at 14. 16 McLeod, *Geography of empire*, p. 13; p. 6. 17 Declan Kiberd, *Inventing Ireland: the literature of the modern nation* (London, 1995), p. 9. 18 Mary Louise Pratt, *Imperial eyes: travel writing and transculturation* (London, 1992), p. 3. 19 I borrow the phrase from Bernhard Klein, who uses it with specific reference to Spenser's *Faerie Queene*; see

'OVERRUN ALL YOUR ENGLISH PALE': REBELLION
FROM THE MARGINS IN 2 *HENRY VI*

The text of Shakespeare's 2 *Henry VI* includes a unique stage direction: 'Enter York and his army of Irish, with drums and colours.' As the only occasion in Renaissance drama where the Irish are collectively staged, this is an extraordinary moment. It is all the more striking because York is newly arrived from Ireland, an offstage location in the play, and is using an army to realize his objective: 'From Ireland thus comes York to claim his right, | And pluck the crown from feeble Henry's head' (V.i.1–2). A dramatic opening to the final act, it is one the play has been moving towards. As early as the first act, York states his belief that he is the rightful king and the play foregrounds the subsequent pattern of civil strife that is the War of the Roses. This is just one example of English self-ruin under Henry VI, who fails to regain France and proves incapable of withstanding powerful factions. The arrival of an army 'so near the court' (V.i.22) is symbolic of the king's weakness and vulnerability. But in marking the culmination of York's plot to seize power, a plot whose success centres on Cade and Ireland, the 'army of Irish' also confirms a fear that the play has gestured towards throughout: danger emanates from Irish space. At issue here are questions of spatial control that capture figuratively English anxieties about securing political hegemony in Ireland in the 1590s. On the one hand, York's strategic deployment of his Irish forces suggests a larger confidence in an 'an English ability to penetrate, master, marshall, and control' Ireland.[20] On the other, its suggests the possibility of 'a reversed conquest', or 'the contamination of England by the material and semiotic traces of Irishness'; in this regard, the play demonstrates the negative consequences of involvement in a territory geographically marginal to the centre of power.[21] As these divergent viewpoints suggest, Ireland in 2 *Henry VI* is much more than the locus of York's aristocratic rebellion against the king. Significantly, the play imagines Ireland simultaneously as a source of strength to Englishmen like York and also 'a source of disaster, war and confusion'.[22] The sense in which the play allows both meanings to come into view has interesting implications for its politics.

Any discussion of textual indeterminacy in the play must, however, take into account alternate versions of the play, which can throw light on the way in which the topical subject of Ireland was broached. Like many of Shakespeare's plays, 2 *Henry VI* exists in two texts: the 1623 folio and also the

---

his *Maps and the writing of space*, p. 74.   **20** Murphy, 'Shakespeare's Irish history', p. 51 (1996), 38–59 at 44.   **21** Highley, *Shakespeare, Spenser*, p. 52.   **22** Klein, *Maps and the writing of space*, p. 120.

quarto text or *The First Part of the contention betwixt the two famous Houses of Yorke and Lancaster* (1594), which is generally regarded as a memorial reconstruction of the former. Along with a number of other differences, these texts contain subtle, though significant, variations in their representation of Ireland. Janet Clare attributes these variations to official censorship, citing the excision of Irish material from the second edition of Holinshed's *Chronicles* as evidence of a more general sensitivity towards discussion of Irish affairs that extended to the play; the quarto, she argues, represents a censored text.[23] Moreover, in view of recent bibliographic work on Shakespeare's plays, it is no longer acceptable to privilege one text over another in this way. Paul Werstine and Laurie Maguire have argued for a move away from the hierarchical separation of textual variants into folio and 'bad quartos' – a process that, as Werstine notes, involved a 'presumption of versional integrity' – towards an appreciation of the 'shifting, merging and diverging identities of these multiple texts'.[24] In what follows, I will argue that although Ireland is figured as an offstage space in both texts, they nonetheless provide alternate perspectives on its effect on the English 'centre'.

One of the ways that a sense of Ireland as an offstage and distant space is achieved and maintained is through the dramatic device of the messenger. This device is often used to convey details of plot or introduce a recently completed event which, for reasons of narrative pace, is not represented on stage. Paradoxically, as it is the messenger who connects the offstage world with events onstage, the device can have the effect of disrupting that sense of distance. This is the case in the folio text of the play, where following a discussion between the queen and her supporters about the best strategy to eliminate the duke of Gloucester, the king's ally, a messenger arrives with a report of rebellion in Ireland:

> POST   Great Lord, from Ireland am I come amain,
> To signify that rebels there are up,
> And put the Englishmen unto the sword.
> Send succours, lords, and stop the rage betime,
> Before the wound do grow uncurable;
> For, being green, there is great hope of help.
>
> (III.i.282–7)

---

23 Clare, *'Art made tongue-tied by authority'*, pp 60–3. 24 Quoted in Patricia Parker, *Shakespeare from the margins: language, culture, context* (Chicago, 1996), p. 327, n. 96. For a thorough revision of the 'bad' quarto theory, see Laurie E. Maguire, *Shakespearean suspect texts: the bad quartos and their contexts* (Cambridge, 1996). Maguire defends memorial reconstruction, arguing that 'in seeking evidence of a faulty memory we should perhaps view it not as memorial error but as memorial variation' (p. 148).

With this news positioning Ireland a close, urgent and present problem, any sense that events there are marginal or unimportant are quickly dispelled. The sense of urgency is conveyed through the use of 'from' – a detail that, as Alan Dessen points out, is often used in plays to denote a recently completed event – and also 'amain', as in swiftly or aloud.[25] The report from Ireland is meant to command the full attention of all the characters present. In a direct and succinct manner, the messenger informs the councillors that Englishmen are being killed in Ireland and urges them to act quickly before the 'rage' spreads. It is the metaphor of the body politic, however, that most clearly conveys the seriousness of this situation, suggestively hinting at the possibility that, if ignored, the Irish wound will endanger the entire English body. Indirectly, therefore, the messenger's report prefigures the arrival in England of York and his Irish army later on in the play. Anxiety about events in Ireland reverberating in England further manifests itself in the cardinal's reaction to the news: 'A breach that craves a quick expedient stop!' (III.i.288). The use of 'breach' here, in the sense of a 'space between the several parts of a solid body parted by violence' or a breakage or injury to the body, continues the corporeal imagery of the report.[26] Its additional meaning of a 'gap in a fortification' is also invoked here, the implication being that Englishmen are dying in Ireland because of the inadequacy of English defences and borders.[27] For 'breach', as Patricia Parker has shown, has the sense in Shakespeare of 'leaky' borders and boundaries, 'of being invaded or breached from behind'. It thus conveys 'the vulnerability of national boundaries to incursions' from the perceived margins.[28] With the added signification of the cardinal's 'breach', it becomes apparent just how insistent 2 Henry VI is about the possibility of events in Ireland spilling over into England.

The play's reference to events in Ireland can be understood in context of the War of the Roses, which as Spenser and others recognized, marked a turning point for English settlement in Ireland. In A View, Irenius explains the significance of this period, noting how areas in Ireland that 'had become planted with English, were shortly displanted and lost'.[29] At issue here is a broader point about reading Ireland in Shakespeare. Willy Maley has recently cautioned against tendencies 'to see Shakespeare's histories as driven by the urgency of the Nine Years War rather than informed by four hundred years of Anglo-Irish history'.[30] Maley's 'long view' is necessary but we must not deny

---

25 Alan C. Dessen, *Recovering Shakespeare's theatrical vocabulary* (Cambridge, 1999), p. 134.   26 Alexander Schmidt, *Shakespeare Lexicon*, 2 vols (London, 1968), i, p. 139. *OED*, p. 503.   27 Schmidt, *Shakespeare Lexicon*, p. 139.   28 Parker, *Shakespeare from the margins*, p. 42; p. 168.   29 Spenser, *A view*, p. 23.   30 Willy Maley, 'The Irish text and subtext of Shakespeare's English histories' in Richard Dutton and Jean E. Howard (eds), *A companion to Shakespeare's works*, ii: *the histories* (Oxford, 2003), p. 99.

how the play's allusion to reversal in Ireland takes on an urgency and force that is bound up with its own historical moment.

Topically charged anxieties about the violation of boundaries, both real and imagined, also surface in the quarto text, which contains a fuller version of the folio report:

Enter a Messenger

QUEENE   How now sirrha, what newes?

MESSENGER   Madame I bring you news from Ireland,
                     The wilde Onele my lords, is up in Armes
                     With troupes of Irish Kernes that uncontrold
                     Doth plant themselves within the English pale
                     And burnes and spoiles the Country as they goe.[31]

The difference in detail and tone between the news from Ireland in the quarto and that in the folio is immediately apparent. Although the Post in the folio brings the troubling news that Englishmen were being killed in Ireland, the quarto's report that the 'wild Onele' have invaded the Pale suggests an intractable situation. As the centre of English administration and power, the Pale was an English colonial enclave in Ireland. As Michael Neill writes: 'no term better encapsulates the anxious bifurcation of Tudor propaganda with its simultaneous stress on defiant separateness and besieged vulnerability'.[32] It was, to borrow a phrase from *Henry V*, 'our Inland' – an England within Ireland – that had to be protected from the 'pilfering borders' (I.ii.142) surrounding it. What is especially interesting about the reference to the Pale in *The Contention* is the suggestion that the wild Irish have not only attacked this space but have in fact taken it over. The text's depiction of the Irish recalls that of the kern in Derricke's *Image of Irelande*: 'Unto the English borders next, | doe take their onward waie | And all in warlike wise, | the borders thei invade: | Supposyng subiectes for to quell, | by force of Irishe blade'.[33] Portraying the kern as boundary violators, the *Image* implies that Ireland is a divided land over which the English have a tentative hold. A similar inference is available in the play. The spatial metaphor 'plant' (in the sense of laying claim to and settling in a space) suggests an inversion of power relations between the English and Irish, because in an Elizabethan context it was the English who were associated with plantation and settlement in Ireland. It is also possible that the additional

31 All quotations are from the facsimile edition, *Shakespeare's plays in quarto*, ed. Michael J. Allen and Kenneth Muir (Berkeley, 1981).   32 Neill, 'Broken English and broken Irish', p. 13.   33 Derricke, *Image of Irelande*, p. 57.

meaning of 'plant' as something vegetative is being invoked here, the implication being that the Irish are wild weeds that will destroy the English Pale.

Thus, when compared with the phrasing of the folio report, the quarto's is not only more detailed and specific but politically subversive too. There are also interesting differences in the response to the news from Ireland: unlike the folio, which stresses an equality of power within the group, the quarto emphasizes the queen's role as council leader.[34] It is she who takes charge of the situation ('What redresse shal we have for this my Lords?'), assuaging the tension between Somerset and York and, in a strategic move, requesting the latter to 'cross the seas | With troupes of Armed men to quell the pride | Of those ambitious Irish that rebell'. Conversely, in the folio the decision that York should take up the Irish commission is presented as a group one. In both texts, however, York proves the best strategist, with his soliloquy revealing how his Irish posting will serve his cause.

A strikingly similar reference to that in the quarto text occurs in Marlowe's *Edward II*, where the increasingly powerful barons confront the king:

> Look for rebellion, look to be depos'd.
> Thy garrisons are beaten out of France,
> And lame and poor lie groaning at the gates.
> The wild O'Neill, with swarms of Irish kerns,
> Lives uncontroll'd within the English pale.   (II.ii.161–5)

It will be noted that compared with Marlowe's play, which I will consider in more detail below, the quarto text has the longer and more pejorative reference, mentioning that, led by O'Neill, the kerns have planted themselves in the Pale and 'burn and spoile the cuntry as they goe'. Nevertheless, the overall verbal and tonal similarity between the allusions is intriguing.[35] Given that Marlowe and Shakespeare were both writing for Pembroke's Men, we could be dealing here with 'a fascinating case of theatrical and stylistic interchange between the two dramatists'.[36] Of greater significance for my purposes here, however, is the context in which the 'wild Onele' is mentioned: commanding an attack on the Pale. Members of the O'Neill family were active during the reigns of both Edward and Henry but neither Marlowe's nor Shakespeare's sources make any mention of the O'Neills undertaking such an enterprise. With the reference being more Elizabethan than medieval, it seems both plays engage in anachronism. Certainly, the O'Neill name would have been familiar to Elizabethan

---

34 On the differences between the two texts in the response to the messenger, see Steven Urkowitz, '"If I mistake in those foundations which I build upon": Peter Alexander's textual analysis of *Henry VI* parts 2 and 3', *ELR*, 18 (1998), 230–56 at 236.   35 On the relationship between the two plays, see Christopher Marlowe, *Edward II*, ed. Charles Forker (Manchester, 1994), p. 35.   36 Forker (ed.), *Edward II*, p. 20.

audiences. War in Ireland accounts for the prominence of the name in the period and also perhaps for the way it exceeded its literal signification. For, while the name brought to mind two of the most powerful and notorious enemies of the state, Shane O'Neill and the earl of Tyrone, Hugh O'Neill, characterized as Elizabeth's 'arch-traitors' in the 1560s and 90s respectively, equally it functioned metonymically for any Gaelic chieftain or rebel. Arguably both meanings – the particular and the general – are simultaneously available or implied in *Edward II* and *The Contention* and I now want to consider the implications of this simultaneity.

Hugh O'Neill was in London in 1590, having being called there to appear before the privy council to explain the murder of a rival claimant to the O'Neillship, Hugh Gavelagh MacShane, whom O'Neill had allegedly murdered with his own bare hands. O'Neill was placed under house arrest at Sir Henry Wallop's London residence for the duration of the investigation.[37] It is tempting to speculate that the presence of the O'Neill in the city, perhaps coinciding with either the composition or even the performance of Shakespeare's play, gave the allusion to the 'wild Onele' ransacking the Pale a direct and immediately recognizable topicality. But O'Neill the murderer and troublesome subject is just one version of the man that could have conditioned a play and its audience. O'Neill was a liminal figure who operated at the seemingly extreme poles of loyal subject and rebel in his relationship with the crown, a relationship governed by mutual distrust and political expediency. In the same year that O'Neill was being questioned by the privy councillors in London, Sir William Fitzwilliam, lord deputy of Ireland, was telling Sir Francis Walsingham how 'the Pale hath felt great good and security by his neighbourhood'.[38] Fitzwilliam, who made representations on O'Neill's behalf, assured Sir William Cecil: 'I think he is sufficiently warned how to incur the danger of any more such hereafter. He desires to submit himself at her Majesty's feet. This maketh me hope well of him that he will increase in his dutiful endeavours to make amends for this fault'.[39] However, the combination of faith in the earl's allegiance, as suggested by the image of him prostrate before the queen, and his own professed loyalty, did little to allay anxieties about the power he possessed. Cecil was also advised that although the prospect of reform in Ulster was now better than ever before, it would be in jeopardy, 'so long as the earl of Tyrone has more territories than three earls can manage'.[40] And Fitzwilliam himself identified the risk involved in using O'Neill, observing that 'when he is absolute and hath no competitor, then he may show himself to be the man which now in his wisdom he hath reason to dissemble'.[41]

---

37 Morgan, *Tyrone's rebellion*, p. 108.   38 *Calendar of state papers, Ireland, 1588–1592*, ed. Hans Claude Hamilton (London, 1885), p. 327.   39 Ibid., p. 312.   40 Ibid., p. 441.   41 Ibid., p. 339.

This assessment of O'Neill as dissembler is re-deployed in Captain Thomas Lee's 'A Brief Declaration of the state of Ireland'. Something of an ambivalent figure himself, Lee here acts as intermediary between O'Neill and the crown.[42]

> There was never a man bred in those parts, who hath done your majesty greater service than he, with often loss of his blood upon notable enemies of your majesty's; yea, more often than all other nobles of Ireland. If he were so bad as they [his adversaries] would fain enforce [...] he might very easily cutt off many of your majesty's forces which are laid in garrison in small troops, in divers parts bordering upon his country, yea, and *overrun all your English pale*, to the utter ruin thereof; yea, and camp as long as should please him even under the walls of Dublin, for any strength your majesty yet hath in that kingdom to remove him [emphasis added].[43]

Defending O'Neill's hitherto demonstration of self-restraint, Lee attempts to persuade the crown not to ostracise the earl. Lee's strategy is to play off O'Neill's positioning as loyal subject against that of potential rebel. The text works by insinuation, for encoded in the powerful spatial image of the Pale being 'overrun' is a warning that O'Neill may prove a threat and could, at any moment, go to war against the crown.

The presentation of O'Neill here provides insight into the force of the quarto's allusion to the 'wild Onele' who 'plant themselves within the English pale'. In Lee's text, the Pale symbolically signifies English power and control in Ireland; thus, the threat of O'Neill's incursion into it, like the possibility of him besieging the city, points toward the instability of the English position. The implicit warning, which uses the trope of the besieged nation, suggests that there is an important, though overlooked, subtext to the quarto's reference. The two referents of 'Onele', the particular and the general, Hugh O'Neill and Irish rebel, become elided, the inference being that O'Neill is a capricious figure, who may well represent the very thing people fear he is: the uncontrollable Irish rebel. From this perspective, the argument that the lines referring to an Irish rebellion in 2 *Henry VI* were censored because of a 'specific contemporary resonance' with Hugh O'Neill becomes more

---

42 On Lee's career, see Hiram Morgan, 'Tom Lee: the posing peacemaker' in Bradshaw, Hadfield and Maley (eds), *Representing Ireland*, pp 132–65. In 1598, Lee was imprisoned in Dublin castle for treasonable communication with O'Neill; in August 1599, he held a secret meeting with O'Neill. Lee was arrested again in 1601, this time in London, for his involvement in a plan to free the earls of Essex and Southampton. See *DNB*.
43 Quoted in Hadfield and McVeagh (eds), *Strangers to that land*, pp 89–90.

compelling.[44] Moreover, the likelihood of interference increases if, as I have being suggesting, the reference signals O'Neill as a present, and, most significantly, a neglected danger.

Considering the potential subtext and generally evocative nature of this reference, it is possible to see why the folio might be regarded as a toned down or censored version of the quarto. A closer consideration of the two texts, however, challenges this position. Despite the detailed and subversive nature of the report in the quarto, there is a definite sense in the text that the crisis will be averted. Responding to the queen's request that he muster troops for York's expedition, Buckingham promises to 'lead such a band | As soone shall overcome those Irish Rebels'. The folio version, however, seems to lack such conviction or assurance:

> CARDINAL   My lord of York, try what your fortune is.
> Th' uncivil kerns of Ireland are in arms
> And temper clay with blood of Englishmen.
> To Ireland will you lead a band of men,
> Collected choicely, from each county some,
> And try your hap against the Irishmen?
>
> (III.i.309–14)

The cardinal's invitation to York is an embellishment of the first report and recalls the post's earlier reference to the rebels 'putt[ing] the Englishmen onto the sword'. It is clear that this reiteration of the immediacy and importance of events in Ireland is part of the cardinal's strategy to get York to take up the Irish commission and thus eliminate a powerful political enemy. However, while the cardinal plays up the trope of Irish barbarity, he is unable to control its implications. His language is emotive and disturbing: the evocative image of bodily destruction, of kern that 'temper clay with blood of Englishmen', reactivates the earlier impression of Ireland as a space of reversal and contamination, where the English themselves are 'overcome'. Consequently, though the folio text is less specific than the quarto in its allusions to Ireland, its suggestive topical allusion is similarly at variance with how the Elizabethan state would wish its Irish policy to be perceived. That the folio text includes such an allusion reveals the limitations of state censorship to shape topical meanings as they unfold in a play.

In *2 Henry VI*, Ireland is imagined as a dangerous and troublesome offstage world, its perceived distance carrying a political significance. Both York and his

44 Clare, *'Art made tongue-tied by authority'*, p. 62.

enemies regard the distance afforded by the Irish commission to be politically advantageous. Whereas the queen, Suffolk and the cardinal think they are removing York from the centre of power by persuading him to go to Ireland, he sees the post as an opportunity to outwit them and further his plan to become king. York's elaborate scheme is foregrounded by Shakespeare: as Jean Howard and Phyllis Rackin note, it is York who 'gets the play's big soliloquy', a point that, they argue, creates an intimacy between York and the audience and makes them 'complicit with his agenda'.[45] However, any bond that the convention of the soliloquy facilitates is outweighed by the action that York proposes. It seems more likely that the monologue conveys to the audience 'the threat of overmighty subjects'.[46] As York urges himself to 'change misdoubt to resolution' (III.i.332) and reveals how busy his mind is with thoughts of tricking his enemies, the audience come to see him as a disruptive element within Henry's kingdom. 'Well, nobles, well: 'tis politicly done', York boasts,

> To send me packing with an host of men.
> I fear me you but warm the starved snake,
> Who, cherished in your breasts, will sting your hearts.
> 'Twas men I lacked, and you will give them me.
> I take it kindly. Yet be well assured
> You put sharp weapons in a madman's hands.   (III.i.341–7)

Revelling in the irony that Ireland is a potential power base rather than a land of political exile, York reveals himself to be a cunning and effective strategist. However, his self-characterization as a serpent seems to exceed the obvious biblical allusion in the context of his imminent departure for Ireland. English writers often remarked on the irony of St Patrick banishing snakes from a land whose human inhabitants were deemed venomous by some. In Derricke's *Image of Irelande*, the narrator asks of St Patrick: 'Thou smotest the serpentes veni- mous | and Furies didst subverte | And yet the fotters of the boggs, couldst thou no whit converte?'[47] The text evinces incredulity that those most in need of transformation, the denizens of bogs, have been passed over. Similarly, in Shakespeare's *Richard II*, the king refers to the Irish rebels as 'rough rug-headed kerns | Which live like venom where no venom else | But only they have priv- ilege to live' (II.i.156–8). And in Dekker's 2 *Honest Whore* (1605), Ireland is referred to as 'a country where no venom prospers | But in the nations blood'

45 Jean E. Howard and Phyllis Rackin, *Engendering the nation: a feminist account of Shakespeare's English histories* (London, 1997), p. 78. 46 Janette Dillon, *Language and stage in Medieval and Renaissance England* (Cambridge, 1998), p. 211.
47 Derricke, *Image of Irelande*, p. 43.

(III.i.202–3).[48] On a symbolic level, York is akin to the rebels that he is meant to oppose in Ireland. Thus, if York's monologue suggests that he has won the power struggle with his enemies, by implication it also suggests his lack of concern for that other power struggle between the English and the Irish rebels.

Christopher Highley has argued that in eliding the categories of royal representative and rebel the play evokes Elizabethan fears that the power attached to the position of lord deputy of Ireland could be abused, thus undermining royal authority there. He writes that 'Shakespeare encodes in 2 *Henry VI* a nuanced analysis of Ireland's role in domestic politics and of the problems of ruling an overseas territory – an analysis that entails a subtle reimagining of the assumptions and stereotypes regarding deputies and rebels'.[49] But such claims about authorial intention on topical matters tend to limit the range of potential resonances a play could have had for its contemporary audience. Rather than seeing a direct parallel between York's misuse of his Irish commission and Elizabethan anxieties about office in Ireland, I would argue that the play's topical inferences operate more generally and also metaphorically. York's recognition that the Irish post is potentially empowering for him and disempowering for the king is a broadly Elizabethan one but not necessarily an instance of Shakespearean intentionality.

In the play, as in Elizabethan culture more generally, Ireland's geographic distance conveys figuratively aspects of the power dynamic between the queen and her subjects (both her deputies and also her Irish subjects) in a way that invites topical inferences. Ireland's offstage status in the play, which is only temporarily disrupted by the messenger, sustains the impression that it is cut off from the political realm. Contemporaries were aware of the implications of Ireland's distance, especially in the way it necessitated the delegation of royal authority. Tudor monarchs, Ciaran Brady notes, showed 'little inclination to visit their kingdom'.[50] Fynes Moryson, secretary to Elizabeth's last lord deputy, Lord Mountjoy, observed that the 'dangerous passages of the sea and the generall affayres of state [gave] the Irish small hope of theire kings frequent presence'. Moryson saw a close relationship between royal absenteeism and political instability in Ireland and argued for a strong representative there: 'And since the Irish are most prone to tumults and Commotions, their nature in generall rather requires a valiant, Active Deputy'.[51] As Willy Maley writes, 'the figure of the lord deputy filled the vacuum created by the absentee

48 *Dramatic works of Thomas Dekker*, ed. Fredson Bowers, 6 vols (London, 1964), ii, pp 134–218.   **49** Highley, *Shakespeare, Spenser*, p. 64.   **50** Ciaran Brady, 'Court, castle and country: the framework of government in Tudor Ireland' in Brady and Gillespie (eds), *Natives and newcomers*, p. 31.   **51** Fynes Moryson, *The Irish sections of Fynes Moryson's unpublished 'Itinerary'*, ed. Graham Kew (Dublin, 1998), p. 30; p. 31.

monarch'.[52] But there were risks attached to exercising authority from a distance, both for the deputy and the crown itself. No deputy in the period underestimated the extent to which he was placing himself in a 'vulnerable position by assuming such a treacherous office so far from the court and its intrigues'.[53] The possibility of material or social advancement that the post offered could translate into corruption, accusations of misconduct and even disgrace. No stranger to the latter was Sir John Perrot, lord deputy from 1584 to 1588; writing from Ireland in 1587, Perrot remarked, 'I remain here in the greatest prison in the world'.[54] Ireland was to prove fatal for Perrot, who found himself the subject of a smear campaign led by Sir William Fitzwilliam, his successor in Ireland, with the support of Sir William Cecil in London.[55] Among the specious allegations against Perrot that led to his trial for treason in 1592 were the easy slurs of conspiracy with Spain, harbouring Catholic sympathies, and favouring the Irish, as well as slanderous words against the queen.[56] It is unsurprising that in 1590 Perrot could describe Ireland as 'the most unfortunate soil of the world' and that 'he never knew a good governor who sincerely served there but was stung, maligned, or bitten by some means'.[57] As Perrot suggests, Ireland could be a metaphorical prison that dislocated men like him from the centre of power, leaving them susceptible to political attack. From the perspective of the crown, its literal distance conferred on the post of lord deputy a disruptive and treasonous capability. With Ireland as 'an alternative to the court in terms of being a site from which the metropolis could be criticized' and 'crucially, an alternative court, viewed as a locus of power and patronage in its own right', there was a fear that the monarch's representative might supplant monarchical authority there or, more worryingly, subvert it.[58] There is in 2 *Henry VI* an indirect consciousness of the subversive potential of the royal deputy, with York's expedient use of his Irish commission demonstrating the political consequences of Ireland's imagined geographic distance. His exit offstage to hatch plots in Ireland symbolizes the danger of distance and functions as a metaphor for the vulnerability of Elizabethan governance in Ireland. Thus, where Sir John Davies envisaged the eventual political and cultural assimilation of Ireland into King James' Britain, predicting that 'there will be no difference or distinction but the Irish sea betwixt us', in the Elizabethan period that geographic separateness registered English insecurities about control over Ireland and Irish alterity.[59]

52 Maley, *Salvaging Spenser*, p. 114.   53 Maley, *Salvaging Spenser*, p. 124.   54 *Calendar of the Carew manuscripts, 1575–1588*, ed. J.S. Brewer and W. Bullen (London, 1868), p. 446.   55 See Hiram Morgan, 'The fall of Sir John Perrot' in Guy (ed.), *The reign of Elizabeth*, pp 109–125. For the suggestion of specific parallels between Perrot and York in 2 *Henry VI*, see Highley, *Shakespeare, Spenser*, pp 58–60.   56 *Cal. S.P.Ire.*, 1588–1592, p. 165; p. 305. See also Morgan, 'The fall of Sir John Perrot', pp 118–22.   57 *Cal. S.P.Ire.*, 1588–1592, p. 350.   58 Maley, *Salvaging Spenser*, p. 99.   59 Sir John Davies, *A discovery of the true causes why Ireland was never entirely subdued, nor brought under obedience of the crown of England, until the beginning of his majesty's happy reign* in James P. Myers (ed.), *Elizabethan Ireland: a selection of*

The potential consequences of an uncontrolled Ireland are further delineated through the figure of Jack Cade, the rebel leader. Cade is first mentioned in the play by York as the 'minister of my intent' (III.i.355), whom he will use to cause domestic havoc for Henry: 'Whiles I in Ireland nourish a mighty band, | I will stir up in England some black storm' (III.i.349–50). [60] Cade will be the cipher for this storm; accordingly, his subsequent lower-class rebellion becomes both a reflex of and also a precursor to York's aristocratic one.[61] York explains how it was in Ireland that he first recognized Cade's subversive potentiality:

> In Ireland have I seen this stubborn Cade
> Oppose himself against a troop of kerns,
> And fought so long, till that his thighs with darts
> Were almost like a sharp-quilled porcupine;
> And in the end, being rescued, I have seen
> Him caper upright like a wild Morisco,
> Shaking the bloody darts as he is bells.
> Full often, like a shag-haired crafty kern,
> Hath he conversed with the enemy,
> And, undiscovered, come to me again
> And given me notice of their villanies.   (III.i.360–70)

In York's composite portrait, Cade is linked to the chaos and turmoil in Ireland that the scene has been reporting. The juxtaposition of Cade with the group of Irish and the emphasis upon his bodily endurance and dexterity produces a display of individual English strength over collective Irish violence, which seems to balance out those earlier reports of 'uncivil kerns' killing Englishmen. With the narrative focus fixed on Cade's animal-like body pierced with 'bloody darts', the image of English blood re-occurs. Wounds seem to function here in much the same way as they do in Thomas Kyd's play *Solyman and Perseda* (1590), where an English knight makes the boast, 'Against the light-foot Irish have I serv'd | And in my skin bear tokens of their kerns'.[62] Like the knight's body, Cade's symbolizes English bravery and capacity to overcome the

writings by Elizabethan writers on Ireland (Hamden, CT, 1983), p. 174.   60 On the connection of York on Cade in terms of verbal parallels see *King Henry VI*, part two, ed. Ronald Knowles (London, 1999), pp 99–100. 61 Shakespeare appears to be embellishing his source material here for although both Halle and Holinshed refer to rumours that York's supporters had a hand in the Cade revolt, neither makes any mention of Cade's service in Ireland nor of York ever meeting him. See *Holinshed's chronicles of England, Scotland and Ireland*, ed. Henry Ellis, 6 vols (London, 1807–8), vi, p. 267; Edward Halle, *Union of two noble houses and illustre famelies of Lancaster and York* [1548] in Geoffrey Bullough (ed.), *Narrative and dramatic sources of Shakespeare* (London, 1960), iii, pp 110–13. 62 Dodsley (ed.), *A select collection of old English plays*, v, p. 264.

kerns but since it is inscribed with the wounds they have inflicted, paradoxically his body also becomes a site of Irish violence and resistance. It thus
denotes, symbolically, the breaching of the body politic that I noted earlier.
However, such are the transformative capabilities of Cade's body, he is able to
move from fighting against the kern, to passing himself off as one of them and
communicating with them too, a trajectory that involves the violation of those
boundaries separating and securing civil Englishmen from 'uncivil kerns'.

As boundary violator, the distinctions between Jack Cade and the wild
Irish become increasingly blurred. For instance, Cade's physical fortitude and
indifference to pain aligns him with his adversaries, whose resilience was
commented on by English writers. York observes of Cade: 'Say he be taken,
racked, and tortured – | I know no pain they can inflict upon him'
(III.i.376–7). Similarly, in Spenser's *View* Irenius admits with grudging admira-
tion that the kern are 'for the most part great indurers of colde, labour, hunger,
and all hardnesse, very active and strong of hand, very swift of foot, [...] very
present in perils, very great scorners of death'.[63] There may be a further hint
at Cade's resemblance to the kerns: the reference to his thighs suggests that,
like the native Irish, he too goes bare legged. Accordingly, it is possible to see
Cade as a 'quasi-Irishman' and also concur with Andrew Murphy's suggestion
that Cade's approximation of an Irish identity amounts to a strategy that the
English associated with the Irish themselves, namely 'the ability to shift into a
different identity'.[64] Cade's power resides in his capacity 'to forge (in every
sense) an Irish strategy as a weapon against the Irish themselves', thus
confirming English superiority.[65] His morphing makes him look at home in
and in control of Irish space.

However, while Cade's appropriation of the signs of Irish alterity certainly
enables him to assume another identity, Murphy fails to consider the risks
involved in identity exchange and cross-cultural encounters. It is not entirely
clear, after all, if Cade is in full control of this transformation or if it his environment that has transformed him. In other words, the transformative
capabilities associated with Irish space cast the shadow of degeneration over
Cade's perfomance as a kern. Degeneration was common to any cross-cultural
encounter in the period but it seemed more acute in the case of Ireland. There
was visible proof of this process in the form of the descendants of the Anglo-
Norman conquest in the twelfth century that had, proverbially, become 'more
Irish than the Irish themselves'.[66] Intriguingly, degeneracy was closely linked to

63 Spenser, *A view*, p. 74.   64 See Highley, *Shakespeare, Spenser*, p. 53; Murphy, 'Shakespeare's Irish history', p. 44.
65 Murphy, 'Shakespeare's Irish history', p. 44.   66 The phrase, which crystallizes the Gaelicization of the
Anglo-Norman settlers, was apparently only coined in the early nineteenth century. See *Oxford companion to Irish*

the War of the Roses; in sketching a history of Ireland, for instance, Fynes Moryson noted how the wars drew powerful English lords from Ireland with devastating effects:

> the English Mortuomares, and after the Dukes of Yorke, neglecting theire Earldom of Connaught in Ireland, the English Irish Bourkes theire kinsmen, and theire Tennants of those landes, imboldned by theire lords [absence] and the troubled State of England, and making friendship and marriages with the meere Irish, possessed that Prouince as theire owne inheritance, and dayly more degenerating from the English, applied themselves to the Customes, manners, language, and apparell of the meere Irish. And the like was done in other parts of Ireland, aswell by the meere Irish, as the English Irish.[67]

Does the sense of historical rupture and cultural transformation occasioned by the wars account for the increasing likeness of Jack Cade to the kern? In order to consider this question, it is necessary to consider the process of degeneration further. Moryson's description of the 'English Irish' (or the old English as they were also known in an epithet that conveyed their apparent lapsed status) registers some of the ways in which they were a source of continuous frustration and anxiety for new English settlers. The subject of old English degeneration is fully interrogated in Spenser's *View*, where the two interlocutors debate its causes and consider suitable remedies. Irenius' revelation that the original settlers have been assimilated into Gaelic culture is greeted with incredulity by Eudoxus:

> What here I? And is it possible that an Englishman, brought up in such sweet civility as England affords, should find such likeing in that barbarous rudness, that he should forget his owne nature, and forgoe his owne nation! how may this bee, or what (I pray you) may be the cause thereof?[68]

Irenius attributes old English degeneracy to their geographic remoteness from the civilised centre, explaining 'so much can liberty and ill examples doe'.[69] But it is his report that the 'great houses [...] of the English in Ireland' have, in addition to intermarrying with the Irish, taken Irish surnames and are 'now growne as Irish, as O-hanlans breech' that is especially troubling. To Eudoxus, such tendencies must 'be reformed with most sharp censures, in so great

history, ed. S.J. Connolly (Oxford, 1998), p. 368.   67 Moryson, 'Itinerary', p. 26.   68 Spenser, *A view*, p. 54. 69 Ibid., p. 67.

personages to the terrour of the meaner': for if the lords and chiefe men degenerate, what shall be hoped of the peasants, and baser people?'[70] That men degenerate regardless of class raises the possibility that there is something aberrant about Ireland; as Eudoxus remarks, 'Lord, how quickely doth that countrey alter mens natures!'[71] Eager to discount this possibility, Irenius makes the general observation that 'no times have beene without bad men'. For him, freedom from the strict code of behaviour that regulated society at home means men 'grow more loose and carelesse of their duty' and, since it is the natural state of man to 'love liberty,' they inevitably 'fall to all licentiousness'.[72] In response, Eudoxus suggests that Irenius' earlier plan to settle English among the Gaelic Irish is flawed 'since the English sooner drawe to the Irish then the Irish to the English'. Irenius is confident that 'where there is due order of discipline and good rule, the better shall goe foremost, and the worst shall follow'.[73]

As Eudoxus' note of caution suggests, however, Irenius' plan to intermingle the English and Irish raises the possibility that the new English could prove just as assimilable as the old English had been. As Patricia Fumerton writes, 'rather than the English drawing the Irish into their centripetal cultural circle, the reverse tended to occur: the Irish absorbed English settlers into the Irish cultural round'.[74] Despite Irenius' claims for new English political and military strength, their distance from home puts them in the same high-risk category as the old English. The text tries to construct a rational explanation for the susceptibility of the English to emasculation in Ireland but the dialogic structure produces irresolution; the question of Ireland's capacity to 'alter mens natures' remains open.

In light of new English perceptions of the Irish and the belief that Irish space had the capacity to transform radically those who entered it, I would argue that to contemporaries Cade's metamorphosis into 'a shag-haired crafty kern' is suggestive of cultural contamination rather than the deployment of an 'Irish strategy'. That Cade is assimilated by the same kerns who have been killing Englishmen is not without significance; his degeneracy is a direct consequence of the English failure to subdue these rebels in the first instance, to defend the borders they attack and limit the wild spaces they inhabit. The maintenance of borders and clearing of the dark corners and hidden spaces associated with the wild Irish was, as noted earlier, seen as an essential mechanism not only in defence of the English position in Ireland but also of English identity itself. For 'unregulated space', as Bruce McLeod notes in a related context, leads directly to 'emasculation, where English [...] identity

---

70 Ibid., p. 70. 71 Ibid., p. 143. 72 Ibid., p. 144. A similar explanation is offered in Fynes Moryson's 'Itinerary', p. 101. 73 Ibid., p. 120; p. 144. 74 Patricia Fumerton, *Cultural aesthetics: Renaissance literature and the practice of social ornament* (Chicago, 1991), p. 47.

slides into something else'.[75] Michael Neill captures the implications of this alteration when he writes 'once outside the pale of culture, it is plain, everyone will discover himself or herself a woodkern under the skin'.[76] That shattering of an essentialist identity, the discovery of the Other beneath the self, is the great fear of degeneracy: as Jean Howard and Phyllis Rackin note, degeneracy 'tellingly reveals the fragility of fictions of racial and national difference. Englishness could not be an essence if it could so easily evaporate through contact with the Irish'.[77] This might explain why 2 *Henry VI* draws an equation between the English failure to control the Irish (evidenced by the reports of Englishmen being murdered in Ireland) and the breakdown of the cultural boundaries separating and protecting the English from Irish difference (seen in Cade's dangerous mingling with the kerns). In dramatic terms, the play uses the idea of a degenerate Cade to elaborate on the state of England under Henry VI; so, the impression of a divided state and ineffectual king is now extended to include the suggestion that Englishness itself is unstable. But it is evident that in touching on the effects of an Irish experience, the play is marked by its own historical and cultural moment. Like *A View*, it reflects an Elizabethan desire to re-constitute Irish space because this offers the best means of preserving English identity from degeneracy and dissolution.

The initial association of Cade with Ireland, degeneration and boundary violation continues with the play's dramatization of his popular revolt, where Cade overruns London just as the kern overrun the Pale. With Cade figured as a lord of misrule, the rebellion is variously portrayed as bringing about social inversion and chaos but Clifford, recalling the recent loss of Henry's French territories, also envisions it as the contamination of England by foreign elements. Addressing the commoners, Clifford notes:

> Were't not a shame, that whilst you live at jar,
> The fearful French, whom you late vanquished,
> Should make a start o'er seas and vanquish you?
> Methinks already in this civil broil
> I see them lording it in London streets,
> Crying '*Villago*' unto all they meet
> Better ten thousand base-born Cades miscarry
> Than you should stoop unto a Frenchman's mercy.
>
> (IV.vii.42–9)

Cade is thus construed as an alien within the kingdom, his rebellion a potential conduit for degeneration. Clifford's words have their desired effect and

75 McLeod, *Geography of empire*, p. 54.   76 Neill, 'Broken English and broken Irish', p. 14, n. 51.   77 Howard and Rackin, *Engendering the nation*, p. 14.

Cade's followers abandon him. The rebel leader is next seen on stage alone, having broken into the garden of Alexander Iden; the contrast between the rebel leader boldly rejoicing in inverting social norms and this intruder speaking directly to the audience could not be more striking. Cade reveals 'These five days have I hid me in the woods and durst not peep out' (IV.ix.2–3). As a temporary denizen of the woods – traditionally thought to be a dangerous space bordering the civilized world but also, in an Irish context, the hiding place for rebels – and now as a vagrant in Iden's garden, Cade fulfils Clifford's earlier observation that 'he hath no home, no place to fly to' (IV.vii.39). The play's treatment of Cade's incursion into Iden's private property and his subsequent death is ambivalent.[78] Cade himself says he is famished, Iden reveals how he does not 'wax great by others' waning' but rather 'sends the poor well pleased from my gate' (IV.ix.21; 24). While Cade's transgressive act of trespass renders him undeserving of Iden's charity, the emphasis on the physical disparity between himself and Iden and on his human suffering – 'Famine and no other hath slain me!' (IV.ix.60) – provides the audience with a different perspective on the rebel leader, one which affords him a degree of dignity.

It is possible to see in Cade's death the symbolic containment of the lower classes and, by extension, the Irish. Christopher Highley suggests that Cade's 'struggle for survival revives memories of the Irish context that introduced him', the broad effect of which is to further demonize the rebel. The 'Irishing' of Cade, Highley contends, is indicative of the tendency in official discourse to conflate various forms of otherness, whether based on race, class or gender, into 'a composite symbolic Other'.[79] Jonathan Dollimore and Alan Sinfield have argued that the 'ideological containment' of the Irish 'was continuous with the handling of the disaffected lower-class outgroup'.[80] They cite a 1594 proclamation 'Ordering the arrest of vagabonds, deportation of Irishmen', which targets the 'great multitude of wandering persons', some of whom are 'exacting money continually upon pretense of service in the wars without relief', while others are 'men of Ireland that have these late years unnaturally served as rebels against her Majesty's forces beyond the sea'.[81] But there were other, earlier instances occasioned by the presence of Irish vagrants in London. As early as 1566, Irishmen were among a list of rogues in Thomas Harman's

78 See Thomas Cartelli, 'Jack Cade in the garden: class consciousness and class conflict in 2 *Henry VI*' in Richard Burt and John Michael Archer (eds), *Enclosure acts: sexuality, property and culture in early modern England* (Ithaca, 1994), pp 48–67.   79 Highley, *Shakespeare, Spenser*, pp 54–5. On the conflation of Irish alterity with class and gender difference in the period, see Sheila Cavanagh, '"The fatal destiny of that land": Elizabethan views of Ireland' in Bradshaw, Hadfield and Maley (eds), *Representing Ireland*, pp 116–31.   80 Jonathan Dollimore and Alan Sinfield, 'History and ideology: the instance of *Henry V*' in John Drakakis (ed.), *Alternative Shakespeares* (London, 1985), p. 225.   81 Paul L. Hughes and James F. Larkin (eds), *Tudor royal proclamations*, 2 vols (New Haven, 1969), iii, p. 135.

Caveat for Common Cursitors, vulgarly called Vagabonds, where it was stated 'there is above an hundred Irishmen that wander about to beg for their living, that hath come over within these two years. They say they have been burned and spoiled by the earl of Desmond'.[82] In 1587, the privy council informed the lord deputy of Ireland that the 'poor Irishe people' were to be deported back to Ireland and instructed him to prevent the further 'transportinge over of anie such poor vagrant persons to this realm'.[83] These measures can be interpreted as both reactive and also pre-emptive forms of social policy occasioned by the wars in Ireland. The scorched earth policies used during the Desmond rebellion in Munster, and indeed intermittent warfare more generally, led to displacement, which in turn produced an Irish population in England. At play in the identification of these 'poor vagrant persons' are implicit ethnic assumptions about the native Irish; Irish vagrant seems to equate to double trouble.

What these contemporary analogues reveal is how vagrancy could crystallize English anxieties about the fluidity of Gaelic Irish society, a fluidity that, as recognized in Spenser's *View*, could lead Englishmen to degenerate. Concerns about the fluid nature of Irish society are conveyed in Spenser's text through discussion of the Gaelic Irish practice of transhumance or boolying, which is presented as a series of wanderings through unregulated space and hence indicative of native failure to harness the natural resources of the land. 'Pasturing upon the mountaine, and waste wilde places', Irenius explains how these 'Irish boolies' provide cover for 'out-lawes, or loose people' and act as catalysts for barbarous and licentious behaviour more generally because they confer on their participants a freedom unavailable in towns.[84] Spenser presents boolying as an example of the Scythian genealogy of the native Irish and draws on classical geography to figure the Irish as vagrants in their own habitat.[85] Mention of towns as the preferred form of spatial organization indicates just how far the Irish are deemed to have diverged from an English norm. At work here, then, are two opposing concepts of space that are, I would suggest, also projected on to Jack Cade, that vagrant who finds himself in Iden's garden. The two men are not only social and physical opposites but also spatially distinct: Cade is a wanderer or vagrant, associated with unregulated space, in contrast to Iden who is associated with an enclosed, regulated space. Accordingly, they read as a metaphor for the relation between Irish space (as it was figured in English representations) and English space.

From this perspective, Cade becomes a signifier of vagrancy, degeneracy

82 *Elizabethan underworld: a collection of Tudor and early Stuart tracts*, ed. A.V. Judges (London, 1930), p. 113.   83 *Acts of the privy council, 1587–1588*, ed. John Roche Dasent (London, 1897), p. 109.   84 Spenser, *A view*, p. 55. 85 On the use of classical precedent in figurations of Irish space, see Bernhard Klein, *Maps and the writing of space*, pp 173–4.

and alterity. His incursion into Iden's garden is more than the characteristic wandering of the vagrant but symbolizes the wild Irishman who simultaneously threatens and defines civilized and regulated English space. Shakespeare employs here the 'conventional political trope that represents England as the idealized Garden of Plenty'.[86] Iden imagines his garden as a pastoral world, free from the corruption of the court and the desire for material possessions which, as Thomas Cartelli notes, has 'encouraged many of [his] social superiors to turn the "garden of England" into a site of fraternal bloodletting'.[87] To Iden, his garden is 'worth a monarchy' (IV.ix.19), a resonant phrase implying that the garden functions not only as an ideal England but also as a microcosm of Henry's troubled kingdom. As a representative of chaos and inversion, Cade must be erased from this garden but his death at the sword of Alexander Iden can look as if he is the lower-class scapegoat for aristocratic dissent. Moreover, on a symbolic level, Cade's death is necessary for the preservation of an English form of spatial organization that affords an already vulnerable English identity some protection from unregulated space and the difference it was seen to embody.

Cade's encroachment into the ordered space of Iden's garden recalls York's recently reported arrival from Ireland and the rebel leader's death would seem to indicate that the threat posed by the king's Irish deputy will ultimately be diffused. The audience cannot fail to see this connection between the two boundary violators for it is also reflected in the dramatic structure. It is surely no accident that slotted between report of York's return (IV.ix) and his arrival on stage (V.i) is the scene of Cade's foray into Iden's garden. This correspondence between their movements and actions – one of several thematic and structural parallels between them in the play – is made explicit as Henry remarks, 'Thus stands my state, 'twixt Cade and York distressed, | Like to a ship that, having 'scaped a tempest, | Is straightway calmed, and boarded with a pirate' (IV.viii.32–4). The king is responding here to the messenger's announcement that

> The Duke of York is newly come from Ireland,
> And with a puissant and a mighty power
> Of gallowglasses and stout Irish kerns
> Is marching hitherward in proud array.   (IV.viii.25–8)

Once more, the framing device of the messenger mediates events offstage to the audience, but whereas previously the device maintained the sense of Ireland

---

86 Neill, 'Broken English and broken Irish', p. 11.   87 Cartelli, 'Jack Cade in the garden', p. 48.

as a distant offstage space, it now implies that Ireland is dangerously near. Interestingly, the quarto text contains no such report, making the arrival of York 'In Armes from Ireland' all the more dramatic because unannounced. As the stage directions in both the folio ('with drum and colours') and the quarto ('with Drum and soldiers') indicate, however, the entrance of York was clearly meant to be powerful in performance. Although it is difficult to precisely determine how the Irish army was represented, the messenger's description demands that the army's Irishness be registered visually.

According to Alexander Leggatt, 'York's return from Ireland is, for a few lines tremendous – but for a few lines only'.[88] While the threat York poses is only momentary and is ultimately diffused (the army is disbanded at line 45), Leggatt underestimates its broader significance. For the presence of York's 'mighty power' of Irish before the king literalises those earlier images of infiltration and contamination associated with Cade. Under the command of a claimant to the throne, the presence of these Irish soldiers makes present and immediate what was previously only reported, and raises the possibility that the violence synonymous with the Irish could now be unleashed. Buckingham expresses official concern when he asks York why he 'should raise so great a power' without permission and 'dare to bring' his 'force so near the court' (V.i.21–2). The proximity of the Irish (already variously associated with destruction, disorder and degeneracy) to the court and hence person of the king, enacts contemporary fears 'about Ireland as a staging post of disruption within England', or 'reversed conquest'.[89] With the army constituting a direct threat to both the English body politic and the corporeal body of the king, the tenor of those spatial metaphors about the Pale being overrun or of rebellion in Ireland as a 'wound' that could prove 'incurable' (III.i.286) is fully revealed.

With York's dismissal of his Irish mercenaries, danger would appear to have been averted but their worrying proximity to court is merely displaced on to the city: 'Soldiers, I thank you all; disperse yourselves; | Meet me tomorrow in Saint George's field. | You shall have pay and everything you wish' (V.i.45–7). It has been noted that 'the pointed irony of Irish soldiers assembling at a place named after England's patron saint is compounded by the alarming prospect of an unpaid and unsatisfied army wandering about London, with the openness of York's "everything" being especially worrying'.[90] In the quarto text, York tells the army to gather at George's Field, where 'you shall receive your paie of me'; nonetheless, this too leaves open the possibility of idle soldiers in London. Recalling Clifford's earlier vision of

88 Alexander Leggatt, *Shakespeare's political drama: the history plays and the Roman plays* (London, 1988), p. 13.
89 Highley, *Shakespeare, Spenser*, pp 49–50.   90 Ibid., p. 49.

reversal, where he foresees Frenchmen 'lording it in London streets', the prospect of an alien, private army at loose in London articulates English domestic loss under Henry.

Working from the chronicle sources, Shakespeare appears to have enhanced his depiction of York as a scheming usurper who uses the Irish commission for his own purely selfish reasons, thus bringing the concept of Ireland as a space from which danger originates and spreads to its logical and dramatically effective conclusion. Holinshed's brief reference to Yorkist supporters inciting Cade into rebellion is, as noted earlier, pointed up in the play. And in dramatizing York's return from his Irish post, Shakespeare once again proves inventive: in both Halle and Holinshed, York returns from Ireland and bides his time before gathering a 'great army in the Marches of Wales'.[91] There is no historical foundation for the play's 'army of Irish'. From his reading of the history of Henry's reign in the chronicles, then, Shakespeare probably would have known that York was something of an anomaly when it came to Ireland, having enjoyed a relatively successful stay there. In Halle's assessment, York's is a welcome presence in Ireland:

> as lieutenant of the king [he] not only appeased the fury of the wylde and savage people there, but also gat him such love and favour of the countrey and the inhabitauntes, that their syncere love and frendly affection could never be separated from him and his lynage.[92]

Similarly, Holinshed also testifies to York's good service in Ireland and quotes a letter from the duke to his agent at court, Salisbury. In the letter, York boasts that 'it shall never be chronicled nor remaine in scripture (by the grace of God) that Ireland was lost by my negligence'.[93] Of course, this is precisely what is 'chronicled' in 2 *Henry VI*. Conversely, in the quarto text, York's service in Ireland is acknowledged. Incorrectly assuming that York is no longer a threat, the king praises him for his lieutenancy: 'And thankes for thy great service done to us | Against those traitorous Irish that rebeld'. So close are the verbal parallels between the king's words here and the queen's earlier request that York 'quell the pride | Of those ambitious Irish that rebell' that the image of the Irish attacking the Pale is balanced out. Irish recalcitrance has been met with English strength. Notwithstanding the portrait of York as a dissembler, his suppression of rebellion in Ireland is registered.

Whereas the quarto can thus be said to bring the problem of Ireland to a close, the folio is more open-ended, being completely silent at this crucial

---

91 Halle, *Union of two noble houses*, p.119.   92 Ibid., p. 110.   93 *Holinshed's chronicles*, p. 268.

juncture on York's successful resolution of the crisis in Ireland. Towards the beginning of the folio version of the play, York is commended for his recent service in France and also in Ireland for 'bringing them to civil discipline' (I.i.193). He himself notes how his fate stands between England, France and Ireland (I.i.232–5). In a play that dramatizes the loss of English possessions in France, the connection between France and Ireland is an especially interesting one. The loss of Anjou and Maine suggests the beginning of a pattern of reversal or inversion, encapsulated in Gloucester's prophetic comment 'Undoing all, as all had never been!' (I.i.100), that will repeat itself in Ireland. The subsequent reports of 'uncivil kerns' participating in English bloodletting in Ireland or of Englishmen like Cade being subsumed by an Irish difference that cannot be effaced serves to confirm this. These images of reversed conquest are never redressed. By omitting York's management of the Irish, the folio text of 2 *Henry VI* exposes the harsh reality of the English failure to transform Irish space and reform its inhabitants. It is a significant lacuna in the play and one that speaks to the Elizabethan problem of Ireland.

'CHAS'D FROM ENGLAND'S BOUNDS':
MARLOWE'S *EDWARD II* AND EXILE IN IRELAND

A similar, though more acute, exploration of inverted power relations can be detected in *Edward II*, where the king's authority is increasingly contested and limited by powerful nobles who hold him accountable for losses in foreign territories and for the domestic implosion such losses signify. The illuminating moment of intertextuality between 2 *Henry VI* and *Edward II* – the verbal echoing in the allusion to the 'wild O'Neill'– thus reflects larger thematic parallels between the two plays. In both, Ireland is a site of reversal and also an offstage space, a location to which discordant elements can be dispatched and, as in the case of York, a potential resource for opportunistic exiles. In *Edward II*, however, the Shakespearean drama of the nation, that broad concern with the condition of England, is overshadowed by a Marlovian drama of desire as the play focuses on the relationship between the king and his favourite, Gaveston. Marlowe's play identifies 'private space as the origin of historical action'.[94] Such an approach involves condensing the reign into a series of accumulative losses and disasters that can be seen to have their origin in Gaveston's influence over the king.[95] This might explain why Marlowe 'scants

94 Joan Parks, 'History, tragedy and truth in Christopher Marlowe's *Edward II*' *SEL*, 39 (1999), 275–90 at 283.
95 On Marlowe's use of his sources, see Vivien Thomas and William Tydeman (eds), *Christopher Marlowe: the plays and their sources* (London, 1994), pp 341–50.

Edward II's affairs in Ireland even more drastically than those in Scotland'.[96]
Nonetheless, this brevity belies Ireland's semiotic importance in the play. It is
the barons' objection to Gaveston that forces Edward to send him to Ireland,
later envisaged as a potential refuge from the barons for Edward himself. With
Ireland figured as a key space for both the king and his favourite, I want to
suggest that the play offers a different conception of Ireland than 2 *Henry VI*
and perhaps even Elizabethan drama more generally.

Gaveston's forced journey to Ireland is just one of several associations he
has with travel or movement. The play opens with him newly arrived from exile
in France, viewing London as if a stranger; shortly afterwards, he is sent to and
recalled from Ireland; and finally, he is pursued through England by the
barons. These journeys convey Gaveston's lack of agency and power, yet his
temporary presence in England is regarded as a threatening one. The tone of
his opening speech, no less than its content, makes it abundantly clear why
Edward's father banished him from the kingdom and why the barons will do
likewise. Gaveston's perception of London 'as Elysium to a new-come soul'
(I.i.11) indicates how out of touch he is with the material realities of England.
He displays distaste for the 'real' London, surely not something to endear him
to the audience, and a disregard for the vagrant soldiers. Gaveston's London is
neither the real urban space nor a theatrical one (as that urban space is
momentarily constituted on stage) but an ideal to be revered because 'it
harbours him I hold so dear' (I.i.13). The return of Gaveston into England is
imagined, then, as a return to the personal space of the king. It is the sense of
privacy and proximity that leads the barons to see Gaveston's presence, which
they increasingly figure as an alien presence, as deeply unsettling. The lexicon
of epithets applied to Gaveston – 'base peasant' (I.ii.6), 'peevish Frenchman'
(I.ii.7), 'Greekish strumpet' (II.iv.16) – suggest his alien status and attest to the
impossibility of him 'stay[ing] within the realm' (I.i.105). What these evince is
the desire among the barons for a pure, homogenous England that requires
Gaveston's absence; and, since Ireland is the location of his absence, it is as if
it becomes a repository of impure, alien elements. Coupled with his perceived
foreignness, Gaveston's relationship with the king marks him out as a threat to
the body politic in both material and political terms. His decadence, exempli-

---

96 Forker (ed.), *Edward II*, p. 47. The absence of a detailed treatment of Ireland might account for the relative
critical silence on its figuration in the play. Two exceptions are Mark Thornton Burnett, '*Edward II* and
Elizabethan politics' in Paul Whitfield White (ed.), *Marlowe, history and sexuality: new essays on Christopher Marlowe*
(New York, 1998), pp 91–107. Burnett glosses the play's allusion to the O'Neill rebellion, noting that they
'rebelled in Ireland against English rule in the 1560s and 1570s' (p. 104). However, his explanation completely
ignores the play's more immediate Irish context of the 1590s. For a corrective to Burnett, see Curtis Breight's
short discussion of the play in *Surveillance, militarism and drama in the Elizabethan era* (London, 1996). Breight suggests
the 'wild O'Neill' allusion anticipates the rise of the earl of Tyrone (p. 138).

fied by his penchant for 'Italian masques by night' (I.i.55), variously suggests distraction, fiscal rectitude and general mismanagement. As an alien figure, or, more specifically one who has been labelled alien, Gaveston is imagined as a catalyst for the emasculation of the king and the contamination of England.

As several critics have noted, the play derives energy here from contemporary anxieties about foreign infiltration of a kind that found expression in anti-foreigner riots in London in the early 1590s as well as more general fears about Catholic and Spanish plots.[97] In this sense, Gaveston might be compared to Cade in *2 Henry VI* as another instance of the tendency of the dominant order to produce a symbolic Other on to which a range of anxieties can be projected. Yet *Edward II* unsettles the positioning of Gaveston as Other and enables the audience to understand how his alterity is, to a large extent, constructed by the barons. Marlowe offers an alternative to the barons' perception of Gaveston by linking him with an attack on Roman Catholicism; which, like Gaveston himself, is presented in the play 'as the diabolical foreign, capable of infecting the English state'.[98] Gaveston becomes the principal agent in the attack on the church, his rough handling of the bishop of Coventry precipitating Edward's question 'Why should a king be subject to a priest? (I.iv.96). While the play capitalizes here on anti-Catholic sentiment in London and, in the process, offers a concession to Elizabeth who had been excommunicated in 1570, the dominant effect is to render both characters popular and, crucially, native. The presumed alien wins the popular vote with the audience by brow-beating a more heinous alien entity than himself.

If Gaveston's actions endear him to a broad constituency of the audience, they also provide the barons with further proof of his influence over the king and therefore of the need to banish him from the kingdom. Mortimer remarks, 'That sly inveigling Frenchman we'll exile, | Or lose our lives; and yet, ere that day come, | The king shall lose his crown; for we have power, | And courage too, to be reveng'd at full' (I.ii.57–60). As the archbishop of Canterbury urges them not to use violence against the king, Lancaster repeats their intention to 'lift Gaveston from hence' (I.ii.62). In seeking Gaveston's banishment, the baronial faction evinces a fixed and hierarchical spatial logic, which privileges centre over periphery. This can be understood in terms of Gillies' 'poetic geography', for the barons sense of England and of themselves is achieved in relation to what, or who, is deemed to lie beyond or outside; however, it is precisely this type of spatial logic that is interrogated and deconstructed in Marlowe's plays.[99]

97 See Burnett, '*Edward II* and Elizabethan politics', p. 103; Thomas Healy, *Christopher Marlowe* (Plymouth, 1994), 76. 98 Healy, *Christopher Marlowe*, p. 82. 99 Gillies, *Shakespeare and the geography*, pp 6–7. See Garret Sullivan, 'Geography and identity in Marlowe' in Patrick Cheney (ed.), *Cambridge Companion to Christopher Marlowe* (Cambridge, 2004), pp 231–44.

The barons believe that by sending Gaveston 'hence' they can fully limit his corrupting influence on the king and also protect England from further contamination. Yet, in proposing Gaveston's banishment, they bring themselves close to proposing the usurpation of Edward, who seems incapable of the political will and decisive action they themselves display. Emily Bartels has argued that Edward is equally adept as his adversaries at exploiting the sexual for political ends, noting how he assumes the guise of a king 'love-sick for his minion' (I.iv.87) in order to defer the threat of deposition and conceal his readiness to fight. To Edward, she argues, Gaveston is simultaneously 'a private subject of desire and a public object of negotiation'.[1] However, in his efforts to prevent the banishment Edward oscillates between a reckless determination and a pathetic desperation. He contemplates the decentring of England itself rather than the de-centring of his favourite: 'Ere my sweet Gaveston shall part from me, | This isle shall fleet upon the ocean, | And wander to the unfrequented Inde' (I.iv.49–50). The imagined dissolution of England is reiterated as Edward proposes the division of his kingdom among the barons 'So I may have some nook or corner left | To frolic with my dearest Gaveston' (I.iv.72–3). The proposed re-configuration of the kingdom emphatically registers Edward's desire for a private space and, by extension, the extent to which the idea of a political centre is slipping. As Edward says, 'Thou from this land, I from myself am banish'd' (I.iv.119).

In view of these images of decentring, Edward's choice of Ireland as the location of Gaveston's exile is noteworthy. In marginalizing Gaveston to a space regarded as peripheral to the English centre, Edward not only concedes to the barons' demands but is also forced to embrace (albeit temporarily) their spatial logic; on a symbolic level, then, the choice of Ireland has the effect of re-centring England. Yet, even as Edward moves to protect his power, the sense that the king's priorities lie elsewhere, that his concern is the primacy of private space, is asserted in the moment of separation:

EDWARD   And only this torments my wretched soul,
That, whether I will or no, thou must depart.
Be Governor of Ireland in my stead,
And there abide till fortune call thee home.
Here, take my picture, and let me wear thine:
They exchange pictures.
O, might I keep thee here, as I do this,
Happy were I! but now most miserable.

1 Emily C. Bartels, *Spectacles of strangeness: imperialism, alienation and Marlowe* (Philadelphia, 1993), p. 170; p. 172.

GAVESTON   'Tis something to be pitied of a king.

EDWARD   Thou shalt not hence; I'll hide thee, Gaveston.

GAVESTON   I shall be found, and then 'twill grieve me more.

(I.iv.124–30)

The king proves he is capable of pragmatic thinking yet also shows himself to be 'love-sick'; he acknowledges the political necessity and inevitability of the exile only to protest against it. As his kingly resolve gives way to private needs, Edward seems divided against himself. He entertains the possibility of hiding Gaveston, a remark that not only recalls that earlier desire for 'some nook or corner' of the kingdom to 'frolic' with his minion (I.iv.72–3) but also indicates how relationships, both political and personal, are figured spatially.

As I have suggested, the play's use of Ireland is not simply a case of historical accuracy but is political and ideological too, a point that raises broader questions about reading historically and the politics of location. Seamus Heaney has drawn attention to the politics of the play's representation of Ireland in an illuminating digression to his essay on Marlowe's 'Hero and Leander'. Addressing the poem's aesthetic pleasure and its politics, or how its 'English pentameter marched in step with the invading English armies of the late Tudor period', Heaney turns his attention to *Edward II* and writes how he was

> conscious of the banishment to Ireland of Gaveston, the king's favourite, as something more than a shift of plot. Inevitably, in the present intellectual climate, it was hard not to read in Gaveston's relegation to the status of non-person an equal relegation of Ireland to the status of non-place. By its inclusion within the realm of English influence, late-medieval Ireland had become at once an annexe of the civil conquerors and the locus of a barbarism that had to be held at bay.[2]

Heaney alerts us to the political unconscious of Gaveston's temporary effacement in Ireland: thinking ahead to the play's allusion to the 'wild O'Neill [...] uncontroll'd within the English pale' (II.ii.164–5), he suggests the play implicitly erases Ireland. In this sense, it offers an attractive fantasy to Elizabethan culture, which needed to conceive of Ireland as an extension of the civilized space of the kingdom rather than a wild and uncontrollable terrain where even

2 Seamus Heaney, 'Extending the alphabet: on Christopher Marlowe's "Hero and Leander"' in *The redress of poetry* (London, 1995), pp 22–3.

the borders of the English Pale could prove vulnerable to native incursions. However, Heaney expresses caution at reading into the subtext of the play, and indeed literature more generally, commenting that it is an 'abdication of literary responsibility' when 'imaginative literature is read simply and solely as a function of an oppressive discourse, or as a reprehensible masking'.[3] Certainly, as Heaney implies, one can make too much of the play's use of Ireland; for instance, it is probably best to avoid seeing any broad significance in the silence concerning Gaveston's responsibilities as royal representative in Ireland. The collective silence says more about character and the political neglect occasioned by desire, favouritism and excess than it does about an ideology in the text. Nonetheless, it is important to recognize the potential force of the play's figuration of Ireland or its Irish images for, at the level of the unconscious, Edward's exile of Gaveston to Ireland does presuppose it is a natural extension of royal space. In legal terms, Ireland had been a kingdom since 1541 but in reality, the extension of English sovereignty there involved the re-constitution of Irish space and, in turn, the displacement or even removal of the native presence. Marlowe's play might be said, if only by implication, to share a similar ideological ground to a text like the 'Discourse of Ireland' (1599), which includes among its proposals for the colonization of Ireland, the re-settlement of the native inhabitants. 'I would not the bloud of them should be extinct', writes the anonymous author, 'but all the race of them to be translated out of Ireland, and English with some Flemmings to be onely planted in their Roomes'. Through the re-settlement of the Irish and the plantation of English and Flemish (whom the author sees as similar to the English), the text concludes, 'her Majesty shall make Ireland profitable unto her as England or mearely a West England'.[4] What is especially striking here, is the 'process of reasoning which enables the writer to "disappear" the Irish and smooth the island out into a "West England"; people and land are brutally deracinated'.[5] That Edward is prepared to send Gaveston to Ireland, and later entertain the idea of it as a safe haven for himself, might suggest that he conceives of Ireland along similar colonialist lines, which would align Marlowe's text with a more extreme policy toward the Irish in the period. As we shall see, however, closer attention to the text reveals different motivations for these movements – both real and intended – to Ireland, and crucially, different implications.

Despite the barons' assumption that the re-location of Gaveston is tantamount to his annihilation, it becomes clear that the relationship of king and

---

3 Heaney, 'Extending the alphabet', p. 24.   4 D.B. Quinn, '"A Discourse of Ireland": a sidelight on English colonial policy', *Proceedings of the Royal Irish Academy*, 46 (1942), 151–66 at 164; 166.   5 Hadfield and McVeagh (eds), *Strangers to that land*, p. 50.

favourite transcends spatial or geographic distance. It is the queen who, confronted by Edward, understands how Gaveston's literal absence will in fact signify nothing. Her husband, she soliloquizes, will 'ever dote on Gavetson' (I.iv.186). In a move that indicates the degree of power he retains, Edward urges Isabella to persuade the barons to repeal their decision. Mortimer initially refuses, hoping that the 'vile torpedo [...] floats on the Irish seas' (I.iv.226–7) but, convinced by the queen, he entreats Lancaster and the other earls to recall Gaveston, explaining:

> Know you not Gaveston hath store of gold,
> Which may in Ireland purchase him such friends
> As he will front the mightiest of us all?
> And whereas he shall live and be belov'd,
> 'Tis hard for us to work his overthrow. (I.iv.260–4)

Even allowing for the about turn Mortimer is advocating here, a tactical manoeuvre set in motion by the queen, there is an acknowledgment of the danger of distance, that phenomenon of the enemy abroad explored in *2 Henry VI*. Mortimer imagines Gaveston procuring his very own network of favourites in Ireland, so that Edward's destructive policy of favouritism will be replicated away from home. The play may be alluding to what one modern biographer of Gaveston sees as the opportunity for power and wealth that came with his role as royal plenipotentiary in Ireland.[6] Certainly, the suggestion that Gaveston's geographic separateness in Ireland could be empowering is corroborated by Edward's earlier assurance to his favourite 'Live where thou wilt, I'll send thee gold enough' (I.iv.114) and also by the general association of Gaveston with financial excess. Mortimer later complains 'that one so basely born | Should by his sovereign's favour grow so pert | And riot it with the treasure of the realm | While soldiers mutiny for want of pay' (I.iv.405–8). This complaint is indicative of how the barons see the Edward-Gaveston relationship in material and monetary terms, with the latter viewed as a drain on the kingdom, a financial burden that must be shaken-off if the king is to regain the support and confidence of the discontented nobility. As Thomas Healy observes, 'the barons' difficulty with Gaveston is a fear that the state's structures of power are being re-arranged'.[7] However, like his willingness to bestow royal monies on Gaveston, Edward's claim that, if his crown's revenue could secure the return of his beloved, he would 'freely give it to his enemies'

6 Pierre Chaplais, *Piers Gaveston: Edward's adoptive brother* (Oxford, 1994), pp 49–51.   7 Healy, *Christopher Marlowe*, p. 75.

(I.iv.311) suggest the impossibility of any reconciliation between the nobility and their king.

It is tempting to see in Mortimer's observations about Gaveston a broadly Elizabethan knowledge about office in Ireland of a kind evident in 2 *Henry VI*. Indeed, Mortimer speaks like an Elizabethan courtier in his appreciation of how an Irish posting could be purposefully misconstrued to damage the reputation of a rival. The case of Sir John Perrot in the early 1590s, like that of the second earl of Essex, Robert Devereux, towards the end of the reign, reveals the risks attached to service in Ireland. However, while *Edward II* is topically allusive, it does not offer as direct a topicality on Irish matters as Shakespeare's play. Rather, I would argue, the play figures Ireland in a conceptual or symbolic way. In contrast to 2 *Henry VI* and *Richard II*, where Ireland's offstage status confers a significant distance on it, in Marlowe's play it is a proximate space by virtue of its association with Gaveston. No sooner does Gaveston exit the stage for Ireland than there is swift communication and talk of his imminent return: Edward instructs 'our warrant forth | For Gaveston, to Ireland!' (I.iv.371–2) and his niece notes that 'My Lord of Cornwall is a-coming over, | And will be at court as soon as we' (II.i.75–6). The king later says that the 'wind is good' and though he fears Gaveston is 'wrack'd upon the sea' (II.ii.1–2) this is less to do with Ireland's geographic distance and more proof of how, in Lancaster's words, Edward's 'mind runs on his minion' (II.ii.4). Mortimer gives expression to Gaveston as a continuous absent presence when he remarks of the king 'If in his absence thus he favours him, | What will he do whenas he shall be present?' (II.ii.47–8), at which point Gaveston re-appears on stage. The barons think they have demonstrated their power over the king's favourite but the opposite is in fact the case: the play intimates that power resides with Edward and Gaveston, whose relationship determines space and time. What this reveals is not only how journeys in the play are, as Lisa Hopkins notes, 'essentially internal ones' but also, by connection, how that transcendent relationship breaks down the centre/periphery divide.[8]

The play offers competing viewpoints as to the implications of the elision of centre and periphery. To the barons, Gaveston's return to England and, more specifically, to the court, signals dissolution and destruction from within. Mortimer notes how there is 'Nothing but Gaveston!' (II.ii.7) from Edward, who dismisses the earl's report of French advances into Normandy as 'a trifle' (II.ii.10). With Gaveston present, Mortimer and Lancaster mock his newly acquired titles and Lancaster tries to stab him but, in a significant role reversal with their nemesis, both are subsequently barred from court by the king. The

8 Lisa Hopkins, *Christopher Marlowe: a literary life* (London, 2000), p. 118.

impression that the nobles are now on the margins looking in on a newly
configured centre is reinforced in the following scene, in which they try to gain
direct access to the king, despite being told that the he is 'dispos'd to be alone'
(II.ii.136). Confronting Edward directly, however, Mortimer and Lancaster
deliver a dual verbal assault that amounts to a damming portrait of the state
of the nation under Edward:

> MORTIMER The idle triumphs, masques, lascivious shows,
> And prodigal gifts bestow'd on Gaveston,
> Have drawn thy treasury dry, and made thee weak;
> The murmuring commons, overstretched, break.
>
> LANCASTER Look for rebellion, look to be depos'd.
> Thy garrisons are beaten out of France,
> And lame and poor lie groaning at the gates.
> The wild O'Neill, with swarms of Irish kerns,
> Lives uncontroll'd within the English pale.
> Unto the walls of York the Scots make road,
> And, unresisted, drive away rich spoils.
>
> (II.ii.157–67)

Defeated abroad, neighboured by the rebellious Irish, bordered by the
powerful Scots and ruled by an ineffective king, England is imagined as a
besieged and vulnerable space, its external difficulties merging with internal
ones. The Scottish incursion is the most imminent – Mortimer has already
asked the king to ransom his father who has been taken by the Scots – but,
like the other problems, it is presented as a direct consequence of Gaveston's
presence and overbearing influence on the king. Mention of English reversal in
Ireland invariably recalls Gaveston's role as royal representative there, the inference being that Gaveston is as ineffective a governor of Ireland as Edward is a
king of England. The centre, it seems, is now dangerously close to the margins,
the kingdom little more than a Pale.

As editors of the play have noted, the reference to Ireland has more of a
sixteenth than a fourteenth century resonance. It arguably shares a topical
weight with the strikingly similar allusion in the *Contention* but the issue of
application remains. Mark Burnett has shown that contemporaries did draw
analogies between Edward and Elizabeth, although in noting that that the
play's treatment of the topical is opaque and diffuse, he cautions against infer-
ring any 'easy correspondences' between the two.[9] Denis Kay argues the world
of Marlowe's play 'is constructed as an admonitory negative example for the

9 Burnett, '*Edward II* and Elizabethan politics', p. 93.

present', with the king's style of monarchy being the opposite of Elizabeth's.[10] With this in mind, it is possible to read in Lancaster's indictment of Edward a veiled warning to Elizabeth about favouritism, the maintenance of domestic stability and, more pointedly, the potential effects of procrastinating about Ireland. Certainly, Lancaster's comment about chaos in the Pale points toward contemporary concerns about political stability in Ireland. In 1589, for instance, the then lord deputy of Ireland told the privy council:

> the men of the Pale are utterly unprepared for armour and weapon, as appeared last summer in all the heat of the approach of the Spanish fleet. It should be remembered when the garrison and the nobleman and gentlemen of the Pale are drawn away, all the bad neighbours who border upon it are not unlikely to make havoc on Her Majesty's good subjects.[11]

The fear of porous borders and unwelcome incursions here should be understood not just in the context of recurrent rumours about another Spanish armada but also the symbolic significance of the Pale itself; as the centre of English governance in Ireland it always reflects in microcosm the English position there. A more general and explicit assessment was provided to the council in 1592: 'Ireland is like to go from Her Majesty and Her successors for ever, with great danger to the state of England, unless the pretence of Her Majesty's enemies be advisedly prevented'.[12] Beneath the alarmist tone so characteristic of official discourse on Ireland, is a depth of concern and a climate of unease that may well have shaped Marlowe's play indirectly. But it should also be noted that what Lancaster says and to whom he says it, reveals how observations about the state of Ireland could be used as a platform to criticize the queen or provide a cipher through which frustrations with royal power might be articulated.

Like the image of Ireland, the trope of the besieged nation is something of an open signifier: while the barons use it to accuse Edward of exposing England to domestic and foreign elements, he also applies the trope to himself. For example, in a characteristic aside, Edward asks 'What care I though the earls begirt us round?' (II.ii.224), a phrase that, with the meaning of 'to surround or enclose,' is richly suggestive of the king's increasingly marginalized position within his own kingdom.[13] The effect of Edward's

10 Dennis Kay, 'Marlowe, *Edward II* and the cult of Elizabeth', *EMLS*, 3.2 (1997), www.shu.ac.uk/emls, accessed November 2005.   11 *Cal. S.P.Ire.,1588–1592*, p. 116.   12 Ibid., p. 493.   13 'Begirt' is from the word 'gird, or girt', meaning to 'surround, encompass' or 'enclose'. The *OED* gives 1608 as the earliest date for the use of 'begirt' (p. 70).

self-characterization is to align Mortimer and Lancaster, and their co-conspirators more generally, with the imagined advances of the three disaffected
groups (the idle soldiers; the Irish; and the Scots). Revealingly, Mortimer and
Lancaster's rhetorical attack on the king ends with the Lancaster warning,
'Look next to see us with our ensigns spread' (II.ii.199). Later, in an attempt
to instil a sense of purpose in the enfeebled Edward, Spenser states: 'Were I
King Edward, England's sovereign [...] would I bear | These braves, this rage,
and suffer uncontroll'd | These barons thus to beard me in my land, | In mine
own realm?' (III.ii.10–15). Although Spenser is keen to gain the king's favour,
the use of 'uncontroll'd' in relation to the barons recalls Lancaster's own reference to the 'uncontroll'd' Irish in the Pale. The effect of such verbal echoing is
to connect the barons to the Irish rebels and Irish Others: the implication
being that it is the barons themselves, not Edward, who reduce the kingdom
to a Pale.

What is apparent here is how Ireland and the Irish become a metaphor or
signifier; their semiotic meaning of rebellion, wildness and alterity is re-
deployed in order to cast the English earls as rebels who enclose the king and
unsettle and de-centre the kingdom. From this perspective, it is possible to
understand why Edward is prepared to send his favourite to Ireland rather than
leave him in England. More importantly, however, the play's figuration of
Ireland suggests that the 'locus of barbarism', to recall Heaney's reading,
'cannot be held at bay' because, as this scene demonstrates, it is not something
'over there' or on the margins in Ireland but at home in England itself. In delineating the power of the barons, Ireland thus becomes a space to explore
England.

Throughout *Edward II*, then, the threat to and violation of borders, territories, and spaces – both physical and also conceptual – conveys the
diminution of the king's power at the hands of the barons. Lancaster and
Mortimer's incursion into the private space of the king not only literalizes the
concept of the enclosed king but also, symbolically, prefigures the ultimate
enclosure of him in the cesspool of the royal palace. Before this ignoble end,
however, Edward has already been the subject of a series of forced journeys, as
he is taken from the Welsh abbey, the place of his capture, to Killingworth,
and eventually to the royal palace, the place of his death. Lisa Hopkins
describes these journeys as 'an inversion of the teleology of the *Odyssey*', in that
they take Edward away from the familiar.[14] However, the point would rather
seem to be that it is England itself that has been rendered unfamiliar to
Edward. Just like Gaveston, Edward is forced into flight in a futile effort to

14 Hopkins, *Christopher Marlowe*, p. 126.

elude capture and, as with his favourite, it is Ireland that is imagined as a potential place of refuge.[15] The symbolism of these journeys is not lost on Edward, as his brief exchange with Leicester illustrates:

> LEICESTER   Your majesty must go to Killingworth.
>
> KING EDWARD   Must! It is somewhat hard when kings must go.
>   (IV.vi.83–4)

Travel and physical movement not only articulate the king's powerlessness, they also lead to and indeed symbolize the barons' act of usurpation and murder. As the rebellious lords pursue the royal party, the Younger Spenser advises the king: 'Fly, fly, my lord! The queen is overstrong! | Her friends do multiply, and yours do fail. | Shape we our course to Ireland, there to breathe' (IV.v.1–3). This is an especially evocative phrase: it is only in Ireland that Edward can have breathing space for, in England, Edward is suffocating; he will of course die of asphyxiation. In imagining Ireland as a potential safe haven for Edward, Marlowe appears to be following his source material quite closely. Holinshed notes that while Edward planned to go to Wales, where he had support, he also considered that 'he might easilie escape over into Ireland, and get into some mounteine-countrie, marish ground, or other streict, where his enemies should not come at him'.[16] The idea of such hidden spaces providing safety and cover inverts the Elizabethan image of the Irish landscape as hostile to newcomers. Indeed, the idea of Ireland as safe haven in *Edward II* is virtually unique in the drama, with the exception of Thomas Heywood's *Four Prentices of London* (1594), where the youngest of the four brothers is 'cast upon the coast of Ireland' and briefly stays 'mongst the Irish kernes'.[17] Of course, neither text should be thought of as exception to representations of Ireland but rather an indication that Ireland could be a malleable image in the period.

Edward's attempt to go to Ireland, like his decision to flee, might be interpreted as a further indication of his abdication of kingly responsibility, a sign that he has absolutely no appreciation of the political realities in either England or Ireland. Yet, the play enables the audience to understand why Edward must 'go', even if it means going to a space previously associated with rebellion. As I have been suggesting, that image of rebellion in Ireland reverberates back on the barons themselves, so that it is England, not Ireland, that

15 See Elizabeth Rambo, *Colonial Ireland in medieval English literature* (London, 1994) on the representation of Ireland in medieval romances as 'a place of safe exile for those fleeing enemies at home' (p. 64).   16 Quoted in William Dinsmore Briggs, *Marlowe's Edward II* (London, 1914), p. 173.   17 *Dramatic Works of Thomas Heywood*, 3 vols (New York, 1964), ii, p. 185.

is a place of danger. After all, it was only in Ireland that Gaveston was safe; once he returns to England, his death becomes inevitable, as Lancaster's wounding of him immediately upon his arrival illustrates (II.ii.79). As news spreads that the king has 'shipp'd but late for Ireland' (IV.vi.69), Mortimer hopes that the Irish seas will 'sink them all' (IV.vi.70), just as he had hoped before that they would consume Gaveston. Kent, in an aside, laments his brother's hasty departure: 'Unhappy is Edward, chas'd from England's bounds' (IV.vi.74). Kent speaks quite literally of Edward's loss of power but in connecting that loss to Edward's departure, he alludes to the powerful association between kingly authority, identity and the geographic space of England, or what Garret Sullivan describes as the 'geography of national sovereignty'.[18] By the terms of this geography —which involves the 'conceptual annexation of distinct cultural spaces in the name of the monarch' — Edward's lordship of Ireland, the place where Edward is being 'chas'd' to, is within his authority and thus England's bounds.[19] Kent's comment points to the collapse of this geography and the fictions of national identity that it sustains as Edward opts for his own private space or geography.

As it transpires, the idea of the king forcibly externalized from the geographic boundaries of his kingdom is more symbolic than literal because, unlike Gaveston, Edward never reaches his destination. Ireland proves to be Edward's final but elusive chance of escape. As Edward and his two associates conceal themselves in the Welsh abbey, one of them explains:

> We were embark'd for Ireland, wretched we,
> With awkward winds and with sore tempests driven,
> To fall on shore, and here to pine in fear
> Of Mortimer and his confederates. (IV.vi.33–6)

It will be apparent that there are a number of similarities between Gaveston's final movements and those of the king. Both are forced into a form of exile, to 'fly and run away' (IV.v.4) and significantly both are associated with Ireland before their deaths, but there are also some intriguing verbal parallels too. Before his capture, Gaveston refers to himself as 'Breathing in hope' (II.v.5) to see Edward again, a remark echoed later when Spenser instructs the king to go to Ireland, 'there to breathe' (IV.v.4). For both men, the idea of a breathing space proves illusory. However, through this subtle verbal connection, the play symbolically reunites the two men. Before their initial separation, the king had

18 Sullivan, 'Geography and identity in Marlowe', p. 241. 19 Garrett Sullivan, *The drama of landscape: land, property and social relations on the early modern stage* (Stanford, 1998), p. 19.

vowed 'I'll come to thee; my love shall ne'er decline' (I.iv.116). Lawrence Normand has argued that Edward's attempt to construct 'a private discursive and geographic space where his relation with Gaveston might be realized' turns out to be 'a politically impossible, utopian space that can only exist in discourse'.[20] Similarly, Judith Haber argues that this private space constitutes 'a place apart, a site of insignificance: it is what is left over after the kingdom has been meaningfully divided'.[21] While the identification of Edward's private space as 'a place apart' is accurate, I would argue that the space is also a site of significance because it is the only space that appears to afford Edward a genuine sense of self-worth. Moreover, as the play intimates throughout, it is the space Edward and Gaveston occupy rather than any 'real' geographic or political space that matters. What Haber and Normand fail to consider is the importance of Ireland to the conception of this site within the play. As Edward unwittingly retraces the steps and fortunes of his beloved, it seems as if, on a symbolic level, he is seeking out that 'nook or corner' where they can be together. In the play's drama of desire, Ireland is figured as a space of safe exile, the potential site for this symbolic reunification. Ultimately, then, the idyllic 'nook' is located somewhere between Ireland and England, an interstice or in-between space where Edward and Gaveston can be free from English barons turned Irish rebels.

'NOW FOR OUR IRISH WARS': HOME AND AWAY IN *RICHARD II*

If *Edward II* suggests the fragility or even pointlessness of national geographies, Shakespeare's *Richard II* – which shares several thematic and stylistic parallels with Marlowe's play – oscillates between a recognition of their power and a considered awareness of their ideological underpinnings. For instance, it is not difficult to see how, for all its nostalgia, John of Gaunt's impassioned vision of England demonstrates the capacity of the early modern stage to produce a poetics of nationhood. England is variously imagined as 'this sceptred isle' (II.i.40), 'this precious stone' (II.i.46), 'this blessed plot' (II.i.50), 'bound in with the triumphant sea' (II.i.61). What occurs momentarily here through the English language, that 'native English' (I.iii.160) that the banished Mowbray speaks of, is a fusion of the geographic space of 'Britain', English sovereignty and an imagined community. Yet, the audience is also aware of Gaunt's rhetorical manipulations, how his words are positioned to condemn

20 Lawrence Normand, '"What passions call you these?": *Edward II* and James VI' in Darryll Grantley and Peter Roberts (eds), *Christopher Marlowe and English Renaissance culture* (Aldershot, 1996), p. 190.   21 Judith Haber, 'Submitting to history: Marlowe's *Edward II*' in Burt and Archer (eds), *Enclosure acts*, p. 173.

King Richard and, perhaps less obviously, how his 'cartographic lyricism' is predicated on omissions and occlusions as the Welsh and Scots are elided in the fashioning of England as island nation.[22] As Andrew Murphy notes, 'the ethnic divisions within the island of Britain itself are simply written over'. Murphy also draws attention to another requisite omission in the Gauntean construction of the 'sceptred isle', observing that the 'the problematic territory of Ireland is excluded, as if simply abandoned to its venomous kern'.[23] However, it is not accurate to say that Ireland is simply excluded, for the play reveals how that 'sceptred isle' is a fiction dependent on 'colonialism of a kind epitomised by [Richard's] Irish expedition'.[24] What this suggests is significant connections between Richard's urgent Irish wars – which take the king, but interestingly not the play, away to Ireland – and concepts of English identity. As Garret Sullivan has astutely observed, the concatenation 'between the physical limits of the nation, English identity, and the limits of Richard's authority is played out geographically through Richard's disastrous relation with Ireland'.[25] More intriguing still, is the figuring of Ireland as 'an absent presence in the dramatic action' of the play.[26] Simultaneously invisible and also in view, marginal but also symbolically central, Ireland occupies a curious position in *Richard II*. I suggest that the text's double take registers conflicting Elizabethan desires towards Ireland: on the one hand, the desire to engage with and reform it; on the other, the desire to occlude it.

Although an offstage space, Ireland nonetheless proves central to the dramatic action of *Richard II*. News of rebellion there and Richard's decision to attend it personally sets everything in motion, from the king's seizure of Gaunt's estate to Bolingbroke's timely return from exile. Richard's departure for Ireland is, then, the originating moment of his downfall. In prioritizing Richard's absence in Ireland as a crucial factor in Bolingbroke's seizure of power, Shakespeare makes dramatic capital of Holinshed's reference to Richard's delay in Ireland.[27] Highley maintains that, in contrast to the source text, the play gives insufficient reason for Richard's decision to go to Ireland, with the effect that Ireland is presented 'as an expensive and dangerous distraction for England's rulers'.[28] But this is to overlook the figuration of Ireland as both a pressing and present problem, from Greene's initial 'Now, for the rebels

22 Neill, 'Broken English and broken Irish', p. 14.   23 Murphy, 'Shakespeare's Irish history', p. 46.   24 Maley, 'The Irish text and subtext of Shakespeare's English histories', p. 104.   25 Sullivan, *Drama of landscape*, p. 115. 26 Highley, *Shakespeare, Spenser*, p. 64.   27 See *Holinshed's chronicles*. Holinshed reports 'it fortuned at the same time, in which the duke of Hereford or Lancaster [...] arrived thus in England, the seas were so troubled by tempests, and the winds blew so contrarie for anie passage, to come over foorth of England to the king, remaining still in Ireland, that for the space of 6 weeks, he received no advertisements from thence: yet at length, when the seas became calme [...] there came over a ship, whereby the king understood the manner of the dukes arrivall' (p. 852).   28 Highley, *Shakespeare, Spenser*, p. 65.

which stand out in Ireland. | Expedient manage must be made, my liege, | Ere further leisure yield them further means | For their advantage and your highness' loss' (I.iv.37–40); to Richard's own 'we will make for Ireland presently' (I.iv.51); 'We will for Ireland, and 'tis time I trow' (II.i.219); and the queen's 'his designs crave haste, his haste good hope' (II.ii.44). Certainly, news from Ireland distracts Richard from concerns about Bolingbroke's popularity but his resolve to quell rebellion and, more particularly, rebellion in Ireland, demonstrates kingly resolve and an adjudged sense of priorities. It is only when viewed retrospectively that his decision appears a bad judgment call.

If Ireland is the originating moment of Richard's downfall, it also captures something of his relationship with the past. Phyllis Rackin notes how Richard moves from an initial association with an idealized feudal past towards an association with the erosion of medieval values, as evidenced by his disruption of the trial by combat and his financial excesses, which are indicative of the emergent money economy.[29] Redefined in the eyes of the audience, the king becomes separated 'from the object of nostalgic desire', that is the lost England recalled in Gaunt's speech, and associated with 'objects of present anxiety'.[30] The dramatic action now takes the form of what Rackin calls a 'disturbing present process' that has the capacity to reach out and implicate the audience. Although Rackin does not mention it, what is intriguing here is that as 'objects of present anxiety', the Irish wars demonstrate Richard's commitment to the immediate present and a break with the past represented by the England engendered in Gaunt's vision. Yet, the Irish wars also involve a link back to the past for in going to Ireland, Richard is, on a symbolic level, endeavouring to prove Gaunt wrong, re-writing his uncle's damning deathbed history of his reign. As Graham Holderness writes, 'it is precisely because the England he sees before him – Richard's England – falls so short of his idealized vision of what he believes England once was, that his poetic vision of national glory is so brightly and vividly imagined'.[31] Gaunt's encomium famously ends lamenting how 'That England that was wont to conquer others | Hath made a shameful conquest of itself' (II.i.65–6). Richard's determination to go to war in Ireland indirectly redresses Gaunt's perception of England as implosive and retractive. By campaigning against the Irish, Richard looks as if he is doing precisely what English kings are supposed to do, that is, to 'conquer others' (II.i.65), in both the grammatical and also the ethnic sense. There is perhaps, then, an implied irony in Richard's appropriation of Gaunt's monies for the Irish wars: 'The lining of his coffers shall make coats | To deck our soldiers for these Irish wars' (I.iv.60–1). Ireland is to be the originary site of Richard's

29 Rackin, *Stages of history*, p. 119.   30 Ibid., pp 121–2.   31 Graham Holderness, '"What ish my nation?": Shakespeare and national identities', *Textual Practice*, 5 (1991), 74–93 at 13.

revisionist act, his determination to counter Gaunt's history: 'Now for our
Irish wars', declares Richard,

> We must supplant those rough rug-headed kerns,
> Which live like venom where no venom else
> But only they have privilege to live.
> And for these great affairs do ask some charge,
> Towards our assistance we do seize to us
> The plate, coin, revenues and moveables
> Whereof our uncle Gaunt did stand possessed.   (II.i.156–162)

Richard's use of 'kern' as a metonym for the native Irish demonizes the inhabitants of his lordship as wild and barbarous, a demonization completed by the
simile; which, in alluding to the reputed absence of snakes from Ireland,
portrays the Irish themselves as serpentine and poisonous. As already noted,
this image of the Irish as quasi-bestial appears to have been relatively
commonplace in the period. However, it is significantly extended here through
its combination with the word 'supplant', meaning to displace or remove (as
in *The Tempest*, with Sebastian's 'you did supplant your brother Prospero'
[II.i.276]). On a metaphoric level, 'supplant' involves the uprooting of the
Irish, an uprooting apparently justified by their innate wildness. With the additional sense of removal or 'dispossession by treacherous or dishonourable
means', it literally denotes a policy of scorched earth, a tactic deployed by
Richard and of course by Elizabeth's military men in Ireland.[32] The speech
prompted John Arden to hold Shakespeare accountable for perpetuating anti-
Irish prejudices but Willy Maley has recently argued that 'the anti-Irish speech
can be read as anti-courtly critique'.[33] Maley points to Ross and
Northumberland's criticism of the king's financial rectitude, which they link
to excessive expenditure at court. Northumberland comments on the mismanagement of the royal treasury, explaining 'Wars hath not wasted it, for warred
he hath not' (II.i.252), and, comparing Richard to his ancestors, adds 'More
hath he spent in peace than they in war' (II.i.255). Maley argues that 'the true
expense is an overblown court, not a neglected colony. That Shakespeare is less
critical of Ireland than of England is something critics cannot grasp'.[34] While
critics may well be culpable of re-inscribing a politics of centre and periphery

---

32 *OED*, p. 249. On Richard's use of scorched earth policy in the early phase of campaign against
MacMurrough, see in J.F. Lydon, 'Richard II's expeditions to Ireland', *Journal of the Royal Society of Antiquaries of
Ireland*, 92 (1963), 135–49 at 145.   33 John Arden, 'Rug-headed Irish kerns and British poets', *New Statesman* (13
July 1979), 56–7; Maley, 'The Irish text and subtext of Shakespeare's English histories', p. 105.   34 Ibid., p. 105.

in interpreting Shakespearean representations of Ireland, Maley's contention
has the effect of downplaying the force of Richard's proposal to deal with the
Irish and deflecting attention from the ideology that underpins the king's rhetoric, an ideology that may not be Shakespeare's own but rather part of an early
modern discourse of Irish barbarism. As Clare Carroll has argued, this is a
proto-racialist discourse where early modern notions of race 'as family lineage
or genealogy and as an inherited disposition imposed on a whole group of
people' intersect to produce an ideology based on the absolute alterity of the
Irish.[35]

It is necessary, therefore, to recognize the contexts that inform and are
possibly encoded in Richard's planned act of supplanting, as well as the anxieties that such an act disguises. The king's 'Now for our Irish wars', like
Greene's 'Now for the rebels which stand out in Ireland', is a call to arms
charged with the energy and demands of the present but the real 'now' at issue
is Elizabethan rather than Ricardian. Shakespeare's *Richard II* dates to late 1595,
the year in which Hugh O'Neill was declared by royal proclamation 'the principal traitor and chief author of this rebellion and a known practiser with
Spain and other her majesties enemies'.[36] Setting out the state's grievances with
O'Neill, including the allegation that he had drawn other northern chieftains
like Hugh Roe O'Donnell into rebellion, the proclamation was 'issued to coincide with the march of the queen's army into Ulster'.[37] O'Neill had already
ambushed and defeated the forces of Marshal Bagenal at Clontibret; such
attacks with well-equipped and sizeable forces marked a new phase in the wars
in Ireland. Although the state negotiated a truce with O'Neill that would last
until 1597, the situation in Ulster remained volatile. Writing from Ireland in
February 1596, Sir Henry Wallop informed Sir Robert Cecil of the new kind
of warfare facing crown forces there:

> The state of the Realm was never so dangerous in the memory of man
> as it is at present, in regard of the uniting of O'Donnell and all the
> chieftains of Ulster and Connacht with Tyrone, and the great combi-
> nation which they have drawn together, stretching itself unto all parts
> of this Kingdom, and the strength of the traitors through Tyrone's
> wealth who is well furnished with all the habiliments of war, and
> [they] have so trained their men, as in sundry encounters that they
> have had with our men, they seem to be other enemies, and not those

35 Carroll, *Circe's cup*, p. 18. 36 'Royal proclamation against the earl of Tyrone' quoted in *Irish history from contemporary sources, 1509–1610*, p. 99. 37 Morgan, *Tyrone's rebellion*, p. 179.

that in times past, were wont never to attempt her Majesty's forces in
the plain field [...] there is great cause in my opinion for her Majesty
to give speedy direction for the suppressing of this rebellion.[38]

Wallop's long service in Ireland meant he was well placed to identify the threat
the confederacy posed and to recognize that royal policy towards Ireland
risked being overtaken by events there. His mention of the Irish wars requiring
'speedy direction' from the queen herself recalls Greene's 'expedient manage' in
Richard II and suggests a topical recognition in Shakespeare's play, although
perhaps there is equal emphasis in the play on the necessity for financial
caution as there is for swift action.

The wars in Ireland presented a number of logistical and financial difficulties for the state, from the maintenance of English garrisons there to the
levying of more forces. Throughout the 1590s, large demands were placed on
shires in England for men to serve in Ireland, a pattern that John McGurk has
shown became widespread towards the end of Elizabeth's reign as the situation
in Ireland grew desperate.[39] 'To fund money for the requirements of the war',
writes Frederick Dietz, 'the queen's ministers literally grabbed at every suggestion which promised a little revenue'.[40] While the financial burden of the Irish
wars reached its apotheosis during 1599, there were signs of a strain on
resources earlier. In 1596, for instance, the queen requested the second earl of
Essex and the lord admiral, both stationed at Cadiz, to send 1,500 men to
Ireland 'because her Majestie is unwilling to burthen the countryes with often
levyes, having bin of late greatly charged'.[41] The following year, when the
quarto text of *Richard II* was printed, there were reports that 'great sums of
money lately sent thither [to Ireland] for our army and garrison there have not
sufficed to supply the wants of our said forces'.[42] The play engages in a
dialogue with these present anxieties for although Richard's financial mismanagement is primarily associated with courtly excesses, it is also linked to his
Irish campaign.[43] As Richard's perceived mismanagement of state finances is
discussed, with reports that 'daily new exactions are devised' (II.i.250), Ross
bluntly states: 'He hath not money for these Irish wars, | His burdenous taxa-
tions notwithstanding, | But by the robbing of the banished Duke'
(II.i.260–2). Such misgivings about the additional financial burden caused by

38 Quoted in *Irish history from contemporary sources, 1509–1610*, p. 185.   39 McGurk, *Elizabethan conquest*, pp 51–108.
40 Frederick Dietz, *English public finance*, 2 vols (London, 1964), ii, p. 89.   41 *Acts of the privy council, 1595–96*, ed.
John Roche Dasent (London, 1901), pp 103–4.   42 *Calendar of state papers, domestic, 1595–1597*, ed. Mary Anne
Everett Green (London, 1869), p. 537.   43 Contrary to what some critics maintain, this is provided for in the
source text, where it is said that 'at his going into Ireland, [he] exacted manie notable summes of monie, beside
plate and jewels, without law or custome', but the way the play foregrounds the two suggests a topical resonance.
See *Holinshed's chronicles as used in Shakespeare's plays* (London, 1927), p. 30.

the Irish venture would have had a particular resonance within the context of increased levies for the war in Ireland. The play also articulates the political and social repercussions of wartime expenditure. Ross observes that 'The commons hath he pilled with grievous taxes | And quite lost their hearts' (II.i.247–8), an observation that is given credence when it is echoed by Richard's own supporter, Bagot, who says of the king's subjects that 'their love | Lies in their purses, and whoso empties them | By so much fills their hearts with deadly hate' (II.ii.130–1). Highley sees here a 'cautionary example, a veiled warning, to the rulers of Elizabethan England of the dangers of embroilment in Ireland', before concluding that the play 'arouses suspicions that Elizabeth's own adventures in Ireland were equally unnecessary and irresponsible'.[44] This is a provocative interpretation but one that fixes what is an ambivalent response to the Irish wars. For, on the one hand, the play demonstrates the domestic costs, both for the king and his subjects, of an the overseas war, while on the other, Richard's appreciation of the urgency of the problem there and willingness to address it personally is an approach that might be emulated. Through Richard's imagined ethnic cleansing and spatial displacement of the Irish, the play enacts a contemporary desire to effect a resolution of the situation in Ireland but it is also suggests an equally contemporary knowledge that 'speedy direction' in Ireland could be costly.

    The play can, however, be interpreted as casting a shadow over Richard's plan for the ethnic purification of the Irish, especially since his effort to re-write history is shown to have disastrous and potentially self-induced consequences. His planned 'supplanting' of the Irish can be included among the pattern of conveyances that Patricia Parker has traced in the play. For it is Richard's intended dispossession in Ireland that leads to his conveyance of 'what Gaunt did stand possessed' (II.i.162), 'an act of conveyance or robbery that has as its consequence Bolingbroke's conveyance of the crown itself'.[45] Moreover, while a temporal urgency surrounds the Irish wars, in going to Ireland Richard begins to look as if he has misread the present, the 'now', in contrast to Bolingbroke's skilful exploitation of it. Newly landed in England, Bolingbroke is asked 'what pricks you on | To take advantage of the absent time' (II.iii.78–9), a query that recalls Northumberland's earlier suggestion that Bolingbroke and his supporters deferred their arrival until '[t]he first departing of the King for Ireland' (II.i.292). Greene, who earlier had given news of rebellion in Ireland as requiring urgent attention, now remarks 'I hope the King is not yet shipped for Ireland' (II.ii.41), an observation suggesting that, like the king himself, Richard's supporters have a flawed sense of timing; so Green vainly hopes against time and reality 'That he, our hope, might have

---

44 Highley, *Shakespeare, Spenser*, p. 64; p. 66.   45 Parker, *Shakespeare from the margins*, p. 151.

retired his power | And driven into despair an enemy's hope | Who strongly hath set footing in this land' (II.ii.46–8). But it is York, the king's uncle, who gives fullest expression to the significance of Richard's absence, remarking to the queen: 'Your husband, he is gone to save far off, | Whilst others come to make him lose at home' (II.ii.80–1). Referring to the king's largess, 'Now comes the sick hour that his surfeit made' (II.ii.84), York apportions blame not on the usurper but on Richard himself, with the mention of timing implying that Bolingbroke's landing in England coincides with and is enabled by Richard's offstage landing in Ireland. Absent from the kingdom and from the dramatic action, the impression that Richard is 'far off' is maintained through references to a breakdown in communication. York asks 'are there no posts dispatched for Ireland?' (II.ii.103), and Bushy later observes that 'the wind sits fair for news to go to Ireland, | But none returns' (II.ii.123–4). This symbolic silence articulates Richard's powerlessness just as his absence in Ireland facilitates Bolingbroke's arrival and presence in England, as York's accusatory question, 'Com'st thou because the anointed King is hence?' (II.iii.95), indicates. Seemingly incidental phrases like 'hence' or 'left behind' (II.iii.96) convey the extent to which the king is dislocated from his kingdom but also render Ireland a world apart.

As we have seen, both *2 Henry VI* and *Edward II* provide examples of Ireland as an offstage space but there is a more pronounced sense of distancing in *Richard II*, which suggests an unconscious movement in the text to efface Ireland and the contemporary problem it presents. So rather than the silencing of the Irish that Richard's expedition promised, we get silence about his 'absent time' there. Such silence draws attention to what is absent from the time of the play itself, in particular why *Richard II* does not include a scene dramatizing Richard's Irish campaign? This is an issue addressed by Plunket Barton who, in *Links between Ireland and Shakespeare*, even goes as far as to 'supply the gap, and to sketch some of the episodes, which might have been fittingly borrowed from the incidents of the Irish expedition', though he does not provide any explanation for the perceived omission.[46] Leaving aside Barton's implicit desire to supplement Shakespeare's text, a desire reminiscent of Restoration and eighteenth century revisions or 'improvements', his reconstruction of this hypothetical Irish scene suggests a possible and intriguing lacuna. Certainly, Shakespeare would have found the material for such a scene in Holinshed's *Chronicles* and, more specifically, its Irish section, which contains a narrative of Richard's two expeditions to Ireland. The text recounts the king's determination to 'voyage thither' to Ireland, suppress 'the unrulie parts and rebellions sturres of the Irishman' and avenge the murder of Robert

---

46 Plunket Barton, *Links between Shakespeare and Ireland* (Dublin, 1919), p. 81.

Mortimer; it also mentions 'the principall rebell' Art MacMurrough, who constituted the greatest threat to the lordship.[47] Richard secured the surrender of MacMurrough and, as noted in the *Chronicles*, he had a successful campaign: 'such was the prowesse of him and his, that the Irish were well tamed, and forced to submit themselves: and yet the kings power made no great slaughter of them'.[48] A carefully planned and costly campaign of military force, the king's first expedition was noted for its scale; 'it is not in memory', wrote the French chronicler Jean Froissart, 'that ever any king of England made such apparel and provision for any journey to make war against the Irishmen'.[49] Richard's second expedition of 1399, however, was compromised by financial difficulties and the threat posed by Bolingbroke; following the king's return into England, MacMurrough was in open rebellion.

Considering the similarity in both scale and purpose between the Ricardian and Elizabethan campaigns in Ireland – a similarity which endows Elizabeth's reputed identification with King Richard an additional resonance – it is not unreasonable to infer that a direct representation of Richard's warring in Ireland in Shakespeare's play would have provoked overt correspondences with the crisis of the late 1590s.[50] McMurrough's rebellion would have suggested topical parallels with Hugh O'Neill. From this perspective, one might connect the omission of this material to Ireland's status as 'a dangerous subject for writers in Elizabethan England'.[51] It is worth remembering, however, that *Richard II* contains a number of direct allusions to the Irish wars and, more generally, that the topical subject of Ireland shaped the drama of the period and was refracted in it. Thus, while it is probable that Shakespeare passed over the Irish material for dramaturgical rather than ideological reasons (with the king's absence in Ireland exploited to good dramatic effect in the play), it is important to recognise the ideological implications that can attach to such structural absences and creative choices. As I have being suggesting, the absence of an Irish scene in the play should be read alongside its distancing of Ireland, a further indication of an unconscious impulse in the text to disengage with Ireland. In order to think further about this, I want to conclude by considering the king's return from Ireland and to the dramatic focus.

47 *Holinshed's chronicles*, pp 850; 259; 851. 48 Ibid., p. 852. 49 Quoted in Lydon, 'Richard II's expeditions to Ireland', p. 142. 50 Elizabeth's exchange with William Lambarde is reprinted in *Richard II*, ed. Peter Ure (London, 1956), p. lix. For a compelling survey of the queen's identification with Richard, an allusion to Essex's reputed appropriation of *Richard II* to announce his coup, see Evelyn May Albright, 'Shakespeare's *Richard II* and the Essex conspiracy', *PMLA*, 42 (1927), 686–720. The wider implications are discussed in David Scott Kastan, 'Proud majesty made a subject: Shakespeare and the spectacle of rule', *Shakespeare Quarterly*, 27 (1986), 459–75. See also Kastan, *Shakespeare after theory*, pp 109–27 and Louis A. Montrose, *The purpose of playing: Shakespeare and the cultural politics of the Elizabethan theatre* (Chicago, 1996), pp 76–98. 51 Joan Fitzpatrick, *Shakespeare, Spenser and the contours of Britain: reshaping the Atlantic archipelago* (Hatfield, Herts., 2004), p. 89.

Just before Richard's re-appearance onstage, the audience is reminded of
his earlier invisibility, with a Welsh captain reporting that "'tis thought the King
is dead' (II.iv.7), a rumour which prompts Salisbury to soliloquize propheti-
cally:

> Ah, Richard! With the eyes of heavy mind
> I see thy glory, like a shooting star,
> Fall to the base earth from the firmament.
> Thy sun sets weeping in the lowly west,
> Witnessing storms to come, woe, and unrest.
>
> (II.iv.18–22)

Bringing to mind the literal storms that will delay the king's return – his 'late
tossing on the breaking seas' (III.ii.3) – and anticipating the havoc he will face,
Salisbury evokes a commonplace metaphor of the setting sun for the fall of
the monarch. The image takes on an added significance in the play, however,
considering its specific association with Richard; for, following his return from
Ireland, Richard employs it himself to give expression to his belief in the
divine right of kings. '[K]now'st thou not', he says to Aumerle,

> That when the searching eye of heaven is hid
> Behind the globe, that lights the lower world,
> Then thieves and robbers range abroad unseen
> In murders and in outrage bloody here;
> But when from under this terrestrial ball
> He fires the proud tops of the eastern pines,
> And darts his light through every guilty hole,
> Then murders, treasons, and detested sins,
> The cloak of night being plucked from off their backs,
> Stand bare and naked, trembling at themselves?
> So when this thief, this traitor, Bolingbroke,
> Who all this while hath revelled in the night
> Whilst we were wand'ring with the Antipodes,
> Shall see us rising in our throne, the east,
> His treasons will sit blushing in his face,
> Not able to endure the sight of day,
> But, self-affrighted, tremble at his sin.
> Not all the water in the rough rude sea
> Can wash the balm from an anointed king.   (III.ii.33–51)

By comparing himself to the sun, the king draws an analogy between its departure to the lower world, when its light is hidden from the earth, and his own absence in Ireland, which robs England of its 'light' and permits treason to prosper.[52] Of course, he has only been in Ireland but on a cognitive level his self-characterization intimates that it is he who has been in darkness, 'far off', out of step with time. It is a self-knowledge that will, however, only be fully realized later when Richard admits 'I wasted time, and now doth Time waste me' (V.v.49). As in three of the other four occasions when it is used in the Shakespearean canon, 'Antipodes' is an image of darkness, but its use here also involves implicit assumptions about Ireland and the Irish which modern editorial glosses do not adequately convey.[53] Richard is referring to 'Antipodes' as a place (the lower world or that which is opposite or below the region of western man) and, as the use of the preposition 'with' suggests, a race too. The two meanings are, however, interdependent since, as John Friedman reminds us, the race 'grew from a misconception of the Antipodes as a part of the world where men walked upside down'.[54] As a race, the Antipodes (opposite footed) would have brought to mind other marvellous races such as the Himantopedes (strap feet) or Anthropophagi (man-eaters) referred to in Pliny's *Natural History*, the thirteenth century *Mandeville's Travels* and, of course, Shakespeare's *Othello*, where the Moor's 'traveller's history' of such curiosities is absorbed by Desdemona with 'a greedy ear' (I.iii.138; 148).[55] The implicit association here of the Irish with this discourse of the fabulous renders them barbarous and incontrovertibly Other, but the play is not unique in drawing such a connection. In Gerald of Wales' *Topographia Hiberniae* (1187), a text that informs much early modern writing on Ireland, the social behaviour and cultural practices of the native Irish are also related to the wonders of the east.[56] Similarly, in his *Short Survey of Ireland*, published in 1609, Barnabe Rich claimed that in writing of Ireland he could 'speak of greater wonders than either Sir John Mandeville in his travel or any other that have passed the most uncouth places of the world are able to truly report'.[57] Despite Ireland's geographic propinquity to its neighbouring island, it could be imagined as analogous to foreign and marvellous lands.

The analogy with the Antipodes constructs an image of Ireland as a strange land populated with barbarous natives that are dangerously close to England.

52 Ure (ed.), *Richard II*, p. 96.   53 Martin Spevack, *Harvard concordance to Shakespeare* (Cambridge, MA, 1969), p. 50.   54 John Friedman, *The monstrous races in Medieval art and thought* (Cambridge, MA, 1981), p. 11.   55 For a full discussion of such races, see Friedman, *Monstrous races*, pp 9–20; for a brief account of *Mandeville's travels*, which perpetuated belief in the monstrous races, see J.R.S. Phillips, *The medieval expansion of Europe* (Oxford, 1988), pp 205–11.   56 Gerald discusses what he sees as the anomalies of Ireland in terms of wonders of the west which, he claims, rival the wonders of the east; see *The history and topography of Ireland*, ed. John J. O'Meara (London, 1982), pp 57–91.   57 Quoted in Quinn, *The Elizabethans and the Irish*, p. 30.

This impression is reinforced by Richard's reference to 'wandering', a word that may have had particular connotations for a contemporary audience. As John Gillies has observed, Elizabethan constructions of the exotic were influenced by the classics and the bible, the combined authority of which produced a set of symbolic equations between 'wandering, diffusion, confusion, degeneration, difference, and remoteness'.[58] Considering these connotations, the king's 'wandering' involves more than a recognition that, relative to events in England, his sojourn in Ireland has been pointless. Rather, it insinuates that he has not only failed to 'supplant' the kern and re-constitute Irish space but, more worry-ingly, that he has been changed by the Irish experience.

It is also possible that another sense of the word 'Antipodes' as 'the oppo-site to a person or thing' is being invoked here.[59] If this is the case then Ireland is being positioned as the spatial or geographic corollary to England, a distant space necessary for the definition of England's boundaries. In this regard, Ireland would appear to take on a similar function to the geographic limits both Mowbray and Bolingbroke are prepared to go to in order to fight each other. Mowbray vows to fight 'wherever Englishman durst set his foot' (I.i.66), while Bolingbroke, employing a cartographic image, boasts that he will fight 'here or elsewhere, to the furthest verge | That ever was surveyed by English eye' (I.i.93–4). Noting how the combatants 'speak as if all the world's an exten-sion of England', Laurie Glover argues that these 'image[s] of dominion' are evocative of English colonial expansion, of the 'European establishing his nation's sovereignty by planting his foot, his standard, or his colonies upon the lands of another'.[60] Conversely, I would argue that, as with the analogy between Ireland and the Antipodes, these images suggest an awareness of boundaries, of spaces not yet subjected to English cartographic knowledge and political control. Like those wild spaces in Ireland, these uncharted spaces perform a crucial function in determining definitions of England and Englishness, because it is in the encounter with such spaces that the seemingly stable categories of nation and self unravel. Thus, the proximate space of Ireland must be construed as an antipodal space so that England's bounds can be defined and its perennial problem imagined as 'far off'.

What is evident in Shakespeare's *Richard II* is a domestic view of Ireland: unlike its king, the play prefers to view Ireland at a distance. This perspective is crystallized in the garden scene where England is examined in microcosm. In an echoing and also literalization of Gaunt's imagery, the gardener's man compares the cultivated space of his garden, 'the compass of a pale' (III.iv.41)

58 Gillies, *Shakespeare and the geography*, p. 32. 59 *OED*, pp 530–1. 60 Laurie Carol Glover, 'Colonial qualms/ colonial quelling: England and Ireland in the sixteenth century' (PhD, Claremont Graduate School, 1995), p. 161; p. 159.

to England, 'our sea-walled garden, the whole land' that is 'full of weeds' (III.iv.43–4). The play exploits the resonance of 'pale', with its Irish associations, to suggest that Richard has not only neglected England but also allowed a process of inversion. As the gardener remarks, 'O what a pity is it | That he had not so trimmed and dressed his land | As we this garden!' (III.iv.55–7), pointing to the irony that the king was 'supplanting' in Ireland for the protection and preservation of England when he should have been doing so at home, in the garden of England itself. Perhaps this insular logic is behind the curious silence about what Richard did in Ireland, for we never here whether the king supplanted the Irish and succeeded in 'these great affairs' (II.i.160). Clearly, the play's interests lie elsewhere, with the focus on Richard's tragically altered state and Bolingbroke's political victory, though the latter is forced to play the role of silent king to the 'unkinged Richard' (IV.i.220). However, as with the absence of Ireland from Gaunt's speech, this silence is significant. The legacy of Richard's campaign in Ireland, implied but never stated in *Richard II*, is of the 'absent King' (V.i.49) and his 'unlucky Irish wars'.[61] The play reveals a desire to confront the urgent Irish problem, holding out the possibility that Elizabeth will not share such a legacy. Yet, its relegation of Ireland to an offstage and then antipodal space, to a world beyond representation, signifies a desire to keep Ireland and its imagined Otherness at bay for fear that it will contaminate England, reducing it to the status of those 'less happier lands' that Gaunt refers to (II.i.49). Beneath these conflicting desires is a recognition that Ireland is a necessary distraction for England, a space that usefully deflects attention from domestic weeds but there is also a recognition that for English kings, Ireland might just prove beyond control.

In tracing the concatenation between early modern assumptions about Irish space and three English history plays of the 1590s, I have demonstrated that spatial imagery relating to Ireland or its spatial displacement in a play can have topical meanings and ideological implications. It is tempting to generalize here, interpreting such figurations of Ireland in a similar way to representations of a journey or travel, where the 'problem of visualizing and defining the Other' turns out to be 'another means of defining the self'.[62] Certainly, Ireland could function as a site of English national imagining or as a symbolic space through which England could be examined. Yet, as the images of reversed conquest in *2 Henry VI* and *Edward II* or the significant silences in *Richard II* suggest, it is also a space where the limits of English identity and power are

61 The quotation is from Worcester in Shakespeare's *1 Henry IV*, V. i. 53. 62 Jean Pierre Maquerlot and Michele Willems (eds), *Travel and drama in Shakespeare's time* (Cambridge, 1996), p. 7.

encountered. The ideological indeterminacy that I have located in these plays should be understood within the context of broader concepts of Ireland in the period. As several critics have pointed out, given Ireland's geographical proximity to Britain, it occupied a liminal position, a curious combination of the familiar and strange, the physically near and the culturally far.[63] As David Baker writes, 'it was not always clear whether Ireland was really there for the viewing, or more disturbingly, whether it lurked, an unrepresentable terrain, just behind the descriptions impressed upon it'.[64] Bernhard Klein notes that because of the long history of contact between Britain and Ireland, Irish space could never be '"empty" or "unknown" to English observers'; instead, he argues, 'it remained riddled with ambiguity'.[65] This liminality is refracted in 2 *Henry VI*, *Edward II* and *Richard II*, particularly in the way the spatial displacement of Ireland in these plays belies its temporal immediacy. The effects of this distancing and visibility varies from text to text for, as in the period more generally, Ireland is a variable image, so that while patterns and moments of intertextuality are discernible, in each text it functions differently and gives rise to different meanings.

By way of an illustration of Ireland's anomalous state, I want to conclude with a description of the Irish landscape by an early seventeenth century traveller, William Lithgow. 'And this I dare avow', he begins,

> there are more rivers, lakes, Brookes, strands, quagmires, Bogs, and Marshes in this countrey then in all Christendome besides; for travelling there in winter all my dayly solace, was sincke down comfort; whiles Boggy-plunging deepes kissing my horse belly; while overmired saddle, Body, and all; and often or ever set a swimming, in great danger, both I, and my guides of our Lives: That for cloudy and fountayne-bred perils, I was never before reducted to such a floting laborinth.[66]

Lithgow's perception of Ireland's topographical features is similar to the moment when the European traveller first sees an unfamiliar landscape, which then comes to define the natives; the Irish are implicitly defined by the rough terrain he has traversed. Such moments, which Mary Louise Pratt has termed the 'monarch-of-all-I-survey' scenario, rapidly become ones of uncertainty and

---

63 On Ireland's proximity, see Murphy, *But the Irish sea*, pp 4–32. 64 David J. Baker, 'Off the map: charting uncertainty in Renaissance Ireland' in Bradshaw, Hadfield and Maley (eds), *Representing Ireland*, p. 82. 65 Bernhard Klein, *Maps and the writing of space*, p. 178. 66 Lithgow, *The total discourse of his rare adventures, and painefull peregrinations of long nineteene yeares travayles, from Scotland, to the most Famous kingdomes in Europe, Asia and Affrica* (1632) quoted in Hadfield and McVeagh (eds), *Strangers to that land*, p. 59. Lithgow's began his travels in 1609; he visited Ireland between 1619 and 1620.

anxiety as the narrative focus shifts from the landscape to its perceived effect on the traveller.[67] The wonderfully evocative metaphor of the 'floating laborinth' expresses the alteration in Lithgow brought about by Irish space. In her study of the labyrinth in history, Penelope Doob has shown that it signifies order and disorder, confusion and clarity: 'what you see depends on where you are'.[68] The viewer and what he views become intertwined: Lithgow internalizes his perception of the landscape, which comes to determine how he sees himself. However, the experience of confusion and entrapment, to carry forward the metaphor, is temporary since there is always a way out of a labyrinth. With its simultaneous sense of a strange, confusing space and one that can be subjected to optical control, the labyrinth provides an appropriate metaphor for English experiences and representations of Irish space more generally. Thus, the labyrinthine doubleness of Irish space and indeed Ireland might go some way towards explaining why on the Elizabethan stage, an easy resolution of the Irish crisis was not always possible.

67 Quoted in Gerry Smyth, *Space and the Irish cultural imagination* (London, 2001), p. 26. 68 Penelope Doob, *The idea of the labyrinth from classical antiquity through the Middle Ages* (Ithaca, 1990), p. 1.

Ireland onstage in *Captain Thomas Stukeley*

In *The famous historye of the life and death of Captain Thomas Stukeley* (1596–7), a character cautions: 'go not to Ireland: The countries rude | and full of tumult and rebellious strife, | Rather make choice of Italy or France'.[1] An Elizabethan audience would probably have shared this impression of Ireland and appreciated the travel advice but it goes unheeded in the play, which transports its audience to the scene of 'tumult'. Whereas in the plays considered in chapter two Ireland is figured as an offstage space, in *Stukeley* it constitutes an onstage location that forms a significant part of the dramatic action. *Stukeley* is a fast-paced play that attempted to build on the fame of the English adventurer turned privateer, already popularized on the stage in Peele's *Battle of Alcazar*.[2] As with that play, there is an similarly impressive geographic range here as the play traces the travels and fortunes of Stukeley from his dissolute days in London to his participation in the campaign against Irish rebels led by Shane O'Neill, his embroilment in Sebastian of Portugal's African wars and, finally, his death following the battle of Alcazar. In terms of its Irish scenes, the play is especially interesting for a number of reasons. With the exception of Thomas Heywood's *Four Prentices of London* (1594), where the youngest of four brothers finds himself 'cast upon the coast of Ireland' and briefly stays 'mongst the Irish kernes', *Stukeley* is the only Elizabethan play to bring Ireland on stage.[3] Considering the recent attribution of *Stukeley* (or portions of it) to Heywood, the connection between the two plays may be more than an instance of intertextuality in Elizabethan drama.[4] *Stukeley* also contains the most detailed and accurate use of Gaelic phrases in the drama of the early modern period.[5] More intriguingly still, in its dramatization of English efforts to repel O'Neill and his cohorts from the town of Dundalk, and their subsequent fatal clash with 'two Scots', the play addresses the 'contact zone' of Elizabethan Ireland.[6] Thus, where *2 Henry VI*, *Edward II* and *Richard II* refer to rebellion in Ireland, *Stukeley* dramatizes it and shows it in full. By bringing Ireland on stage

---

1 *The famous history of Captain Thomas Stukeley*, ed. Judith C. Levinson (Oxford, 1975), lines 538–40. 2 On the play's genre, see Candido, 'Captain Thomas Stukeley', 50–68. 3 *Dramatic works of Thomas Heywood*, ii, p. 178; p. 185. 4 See Edelman (ed.), *The Stukeley plays*, pp 38–42. 5 Bartley, *Teague, Shenkin and Sawney*, p. 42. 6 On the concept of a 'contact-zone', see Pratt, *Imperial eyes*, pp 3–5.

in this way, the play effects an interesting conjunction between the temporal and the spatial to produce a conspicuous topicality with the Irish wars. This chapter focuses on representations of the Irish rebels, treason and language in *Stukeley* and explores to what extent the text advances and sustains an ideological position on the crisis in Ireland.

Before addressing the play's representation of Ireland, a consideration of the provenance of the text itself is necessary for, as noted in relation to *2 Henry VI*, dating and textual issues do have a bearing on topical meanings. Thomas Pavier entered the play into the Stationers' register in 1600 – thereby claiming copyright and declaring his intention to print the play – and published the quarto text in 1605.[7] The title page gives no details about the play apart from the standard 'As it hath beene acted'. The condition of the text itself has been described as 'disordered', perhaps indicating that the conflation of at least two plays.[8] Critics have disputed the provenance of the conflation but there is consensus that the 1605 text combines elements from two lost plays.[9] These are the 'Stewtley' play mentioned by Henslowe as a 'new' play in the repertoire of the Admiral's men in December 1596 and also a play about the battle of Alcazar and its aftermath, possibly *Sebastian and Antonio*.[10] The available evidence for the 'Stewtley' play suggests that it was not a great commercial success: Henslowe's records reveal that it was performed ten times between December 1596 and June 1597. As Carol Rutter notes, there is 'an air of desperation' to this and other plays in the repertoire of the Admiral's men at the time 'as though the company was trying to find something, anything that would work with audiences'.[11] It would seem the story of the English adventurer and pirate – although of likely appeal to the patron of the Admiral's men, Charles Howard, the lord admiral – did not excite Elizabethan theatregoers.[12]

However it is possible that this 'Stewtley' play was revised between 1598 and 1600 to capitalize on the growing interest in the myth that Sebastian had survived the battle of Alcazar and would reclaim the Portuguese throne. In the quarto text, an awkwardly introduced chorus refers to 'Stukleys life in comicke historie | Bin new revivde' (lines 2421–2). John Yoklavich argues that the work of a reviser is clearly evident in the 1605 quarto. The reviser retained the first three acts of 'Stewtley' (dealing with the adventurer's London prodigality, service in Ireland and exploits in Spain) but omitted the scene showing Stukeley in Rome. In the text, the chorus refers to the papal appointment of

7 Levinson (ed.), *Captain Thomas Stukeley*, p. v.   8 Ibid., p. vi.   9 Levinson (ed.), *Captain Thomas Stukeley*, p. vi; J.Q. Adams, 'Captain Thomas Stukeley', *JEGP*, 15 (1916), 107–29.   10 Yoklavich (ed.), *The Battle of Alcazar*, pp 257–8; Levinson (ed.), *Captain Thomas Stukeley*, p. viii; Edelman (ed.), *The Stukeley plays*, p. 38.   11 Carol Chillington Rutter (ed.), *Documents of the Rose playhouse* (Manchester, 1985), p. 108.   12 Jowitt, *Voyage drama*, p. 65.

Stukeley as 'Marqusse of Ireland' (line 2429), yet the audience has not seen any such scene.[13] What is important for my purposes is that the 1605 quarto does give an indication of what audiences saw on the Elizabethan stage in late 1596 to early 1597, that is the 'Stewtley' play recorded by Henslowe. Moreover, since the quarto can be said to constitute a revised version of 'Stewtley', it may also reflect what audiences saw between 1598 and 1600, which further substantiates my contention that the Irish wars were being refracted contemporaneously in Elizabethan drama.

The condition of the text is of further relevance to the play's engagement with Ireland because the scene detailing the siege of Dundalk by the Irish rebels appears in two consecutive versions. As they appear in the text, the first version (viia) is in blank verse, as with the play in general, and contains a few Gaelic phrases. By contrast, the second version (viib) is in prose and the characters speak in an English dialect interspersed with a number of Gaelic phrases.[14] Ostensibly, the scenes narrate the same events, albeit in a somewhat different sequence; in both, Shane and his men discuss strategy, advise each other to be quiet in case the English soldiers hear them advancing, await a sign from their lookouts within the town and, when it does not materialize, decide to postpone the siege until the arrival of their compatriots. As with irregularities in the text as a whole, there is no definitive explanation for the linguistic and tonal differences between the scenes.[15] J.O. Bartley argues that the prose or Gaelic version represents the original and indicates first-hand knowledge of the Irish language on the part of the dramatist, perhaps stemming from direct experience in Ireland. Based on the use of names in the Irish scene, however, the argument that the playwright was working from local knowledge is not entirely persuasive.[16] Bartley maintains that this prose version was subsequently rewritten in verse in order to render it 'more intelligible and more in keeping with the rest of the play'.[17] This raises the scenario of different playwrights or hands, with Thomas Dekker a possible candidate for the Gaelic version of the scene.[18] Based on the topical nature of the scenes, the question of censorship

13 Yoklavich argues that the Roman scene is substituted by material from 'at least one older drama about Sebastian, Don Antonio and the battle of Alcazar' but there are no direct interpolations from Peele's *Battle of Alcazar*; see Yoklavich (ed.), *The Battle of Alcazar*, pp 259–60. For a sceptical response to Yoklavich's 'reviser-theory', see Edelman (ed.), *The Stukeley plays*, pp 42–4.   14 I follow Levinson (ed.), *Captain Thomas Stukeley*, in labelling the scenes viia and viib.   15 Edelman (ed.), *The Stukeley plays*, p. 42. Oddly enough, in his recent Revels' edition of the play (*The Stukeley plays*), Charles Edelman relegates the prose version of the Irish scene to an appendix in the interests of producing a coherent text out of the 1605 quarto.   16 As Edelman notes, 'the dramatist appears to have chosen Irish families that had some association with him [O'Neill], regardless of actual significance' (*The Stukeley plays*, p.135). For instance, in both versions of scene vii, Brian MacPhelim and Teague Magennis are mentioned as being among Shane's allies (line 882; line 901) when they were in fact his antagonists.   17 Bartley, *Teague, Shenkin and Sawney*, p. 14.   18 See Bartley, *Teague, Shenkin and Sawney*, p. 42; Levinson (ed.), *Captain Thomas Stukeley*, p. vii.

might also be considered, with the verse scene suggesting a toned down version of the prose scene and its Gaelic phrases. However, the similarity in content and the overt topicality of both versions, limits the likelihood of interference. The variant Irish scene is best explained with reference to the condition of the 1605 quarto; thus, scene viia and viib can be said, respectively, to reflect the 'Stewtley' play performed in late 1596 and early 1597 and that play as it was revived for performance between 1598 and 1600. By this stage, perhaps coinciding with, or following on from, the appearance of Irish characters in *Henry V* and *Sir John Oldcastle* in 1599, the playwright may have endeavoured to augment the representation of Irish characters by demarcating their difference linguistically and phonetically through the use of Irish phrases as in later Jacobean plays like Jonson's *Irish Masque* (1613) and the *New Inne* (1629).[19]

'THY HEAD FOR TREASON': THE FALL OF THE IRISH REBEL

The play's use of Ireland as a location is established as early as the opening scenes, which are set in London and which serve, primarily, to delineate Stukeley's character. In his domestic setting, Stukeley is variously characterized as a prodigal, spendthrift, a potentially valiant soldier and a self-seeking opportunist. This concern with establishing character is to be expected from a biographical play where history 'functions as the panoramic backdrop against which the life of the central character is brought into salient relief'.[20] The wars in Ireland can, initially at least, be understood in these terms as they form little more than a subtext to the London scenes and are introduced through Stukeley's friendship with Vernon. Providing dramatic counterpoint to Stukeley himself, Vernon is presented as a selfless and morally upright character. He sacrifices his own feelings for Nell Curtis in the interests of Stukeley's, explaining 'I had rather chose to benefit my friend, | whereby two might be pleasd: than greedille | assuming what I might, displease all three' (lines 515–7). Earlier he has described Stukeley as 'the substance of my shaddowed love, | I but a cipher in respect of him' (lines 60–1), his sense of Stukeley's superior claim conveying, on a metradramatic level, the extent to which the titular character dominates the dramatic action and upstages other characters. Vernon subsequently determines to leave England and though he claims his decision is unrelated to Stukeley (line 519), it becomes clear that it stems from an unconscious desire to distance himself from his friend's domi-

---

19 On the use of stage dialect to delineate nationality, see Bartley, *Teague, Shenkin and Sawney*, pp 42–3.
20 Candido, 'Captain Thomas Stukeley', p. 51.

nating presence. Indeed, it seems as if Stukeley's presence has made England odious to Vernon:

> yet whilst I breath this native ayre of mine,
> Methinks I sucke in poison to my hart:
> and whilst I tread upon this English earth,
> It is as if I set my careless feet
> Upon a banke, where underneath is hid
> a bed of crawling Serpents: any place
> but only here (methinks) could make me happy
>
> (lines 520–6)

Vernon's remarks, made here to his friend Ridley, are especially interesting in view of his subsequent decision to go to Ireland. Ridley cautions him against going: 'the countries rude | and full of tumult and rebellious strife' (lines 538–9). His remark points to the irony of Vernon fleeing a supposedly poisonous England for a supposedly serpent-free Ireland (as legend would have it) that in the Elizabethan mind was, metaphorically, full of venomous natives. Vernon cannot be dissuaded, explaining how he is 'fired with a desire to travell | and [to] see the fashions, state, and qualities | of other countries' (lines 533–5). Having given his word to Captain Jack Harbart, who has previously quarrelled with Stukeley over the latter's hasty marriage to Nell, Vernon commits to the Irish campaign. It transpires that Stukeley has also signed up for service in Ireland, with an unnamed captain advising Harbart to reconcile his differences with Stukeley because he 'is to have a charge in this our Irish expedition' (line 551). This is the first direct reference to war in Ireland. Its introduction at this point not only establishes Ireland as a location but also lays the foundation for the 'structural spine' of the play, whereby Vernon repeatedly, but unsuccessfully, attempts to distance himself from his former friend.[21] Vernon alludes to Stukeley's shadowing of him on several occasions. 'Must he needs to Ireland follow me', he says as Stukeley arrives there, 'I will not draw that ayre wherein he breaths, | one kingdom shall not hold us if I can' (lines 1034–6). Later, as Stukeley's presence leads him to abandon the campaign against the Irish rebels, Vernon describes his former friend as a 'monster' in what amounts to a reversal of those earlier images of Ireland: 'therefore Ireland now farewell to thee, | For though thy soile no venime will sustaine, | There treads a monster on thy fruitfull brest' (lines 1109–11). But, encountering Stukeley in Spain and finally

---

21 Martin Wiggins, 'Things that go bump in the text: *Captain Thomas Stukeley*', *Papers of the Bibliographical Society of America*, 98 (2004), 5–20 at 12.

in Africa, Vernon is ultimately reconciled with him, noting 'there is no parting but by death' (line 2935).

What Vernon provides is a subjective and critical viewpoint on Stukeley, which enables the audience more keenly to evaluate his character and, more importantly, determine what lies behind his self-representations and rhetorical flourishes. By constantly juxtaposing Stukeley's claims with various subjective viewpoints, the play confers on the audience considerable powers of interpretation and judgement in its presentation of Stukeley. This is particularly evident in the scenes detailing Stukeley's decision to join the Irish campaign. As he pays off his creditors, he says, 'had I now as many | shot and piks, I would with a valiant band | of mine owne subiects march among the Irish' (lines 591–3). The comparison suggests a martial responsibility on the part of Stukeley but his apparent sense of priority is compromised by the fact that we already know that the monies being doled out are from the dowry of Nell, his recently betrothed, whom he has expediently married. The scene subsequently counters the impression of Stukeley as a spendthrift as three soldiers discuss his military ability and his concern for his peers. With one soldier noting that he 'goes not to the wars | to make a gaine of his poore Souldiors spoile | but spoile the foe to make his Souldiors gaine' (lines 741–3), Stukeley is presented as a potential asset to the prescient Irish campaign. As Stukeley prepares to leave for Ireland, however, this character-assessment is unsettled, particularly in his departing exchanges, the first with his wife, the second with his father and father-in-law. Stukeley rejects his wife's entreaties that he stay, claiming that his aim is to 'make thee great' (line 763). His overriding motivation in going to war quickly reveals itself: 'I must have honour, honour is the thing | Stukly doth thirst for and to clime the Mount | Where she is seated gold shall be my foot-stoole' (lines 771–3). This feminization of honour leads Stukeley to exhibit what Claire Jowitt describes as a 'hypermasculine behaviour' as 'he begins chasing female honour through his demonstrations of masculine prestige and glory'.[22] Stukeley makes no apology for taking his wife's jewels (line 787) to fund his journey, excusing his act of appropriation on the basis that she has a wealthy father. As Nell resigns herself to death – 'That name of death alreadie martirs me' (line 783) – Stukeley's only concern is that his delay in marching with his fellow soldiers will tarnish his military reputation, making him resemble one that 'went unwillingly into wars' (line 799).

The extent to which Stukeley's abandonment of Nell casts a shadow over his pursuit of honour is especially evident in the second of his departing exchanges as his father reprimands him for leaving London unannounced and

---

22 Jowitt, *Voyage drama*, p. 85.

in such haste. News of Stukeley's departure comes second-hand, with Curtis, his father-in-law, being 'sent for in all haste [...] about the Souldiers | That are to be dispatcht for Ireland' (line 705). Stukeley justifies his actions, saying he would not risk being 'thought a traitor to her Majesty, a coward | a sleepy dormouse' (lines 819–20). His father accepts his 'vertuous action' but berates him for his 'lack of husbandry | And the unthrifty courses thou hast usde' (lines 824–5). Stukeley's resolve that he 'vowd in hart | To be a soldier, and the time now serves' (lines 831–2), with the emphasis on the immediacy of the Irish wars, seems to persuade Curtis but he too raises doubts about Stukeley. Reflecting on the losses he has incurred as a result of his daughter's choice of husband, he says, 'So large a sum | Is more then I had thought should fly with wings, | Of vaine expences into Ireland' (lines 859–60). What occurs in the play here is a delineation of the emotional and personal costs of war as seen through the protestations of Stukeley's wife, father and father-in-law. Yet, the scene also insinuates much about Stukeley's protestations and intentions. Joseph Candido argues that 'the veracity of his rhetoric is constantly called into question'.[23] Similarly, Claire Jowitt notes how the implications of Stukeley's abandonment of his wife in the pursuit of honour are drawn out: 'Stukeley is disingenuous and self-interested, and will turn against Elizabeth – deserting his national allegiance – in the same way that he casually abandons his wife.'[24] The play's depiction of Stukeley as a rebel in the making may indeed be a concession to the queen, who disapproved of Stukeley and had blocked his attempts to secure the post of seneschal of Wexford. Stukeley was reputed to have said of Elizabeth that he would 'teach hyr to displace a soldior', as if anticipating his later involvement with those enemies of the Elizabethan state, the papacy and Spain.[25]

It is on location in Ireland that the audience gradually sees how Stukeley's inherent moral ambivalence and contradictions unfold. As he makes for Ireland, the audience is left to ponder whether Stukeley will live up to his boasts or in fact prove a hindrance to English efforts against the Irish rebels. Jowitt argues that the Irish scenes quickly establish that Stukeley's rampant individualism may compromise the interests of queen and state. She suggests that the introduction of the '"real" traitors to the English state' in the form of the Irish rebels and the two Scottish rebels, implicitly invokes a comparison with Stukeley, whose 'rebelliousness starts to appear as little different from that of England's enemies'.[26] While such a comparison is available in the scene on a symbolic level, there are, however, important differences in the portrayal of these groupings. Most notably, acts of treason are racialized in the scenes set

23 Candido, 'Captain Thomas Stukeley', p. 60.   24 Jowitt, *Voyage drama*, p. 86.   25 Quoted in Edelman (ed.), *The Stukeley plays*, p. 7.   26 Jowitt, *Voyage drama*, p. 86.

in Ireland, so that Stukeley's disruptive presence and eventual rebelliousness is regarded as less heinous than the recalcitrance of the Irish or Scots. Moreover, Stukeley's comical egotism has the effect of excusing his behaviour in the eyes of the audience.

As the dramatic action shifts from London to Ireland, the play's biographical focus is temporarily displaced by a broader interest in history, with attention turning to war and cross-cultural encounters. Stukeley is offstage for two full scenes as the Irish and English camps are represented with some attention to detail. The initial impression of Ireland in the play as 'full of tumult and rebellious strife' is sustained here: Shane and his two accomplices, Mackener and OHamlon, are shown approaching the defensive walls of Dundalk, which they intend to 'surprise' (line 874). In dramatizing the siege of Dundalk, the play addresses the crown's efforts to limit the power of Shane O'Neill in Ulster in an earlier part of Elizabeth's reign in ways that resonate with contemporary moves to deal with Hugh O'Neill towards the end of the reign. It is possible that Hooker's Irish history – which formed part of the second edition of Holinshed's *Chronicles* and delved into recent history – provided the *Stukeley* playwright with his source material, although clearly he exercised dramatic licence and historical revision in his treatment of the known facts. In Hooker's narrative, the *Stukeley* playwright would have found a character-portrait of Shane to draw on in representing him on stage:

> his pride joined with wealth, drunkenesse and insolencie, he began to be a tyrant, and to tyrannize over the whole land. He pretended to be king of Ulster [...] and affecting the manner of the great Turke, was continuallie garded with six hundred armed men [...] and had in readinesse to bring into the fields a thousand horsemen and foure thousand footmen.[27]

Included within Hooker's figuration of Shane as rebel and Other are both elements of the history of contact between him and the state, and also the historical background to the play's Irish scenes. Whereas O'Neill had initially proved amenable to negotiating with the crown (as evidenced by his 1562 visit to court) by 1566, the queen had determined that the 'cankred dangerous rebel' should be 'utterly extirped'.[28] Responsibility for limiting O'Neill's dominance in Ulster fell to Sir Henry Sidney, then lord deputy of Ireland. Initially, Sidney had employed Stukeley, who had apparently befriended Shane during the

---

27 Hooker, 'Supplie of the Irish Chronicles', p. 331.   28 Quoted in T.W. Moody, F.X. Martin, and F.J. Byrne (eds), *A new history of Ireland*, 9 vols (Oxford, 1976), iii, p. 85.

latter's court visit, to act as an intermediary between the state and O'Neill as it tried to reach terms with him.[29] Significantly, the play's inclusion of Stukeley at the siege of Dundalk may be apocryphal just as its overall representation of him in the Irish scenes may be, as we shall see, an instance of ideological revisionism, with Stukeley cast as Shane's nemesis. With the failure of negotiations, Sidney subsequently resorted to a military campaign and also that favourite of crown strategies for dealing with Irish 'rebels': playing off one local power magnate against another; thus, Sidney supported the interests of Calvagh O'Donnell in his long struggle with Shane in Ulster. However, the crown itself did not succeed in subduing Shane, who was defeated by Hugh O'Donnell in 1567 and, after taking refuge among the Scots in Ulster, was subsequently murdered by them. Shane's head was dispatched to Dublin castle, where it was displayed above the castle gates.[30]

While the play focuses on Shane's attempt on Dundalk, in reality it was not a focal point in Sidney's campaign compared with Derry and Carrickfergus. Hooker briefly mentions how Shane 'besieged hir highnesse towne of Dundalke', adding that 'his pride and treason were justlie scourged'.[31] Similarly, Sidney himself commented on O'Neill's unsuccessful raid on the town, which was, he noted, 'so ruinous it was scarcely guardable'; O'Neill and his men, Sidney wrote, 'entered the town [...] but such was their repulse that he could not procure any more of his men to follow the enterprise'.[32] These contemporary accounts of Shane's failure might explain, in part, the playwright's use of Dundalk as the location of the Irish scene; its association with his defeat being appropriate to the overall portrayal of Shane that the play is concerned with producing. The use of Dundalk in *Stukeley* also bears comparison to the allusions to the Pale in *2 Henry VI* and *Edward II* for, as with these examples, it denotes a spatial limit to English influence in Ireland. The town marked an entry-point into Ulster, that most recalcitrant of territories in the period and the originating locus of the Nine Years War. To an Elizabethan audience, then, Dundalk could be said to carry a general resonance as an English garrison town in Ireland marking the border of the Pale, bringing to mind those spaces in Ireland associated with English militarism and administration. As with the Pale more generally, towns in Ireland were frequently viewed by successive Tudor governments as 'little bastions of Englishness in a sea of Irish barbarism'.[33] In this sense, the play's depiction of a town besieged

29 On Stukeley's association with Shane O'Neill, see *DNB*; and Edelman (ed.), *The Stukeley plays*, pp 6–7. 30 *A new history of Ireland*, iii, pp 82–5. 31 Hooker, 'Supplie of the Irish chronicles', p. 337. 32 Sidney to Robert Dudley, earl of Leicester, quoted in Padraic Dubhthaigh, *The book of Dundalk* (Dundalk, 1946), p. 7. 33 Anthony Sheehan, 'Irish towns in a period of change, 1558–1625' in Brady and Gillespie (eds), *Natives and newcomers*, p. 111.

captures an aspect of warfare in Ireland throughout the 1590s as English positions were defended from guerrilla style sorties by Gaelic confederates.

However, in the late 1590s, when *Stukeley* was performed, mention of Dundalk may have resonated more pointedly with London theatregoers. On several occasions, the town constituted a point of contact and negotiation for the state and Hugh O'Neill. In June 1593, for instance, O'Neill met with lord deputy William Fitzwilliam and other representatives of the Irish council at Dundalk. In March 1596, this time on the outskirts of the town, royal commissioners met O'Neill and other Gaelic confederates, and secured a cessation to the war.[34] Peace was temporary, however, and by early December 1596 there were reports that some of O'Neill's 'forces [are] on the borders near Dundalk, spoiling, burning and wasting with assured expectation of the arrival of the Spanish army'.[35] The town, once again, served as a contact-zone in 1597 when O'Neill met the earl of Ormond there, 'submitted humbly enough to him' and agreed a two-month truce.[36] Even if such knowledge of the town's political significance lay outside the conceptual possibilities of the audience or even the playwright, the effect of the localized and specified Irish location, combined with the representation of rebel leader Shane, is to endow the play's Irish scenes with an overt topicality.

The sense of Dundalk as a border space where the English and Irish converge in an antagonistic dynamic is established in the first scene set there. Shane and his cohorts are first heard strategizing about how best to approach the town. The rebel leader instructs his men, OHamlon and Mackener, to 'tread softlie on the stones | The water tells us we are neere the towne' (lines 868–9) and to direct their eyes 'upon the walles of this bewitched towne | That harbors suth a fort of English churles' (lines 871–2). In the absence of stage directions, these instructions also serve as verbal pointers from which stage action can be inferred. The scene develops with the Irish discussing their own military tactics and those of the English, and this allows for some differentiation in character among the rebel camp. While Mackener urges Shane to 'speak softly' because 'the English sentinells do keepe good watch' (lines 875–6), OHamlon fears that 'our labour [is] lost' (line 878) as no sign is forthcoming from 'our spies within' (line 880). Shane displays a sense of purpose but is far more impetuous than either Mackener or OHamlon; it is they who advise him and keep him in check. Thus, as Shane curses his men within – 'A plague upon the drowsie drunken slaves | Bryan Mac Phelim and that Neale O Quyme | Who being drunk or sleeping with his drabs | Forget the business that they have in hand (lines 881–4) – OHamlon reminds his chieftain

34 Bagwell, *Ireland under the Tudors*, iii, p. 261.   35 *Calendar of state papers, Ireland, 1592–96*, ed. Hans Claude Hamilton (London, 1890), p. 189.   36 Bagwell, *Ireland under the Tudors*, iii, p. 291

that they may be unable to give a signal because the English 'will be more watchful then their custom is' (line 891). Any faith in English military surveillance is quickly dispelled, however, as Shane boasts that, inside the town, he has 'ten frends to one the English have' (line 896) and that with additional forces, 'we might cut of all the English heads, | Of thers that watch and thers that sleepe in beds' (lines 898–9). He proposes to postpone the siege until the arrival of reinforcements, vowing 'then will we not come miching thus by night, | But charge the towne and winne it by daylight' (lines 903–4).

In representing Shane, the play 'brings the bogeymen of the period, the rebellious Irish kerns, on stage'.[37] By associating him with throat cutting, it invokes and reinforces the stereotype of the pugnacious Irish rebel always on the verge of violence. It is a stereotype that re-occurs in Elizabethan drama, from the 'wild Irishman' of *The Misfortunes of Arthur* to Mackmorrice in *Henry V* and Mack Chane in *Sir John Oldcastle*.[38] Thus, Shane's remark as he overhears an English soldier coughing: 'Some English Soldior that hath got the cough | Ile ease that griefe by cutting off his head' (lines 909–10). Shane's claim is followed by Mackener's observation, clearly for the benefit of the play's London audience, that 'These English churles die if they lacke there bed, | And bread and beere, porage and powdered beef' (lines 911–12). The irony of the Irish commenting on the dietary peculiarities of the English is pointed up by the playwright, who has OHamlon respond with incredulity 'nor bonny clabbo, nor greene Water-cresses, nor our strong butter, nor our sweild oatmeale' (lines 914–16) in what amounts to an inventory of stereotypes of the Irish diet in the period.[39] In Jonson's *Irish Masque*, for instance, Irish diet is alluded to as Dennis, one of the four Irish footmen, says 'I will give tee leave to cram my mouth phit shamrokes and butter, and vater creeshes.'[40] The darker purpose of English perceptions of Irish diet is evident in Spenser's *View* where, as part of the infamous description of the effects of famine in Munster, Irenius refers to the native Irish as 'anatomies of death' reduced to cannibalism, the consumption of 'water-cresses or shamrocks' and, ultimately, self-destruction.[41] In *Stukeley*, Mackener concedes that when it comes to drinking, some of the English 'can fare as hard as we' (line 918). While the effect of these comical exchanges among the rebels is to diffuse Anglo-Irish differences, ultimately it is only temporary: abandoning its comic mode, the scene ends with Shane wryly remarking 'One coughes againe, lets slip aside unseene, | To morrow we will ease them of their spleen' (lines 922–3).

37 Leerssen, *Mere Irish and fior Ghael*, p. 83.   38 On pugnacity as a characteristic of the 'stage Irishman', see Bartley, *Teague, Shenkin and Sawney*, p. 26.   39 Bartley, *Teague, Shenkin and Sawney*, pp 32–3.   40 *Ben Jonson*, viii, p. 182, lines 37–8.   41 Spenser, *A view*, pp 101–2.

While the threat is deferred and ultimately functions as a reminder of the fate the rebel himself will meet, it nonetheless conditions audience response to Shane. For the association of the Irish with excessive violence was almost proverbial in the period. In 1596, Sir Robert Cecil was reminded of the desire among the native Irish,

> to expel of might out of their country all foreign government, and to be governors themselves, which they are persuaded shall or long be brought to pass, and no doubt their fingers do tickle till time serve them to be cutting all the English men's throats in Ireland.

The correspondent went on to enlist 'God in heaven to prevent them and to turn the mischiefe they intend upon their own heads'.[42] From an English perspective, such prophecies of native ferocity were realised in 1598 when new English planters in Munster were attacked; a contemporary described the scene in Youghal where Englishmen were left with 'their throats cut [...] their tongues cut out of their heads, others with their noses cut off'.[43] These atrocities were an inevitable aspect of warfare in the period but, as illustrated by the above report to Cecil and indeed *Stukeley* itself, it is necessary to recognize how 'bodily dismemberment and gagging were familiar elements in an imaginary repertoire of Gaelic violence constructed by the new English'.[44] We are reminded here that however typical 'descriptions' of native Irish violence might be of warfare in the early modern period, they are implicitly informed by a discourse of barbarism that continued into the Jacobean period. Thus, in 1610, when Barnabe Rich considered 'that the Irish by nature are inclined unto cruelty', there was only one real answer. The innate violence of the native Irish was a truism: 'It cannot be denied but that the Irish are very cruel in their executions and no less bloody in their dispositions; the examples are too many and too manifest to be by any means contradicted'.[45] *Stukeley* can be said to partake in such a discourse and to reinforce ethnic stereotyping in its representation of Shane.

As if emphasizing the polarization of the Irish and English, attention now shifts to the English camp, where the audience is re-introduced to Vernon and Harbert, who are entrusted with the defence of the town. As they discuss Shane's attempt to breach the walls, it becomes apparent that distinctions

---

42 *Calendar of state papers, Ireland, 1596–97*, ed. George Ernest Atkinson (London, 1893), p. 202.   43 'William Saxey, Chief Justice of Munster, to Sir Robert Cecil' (26 October 1598) quoted in *Irish history from contemporary sources*, p. 212.   44 Highley, *Shakespeare, Spenser*, p. 101.   45 Barnabe Rich, *A new description of Ireland, together with the manners, customs and descriptions of the people* in Myers (ed.), *Elizabethan Ireland*, p. 132.

between the Irish and English may not be entirely stable. Harbert mentions that 'the townsmen are spies | And help and store them with provision | And love them better than us Englishmen' (lines 995–7), confirming Shane's claim in the previous scene about having spies inside the town. Vernon advises Harbert 'It behoves you therefore to be circumspect' (line 998), a comment that extends beyond its immediate meaning of greater defensive vigilance to suggest that the native Irish and Ireland itself necessitate continuous observation and surveillance. Increasingly, the scene gives the impression that the English occupy a defensive position and that Dundalk is a frontier protecting them from native space; for example, as Harbert eagerly awaits fresh supplies from England to strengthen his vulnerable garrison, he notes 'we must bear the brunt of all the north' (line 1005). With the arrival of reinforcements, however, the English camp looks less vulnerable. Stukeley resumes his central role in the dramatic action and, in a return to its biographical focus, the play intimates that the fate of Shane will rest with the English adventurer. In a Tamburlaine-like vein, he demands of Gainsford, the English captain, 'why doe ye not beat them home into their dens' (line 1062), only to be informed that 'We have enough a do to keepe the towne' (line 1063). In response, Stukeley calls for decisive action: 'hang them savage slaves, | Belike they know you dare not issue out' (lines 1066–7). Implicit in Stukeley's metonymic representation of the Irish as savages, the inhabitants of 'dens', is the assumption that they belong to a specific type of space or habitat. Such spatial binarism reveals just how far the rebels are deemed to have transgressed in making a direct 'assault' (line 1065) upon the town. The English position in Dundalk is shown in the play to have a wider application: functioning as a microcosm for Ireland or, more particularly, those spaces nominally under English control, it recalls those images of the besieged nation in *2 Henry VI* and *Edward II*. Compared with the more abstract notion of Irish space in these earlier plays, however, the naming of a specific location here endows *Stukeley* with a degree of verisimilitude and reinforces its point about the diminution of English control in Ireland. Consequently, in its representation of a particular English space under siege, the play points towards England's tentative hold on Ireland and to the dangers posed by its native inhabitants.

Once again, Stukeley's rhetoric seems out of step with his actual conduct; his attention is quickly diverted from his stated intention to engage directly with the Irish rebels towards those private quarrels that originated in London. That Stukeley's impact on the campaign might be a negative one is suggested both by Vernon's departure from Ireland (to escape what he perceives to be his former friend's ominous presence) and also Stukeley's challenging of Harbert to a duel. Stukeley seeks redress for Harbert's comments about his expedient marriage. Yet, Harbert's reference to 'the discipline of war' (line 1145) and his later question 'Thou seest the publique enemie is at hand, | And we shall fight about a private brall' (lines 1149–50) illuminates Stukeley's flawed value system. His subsequent fight with Harbert is halted only by news of the enemy's approach as Harbert says 'Hark the enemies charges we must to the walles' (line 1168). However, although the play gestures towards the consequences of Stukeley's disregard for military protocol, it also shows him to be an eager soldier. Stukeley pursues the Irish rebels, with the stage direction noting 'after a pretty good fight his Lieftenannt and Auntient rescue Stukeley, and chace the Ireshe out' (lines 1172–3). There is a sense here that the audience probably expects to see Stukeley engage with this Irish enemy of the state, and the play does not disappoint. Stukeley's actions are in contrast to those of Harbert and Gainsford, both of whom are dismayed at the advance of the Irish. As Harbert orders a retreat, he comments 'Who would have thought these naked savages, | These Northerne Irish durst have been so bold, | T'have given assault unto a warlike towne' (lines 1178–81). Anxiety about the mobility of the Irish rebels – again figured metonymically as barbarous – is compounded by Gainsford's complaint that English policy is insufficiently proactive: 'Our sufferance and remissenes gives them hart, | we make them proud by mewing up our selves, | In walled towns, whilst they triumph abroad | and Rebell in the countrey as they please' (lines 1182–5). Harbert tires to reassure Gainsford that despite the defensive, entrenched position of the English forces, they have managed to 'cut three hundred rebells throats at least' (line 1188). But with Gainsford now articulating the kind of tactics that Stukeley had earlier advocated, praising him as 'lustie Stukeley [...] eager to pursue the foe' (lines 1194–5), the play suggests that his resolve and energy, despite their unpredictability, are the requisite responses. Indeed, by portraying a garrison town subjected to the charge of the enemy, the play seems to be arguing for a much tougher, more proactive line towards the Elizabethan Irish wars.

While Stukeley is successful against the rebels, boasting to Harbert 'we have slaine | Two hundred Irish sine yo left the chace' (lines 1222–3), his refusal to obey the retreat prompts Harbert to refuse him entry into the town. 'If all your throats be cut you are well servd', he tells Stukeley, 'To teach ye know the discipline of warre' (lines 1228–9). Throat cutting is once again associated with the Irish rebels, except in this instance responsibility would fall partly on the English commander Harbert. Apart from Harbert agreeing to admit Stukeley's booty, the stand-off between the two men cannot be resolved; the broader implication is that both are justified in their actions, Stukeley having been effective against the Irish and Harbert delivering just punishment for the disobedience of an inferior officer. Stukeley states clearly the consequences of

his exclusion from the town, vowing that whoever 'shut mee out by night, |
Shall never see me enter heere by daie' (lines 1239–40). He agrees to defend the
walls but his hubris overrides concerns about the enemy; thus, he claims that
'Tom Stukely | Can not brook the least disgrace' (line 1259). Stukeley is
presented as a liminal figure who is quite literally situated 'in the hinterland
between rebel and patriot'; his decision to 'shippe from hence to seke a better
coast' (line 1268), abandoning his Irish post, marks his move towards rebellion
as he treasonously aligns himself with Spain. If Shane is the most obvious
manifestation of treason in the play, Stukeley is in fact the most destructive.[46]
Certainly, as we have seen, Stukeley oscillates between loyalty and selfish expediency before he leaves Ireland but he is figured as Shane's nemesis rather than
his symbolic associate. The play further differentiates between Stukeley and
the Irish rebel by portraying the former's rebellious spirit as indicative of his
comical egotism. Moreover, it leaves open the possibility that circumstances
might have led Stukeley to act differently. Thus, in keeping with his preten-
sions, he declaims, 'Farewell Oneale, if Stukly here had staid, | thy head for
treason, soone thous shouldst have paied' (lines 1277–8).

The departing boast is quintessential Stukeley but, more significantly, it
proves prophetic, for it is immediately followed by Shane's re-appearance on
stage: 'Enter Oneale with a halter about his neck' (line 1279). Following on
from his treasonous acts, Shane's transformation on stage, from rebel storming
the town to repentant subject, seems designed to gesture towards his imminent
demise and suggests the emergence of an ideological position towards the Irish
wars within the text. The stage produces the spectacle of the symbolically
submissive Irish rebel. However, as Mackener asks what 'the great Oneale
intends by this' (line 1281) and Shane replies, the symbolic power of the
moment appears to be compromised:

> ONEALE   Neale Mackener, I do not weare this cord,
> as doubting or fordooming such a death,
> but thou who art my Secretarye, knowst
> that my unkind Rebellious merite more:
> Therefore I beare this hatefull cord in signe
> of true Repentance, of my treasons past,
> and at the Deputies feete on humble knees
> will sue for pardon from her maiesties:
> Whose Clemencie I grieve to have abus,
> What sayest thou: is it not my safest course.

---

46 Jowitt, *Voyage drama*, pp 92–3.

> MACK   Can I believe that mighty Shane Oneale:
> Is so defect in corage as he seemes
> or that his dauntles dragon winged thoght,
> can humble them at any Princes feet.

(lines 1283–95)

In one sense, the play is performing a similar textual manoeuvre here to Derricke's *Image of Irelande*, where, speaking in the first person, the rebel Rory Og foretells his own demise and that of his clan. His grafted tongue serves a single purpose: to 'teach other impes to flye | From treasons lure' and, in a final move, the text has Rory's 'trunklesse head', spitted on a stake over Dublin castle, body forth more didactic utterances.[47] With the talking head confirming what the broken body has already made manifest, Derricke's marginal gloss wryly notes that the rebel 'giveth wholsome counsel more better then he ever could take'.[48] It has been suggested that such textual strategies endow the stigmatized enemy with a voice that has the capacity to elicit understanding and empathy but, as in *Stukeley*, the rebel's words serve only to condemn him further.[49] Shane's words here are loaded with dramatic irony: the audience is left in no doubt that his plan to 'sue for pardon' as the 'safest course' amounts to an expedient and tactical manipulation of royal mercy rather than a sign of genuine remorse. Mackener's insistence that Shane avoid such a humiliating course of action further suggests a misplaced confidence on the part of the rebels that will ultimately be stamped out. However, in another sense, the play offers Shane's words less as a sign of the perfidy of rebels that must be punished than an advertisement that royal mercy is available. As Shane explains to Mackener, 'If the Queenes power pursue I am but dead | If I submit she is mercifull' (lines 1299–1300). The play can be said, then, to open up two possibilities for rebels like Shane, one where Elizabethan clemency is offered for the truly repentant rebel and another that, as suggested by Shane's wearing of the cord, insinuates the suppression of rebels through violence and force. Ultimately, it seems it is the latter position that is advanced in *Stukeley* as it moves towards dramatizing Shane's violent end.

Among the shaping influences on the play's representation of Shane in the role of repentant rebel are frustrations with Hugh O'Neill who, like his blood relative, was regarded as being particularly adept at exploiting Elizabeth's clemency to his own advantage. The royal proclamation issued against O'Neill in 1595 noted that he had been 'advanced' by the queen only to become the 'principall traitor and chief author of this rebellion, and a known practiser

---

47 Derricke, *Image of Irelande*, pp 81; 92.   48 Ibid., p. 97.   49 For the argument that the 'dialogic impulse' in the text serves to humanize Rory, see Highley, *Shakespeare, Spenser*, p. 57.

with Spain and other her majesty's enemies'.[50] Similarly, in Spenser's *View*, Irenius describes how O'Neill was 'lifted up by her majesty out of the dust' but now 'playeth like the frozen snake, who being for compassion releived by the husbandman, soone after he was warme began to hisse, and threaten danger even to him and his'.[51] The text's image of the 'frozen snake' articulates an explicit distrust of O'Neill, who throughout the 1590s simultaneously maintained contact with the state while also pursuing his own objectives in Ulster.[52] Government intelligence sources indicated that 'in spite of his outward show of neutrality', he was engaging in military operations.[53] Nonetheless, from the state's perspective, awareness of the costs of defeating the Gaelic confederacy, combined with the real threat of Spanish involvement, meant that negotiation continued to be an element of official policy.[54] As part of this policy, in March 1596 Commissioners Wallop and Gardiner travelled to Dundalk, the English garrison town and location of the Irish scene in *Stukeley*. O'Neill refused to enter the town, preferring instead to meet with the commissioners on the outskirts:

> The forces of either side stood a quarter of a mile distant from them, and while they parleyed on horseback two horsemen of the commissioners stood firm in the midway between the Earl's troops and them, and likewise two horsemen of the Earl's was placed between them and her Majesty's forces. These scout officers were to give warning if any treacherous attempt were made on either part.[55]

The symmetrical arrangement of the two parties, which is similar to the division of the camps in *Stukeley*, conveys their mutual distrust and suspicion. O'Neill's refusal to enter the town no doubt stemmed from pragmatism but in light of what we know about him and his relations with the state, his decision to occupy a liminal or border space is also richly symbolic. On an earlier occasion in 1594, when the earl went to Dublin to make a submission before the council, the queen expressed frustration that her Irish government had not used the opportunity to arrest him. 'This slight manner of proceeding', she complained, 'both eclipsed the greatness of our estate there and served to glorify him, to the comfort of all his followers and to the amazement of all those who have opposed themselves against him'.[56] By late 1596, the privy council had

50 Quoted in *Irish history from contemporary sources*, p. 99.   51 Spenser, *A view*, p. 110.   52 On the limits of Spenser's figuration of O'Neill, see 'Gold lace and a frozen snake: Donne, Wotton and the Nine Years War', *Irish Studies Review*, 8 (1994), 9–11.   53 Hiram Morgan, *Tyrone's rebellion*, p. 173.   54 Steven Ellis, *Tudor Ireland: crown, community and the conflict of cultures, 1470–1603* (London, 1985), p. 339.   55 Quoted in Bagwell, *Ireland under the Tudors*, iii, p. 261.   56 Quoted in Morgan, *Tyrone's rebellion*, p. 172.

arrived at the opinion that 'no hope of favour' could be offered to Tyrone, for he was 'so far rooted in treason' that he would 'not yield to submit himself personally to the state'; the memorandum went on to note that 'it would be a dishonour for her Majesty to have her favour rejected'.[57] The perceived elusiveness of O'Neill and his apparently functional ambivalence that these anecdotes attest to, were a real source of frustration for Elizabeth's government and indeed a potential source of embarrassment for her personally.

By incorporating the narrative of Shane's fall into its biographical frame, *Stukeley* offers a fantasy of closure, and works symbolically to mollify tensions about Hugh O'Neill and the Irish crisis. Accordingly, as with Shane's threats of violence earlier, the play implies that his cynical manipulation of royal mercy will prove counter-productive. On the advice of Mackener, the rebel leader abandons his plan, significantly removing his halter (line 1317), and decides to seek refuge among the Scots, a decision that Shane himself recognises as ominous. Alexander Oge remarks that 'the news are true of great Oneale. | Dundalke hath dasht his pride and quelld his power' (lines 1318–19) and Buske recognises that they now have an opportunity to take revenge on Shane for a previous grievance. While the play is broadly accurate in its dramatization of Shane's death (he was murdered by the Scots at Cushendun), it telescopes the last months of his career into a sudden clash between him and the Scots, on to whom the violent work of subduing the queen's Irish rebel is projected. Shane pleas for assistance from the Scots, explaining how 'fortune hath fround upon your frend Oneale, | My troups are beaten, by the English power' (lines 1328–9). In a response that is beyond the demands of his character, Alexander says: 'How can a Rebell or a traitor hope | Of good successe against his soveraigne: | Awhile perhaps he may disturbe the state | And dam himselfe but at the last he falls' (lines 1335–8). These words carry extra-dramatic weight, exemplifying what seems to be the play's ideology. Insisting on the futility of rebellion in the face of an omnipotent monarch, the text endorses the hegemonic capacity of the Elizabethan state to control those Shane Oneales of the 1590s. It seems as if the play has represented Shane's rebellion in order to stage its powerful containment. Mackener's observation 'I thought thou hadst despisd the English churles' (line 1338) conveys the extent to which both Shane and himself have misread the situation in assuming they and the Scottish rebels share a common enemy in the English. A fight ensues and, as in his earlier encounter with Stukeley, Shane now finds himself being chased across the stage by Alexander. While Busk kills Mackener onstage, Shane's death at the hands of Alexander occurs offstage but the play does not

---

57 'Opinions of the privy council', quoted in Bagwell, *Ireland under the Tudors*, iii, p. 189.

hold back from providing the audience with the spectacle of the defeated rebel: the stage direction reads 'Enter Alex. with Oneales head' (line 1359). At this point in performance, the majority of the audience probably experienced a sense of satisfaction that the play's Irish rebel had finally met his end, a response arguably intensified because the audience could perhaps imagine Irish rebels beyond the play meeting a similar fate. The decapitated head of the Irish rebel becomes the cynosure on stage as, presumably holding it aloft, Alexander explains

> this head for present will I send,
> To that most noble English deputie,
> that ministers Justice as he were a God
> and guerdons vertue like a liberall king,
> This gratefull present may procure our peace
> And to the English fight and our feare may cease.
>
> (lines 1363–8)

Arguably, Alexander's claims complicate the symbolism of the moment, just as Shane's tactical deployment of clemency rendered his appearance in a halter ambivalent. The obsequious reference to the lord deputy, possibly an allusion to Sir Henry Sidney who had Shane murdered by Scottish mercenaries, potentially displaces Elizabeth's female rule in its evocation of male authority figures. Similarly, his hope that the rebel head will act as a bargaining tool for the Scots in their relations with the English, aligns them with the very expediency and strategizing practised by Shane himself. Nevertheless, the inference of the scene is always clear: in the possession of the deputy, the rebel head is to become an unambiguous signifier of Irish recalcitrance subdued and contained. To locate ambiguity here is to ignore the will to do violence with which the scene ends. For, as if to remove the possibility of any confusion, the scene closes with an unequivocal and general pronouncement by Buske: 'And may all Irish that with treason deale, | Come to like end or worse then Shane Oneale' (lines 1369–70). The closing couplet recalls the one from the previous scene where Stukeley boasted about defeating Shane but in this instance, there is a syllogistic logic that serves to racialize treason; Irish rebelliousness is signalled out for specific and extreme punishment. It is possible to see in this moment the influence of a text such as Hooker's Irish history on the play. Describing the display of Shane's head over Dublin castle, Hooker writes: 'A fit end for such a beginning, and a just reward for such a wicked traitor and sacrileger: who began his tyrannie in bloud, did continue it with bloud, and ended it with bloud.'[58] The rebel, the narrative implies, has been justly

---

58 Hooker, 'Supplie of the Irish chronicles', p. 338.

punished. But with Hooker's narrative representing virulent, racialist new English attitudes towards the Gaelic Irish, what we are seeing in these texts are culturally inflected and historically determined figurations of violence. This is apparent in *A View*, where in response to the likening of Hugh O'Neill to a 'frozen snake', Eudoxus remarks: 'He surely then deserveth the punishment of that snake, and should worthily be hewed to peeces'.[59] In *Stukeley*, it is in the suggestiveness of the alternative, 'like end or worse than Shane Oneale', with the syntax hinting at endless possibilities, that reveals how the play is reacting to the demands of its historical moment. The playing out of Shane's murder becomes a fantasy for the annihilation of Hugh O'Neill. However much the play might attempt to displace violence on to others, or keep the concept of royal mercy in view, the final wish for force against the Irish connects its dramatic and theatrical representations with real violence in the field.

'REBBELL TONGE': SIGNIFYING IRISH WORDS

The death of Shane is not the play's final word on Ireland. Stukeley's search for honour brings him into a treasonous alliance with King Philip of Spain and ultimately into the Portugese king's African wars but in scene twenty, the chorus refers to his papal appointment as 'Marquess of Ireland' (line 2429). Having survived the battle of Alcazar, Stukeley is reconciled with Vernon in the play's final scene, only to be murdered by Italian soldiers as revenge for redirecting the papal forces destined for Ireland to Africa. 'We had been safe in Ireland', remarks one of the soldiers, 'where now | We perish here in Aphrick' (lines 2967–8). The play ends with the dying Stukeley bidding 'England farewell' and accusing fortune, which 'By treason suffers him to be overthrowne' (lines 2980–2). It seems the man who had earlier boasted of subduing the Irish rebel must, like his former nemesis, learn the consequences of treason but, by extension, the play intimates that Catholic schemes against Elizabethan sovereignty in Ireland have also been overthrown.

Before making conclusions about the play's relation to the Irish wars and, by extension, its politics, I want to consider the second, prose version of the scene depicting the siege of Dundalk. In this version, Shane and his men converse in English but their enunciation registers their difference in a much more pronounced way than the first scene. On the stage, Irish characters speak in what Bartley describes as 'broken English', that is a 'competent – and exaggerated – mimicry' of Irish pronunciations of English.[60] Regarding such

59 Spenser, *A view*, p. 110.   60 Bartley, *Teague, Shenkin and Sawney*, p. 43; p. 40.

fractured speech as a dialect, Paula Blank notes how it is 'characterized primarily by phonological deviation from a "common" English' that in fact
constitutes a 'racial difference embodied in words'.[61] Language makes difference
audible. Of significance in this scene from *Stukeley* is the fact that English
speech is interspersed with a number of Irish language phrases, thus height-
ening the difference of the Irishmen. For the most part, these phrases take the
form of expletives that Shane directs at his men. For instance, addressing
Mackener, he says 'bodeaugh breen' (*bodach brean*), meaning 'stinking lout'.[62]
Later, fearing that the English guards will overhear them, Shane instructs
Mackener to be quiet, saying 'Esta clampar' (*éist do chlampar*), or 'shut your
mouth', and 'feagh bodeaugh' (*féach bodach*), or 'look, you lout' (lines 933; 940–1).
While these phrases are used exclusively by the rebel leader and indicate a hierarchy within the rebel camp, the overall tone of the scene suggests that they
are a regular mode of address rather than terms of abuse aimed at specific
individuals. For example, on hearing a cough from inside the walls of the
town, an indication to the rebels that the English watch is present, Shane hurls
a series of curses at Mackener: 'Mack Deawle' (*mac diabhal*), or 'son of the
devil'; 'marafassot art thou' (*marbhfhaisc ort*), or 'shrouding death on you'; and
'kana' (*cana*), or 'you whelp' (lines 947–8).

How, one might wonder, did a contemporary audience hear these phonetic
versions of Gaelic phrases? It is possible that they would have agreed with the
assessment of Irish by Felicea in Edward Sharpham's *The Fleire* (1606) and
concluded: 'That's a wild speech.'[63] I think it is fair to assume that the *Stukeley*
audience would have heard in Shane's speech elements of a foreign language
but whether of not they understood the Gaelic phrases is another matter.
Addressing the representation of foreign languages in early modern drama,
Janette Dillon argues that it was possible to 'invoke deep resonances that
bypassed engagement with the sense of the words'.[64] It follows that dramatists
would have been all too aware that while an audience might not make full
semantic sense of an alien language, the sound of that language could have an
impact on them. One potential effect of foreign words was to give definition
to the English language and, by extension, English identity.[65] But their presence

---

61 Paula Blank, *Broken English: dialects and the politics of language in Renaissance writings* (London, 1996), p. 128; p. 130.
62 The following translations are from Bartley, *Teague, Shenkin and Sawney*, p. 272.   63 *A critical old spelling edition of
the works of Edward Sharpham*, ed. Christopher Gordon Petter (New York, 1986), I.ii.115. There is also reference in
the play to 'Maister Oscabath, the Irishman and Maister Shamrough his lackey' (III.iii.73). The editor glosses the
former 'as a word non-existent but probably onomatopoeic on the proper name O'Scabeth' and also suggests the
English word 'scabbed' (p. 339). I think a far more likely explanation is that it is the phonetic version of the Gaelic
'uisce beatha' or 'water of life' (i.e. whiskey).   64 Dillon, *Language and stage*, p. 154.   65 See Dillon, *Language and
stage*, pp 162–82. Dillon cites Bakhtin's assertion that 'one language can, after all, see itself only in the light of
another language' (p. 5).

might also suggest the infiltration and contamination of the otherwise anglo-phone world of a play.[66] Certainly, playwrights could exploit the comic potential of language confusion and even make comic capital of audience incomprehension. In a scene from Dekker's *Honest Whore, part 2* (1605), for instance, the exaggerated dialect of the Irish footman Bryan is used by three courtiers to mock the linen-draper Candido. Confronted with Bryan's broken English and their deliberate mistranslation, he says 'I understand no word he speakes' (III.3.108).[67] Of course, it is the Irish servant's speech that creates the comedy. The sound of Shane's Gaelic in *Stukeley* may have been intended to produce an effect similar to the sound of Bryan's comic dialect, and we could be dealing with soraismus, or the mixture of terms from different languages. This can have ambivalent repercussions, as in *The Irish Masque*, where the reiter-ated call 'king Yamish' (line 3) by the Irish footmen to King James seems designed to elicit laughter. The characters' indecorum works in two directions, however, pointing not just at themselves and their historical old English coun-terparts but also at the object of their address, to produce a moment of *lèse-majesté*.[68] Elsewhere in Jacobean drama, in plays such as Beaumont and Fletcher's *Coxcomb* (1609) or Dekker's *Welsh Embassador* (1623), where characters disguise themselves as Irishmen, Irish stage dialects are largely and indeed consciously comic. In *Stukeley*, the use of Gaelic phrases and the context in which they are used, during the siege of an English garrison town, would appear to indicate that it is not included merely for comic effect. Compared with Dekker's broken English and inaccurate Irish, moreover, the Irish in *Stukeley* is used with 'remarkable correctness', as Alan Bliss points out.[69] OHamlon, one of the Irish rebels, uses the correct salute 'Slan haggat' (*slán agat*), literally meaning 'health at you', as in 'goodbye' and Mackener gives the appropriate response, 'slaue lets' (*slán leat*) or 'health with you', as in 'farewell' (lines 968–9).

Despite the accurate use of the Gaelic forms of address and farewell, as well as the phrases mentioned above, it could be argued that *Stukeley* reflects a larger pattern in the period: the reduction of Irish utterances to a series of stock phrases or English paraphrases. For, as Patricia Palmer argues, although the majority of the population of Ireland spoke Gaelic, the language was largely elided from English discourse in the period, entering this discourse 'only as bursts of irrational disorder: fragmentary, inexplicable and perverse'.

66 See Emma Smith, '"Signes of a stranger": the English language and the English nation in the late sixteenth century' in Philip Schwyzer and Simon Mealor (eds), *Archipelagic identities: literature and identity in the Atlantic archipelago, 1550–1800* (Aldershot, 2004), pp 169–79. 67 *Dramatic works of Thomas Dekker*, ed. Fredson Bowers, 6 vols (London, 1964), ii, 134–218. 68 On the politics of the masque, see James Smith, 'Effaced history: the colonial contexts of Ben Jonson's *Irish Masque at court*', *ELH*, 65 (1998), 297–321. 69 Alan Bliss, 'The English language in early modern Ireland' in *A new history of Ireland*, iii, p. 551.

Equipped with a 'colonial word-list' with which to label the peculiarities of native society and culture, new English writers demonstrated a philological ignorance towards Irish and evaluated it 'not as a language but as a sign'.[70] As such, Irish was 'less a language, than the dissidence and contrariness it encoded. To speak Irish – or not to speak English – is seen less as a linguistic fact than a symbolic action'.[71] This view is echoed by Tony Crowley, who writes that in the period, 'Irish had become another word for trouble.'[72] It is within the context of the elision of language, treason and race that we need to understand the inclusion of Irish language phrases in *Stukeley*. Palmer's observation that in new English texts 'Irish was usually admitted only when disclosure was strategically useful' can be applied to the play too. *Stukeley* allows the audience to hear Irish rebels utter Gaelic phrases, to speak fragments of their native tongue – the 'rebbell tonge' as Antonio, in Irish disguise, describes it in *The Coxcomb* – primarily as a signifier of treason and difference, as something that must be identified and then translated.[73] The play's incorporation of Gaelic phrases is, therefore, of a piece with its dramatization of the rebels themselves, an act of containment whereby Irish words are heard as a series of fractured utterances that are ultimately drowned out by Shane's English. Stanyhurst cited Shane O'Neill as an example of Irish hostility towards English: 'One demanded merrily why O'Neill that last was would not frame himself to speak English? What (quoth the other) in a rage, thinkest thou that it standeth with O'Neill's honour to writhe his mouth in clattering English?'[74] Of course, this is precisely what occurs in *Stukeley*. The play's act of containment, where Irish rebels are not only defeated but also translated, is an act of linguistic imperialism, which asserts the primacy of English.

Once again, what is evident here is the extent to which *Stukeley* is shaped by and is also responding to the demands of its contemporary moment. The play's desire to record and then efface Irish should be understood in relation to the importance of language in debates about the political and religious reform of the native Irish. For, in the rebels' use of Gaelic idioms, a coded form of communication, the play insinuates difference and, as with their threatened violence, gestures towards the difficulty of reforming the indigenous Irish more generally. Within the issue of language choice, 'the very future of English rule in Ireland was in play'.[75] Elizabethan efforts to defend the use of English can be traced as far back as the statutes of Kilkenny (1366) and the

70 Patricia Palmer, *Language and conquest in early modern Ireland: English Renaissance literature and Elizabethan imperial expansion* (Cambridge, 2001), p. 74; p. 88. See also Brian Ó Cuív, 'The Irish language in the early modern period' in T.W. Moody et al. (eds), *A new history of Ireland*, iii, pp 509–45. 71 Palmer, *Language and conquest*, p. 96. 72 Tony Crowley, *Wars of words: the politics of language in Ireland, 1537–2004* (Oxford, 2005), p. 19. 73 *Dramatic works in the Beaumont and Fletcher canon*, ed. Fredson Bowers (Cambridge, 1966), i, 297. 74 Stanyhurst, 'Historie of Ireland' in *Holinshed's Irish chronicle*, ed. Miller and Power, p. 35. 75 Crowley, *Wars of words*, p. 25.

Henrician ordinance of 1537, which observed 'there is again nothing which doth more contain and keep many of his subjects of this his said land, in a certain savage and wild kind and manner of living, than the diversity that is betwixt them in tongue, language, order, and habit'.[76] Stanyhurst, writing forty years later, remarked that if these elements were absent, 'doubtless the conquest limpeth'; he had already delineated the dangers of such absence in narrating how the old English 'have so acquainted themselves with the Irish, as they have made a mingle mangle or gallimaufry of both languages'.[77] What had initially been defensive measures, aimed at establishing linguistic buffer-zones between settlers and native-speakers, became offensive ones, which 'set in motion a transformative project of its own, anglicization'.[78] Thus, among Sir Henry Sidney's proposals for bringing Ireland 'from barbarism to a godly government' was the enactment of laws establishing 'Irish habits for men and women to be abolished, and the English tongue to be extended'.[79] The influence of such new English attitudes was still evident in the Jacobean period, where Barnabe Rich's *New description of Ireland* claims 'that the conquered should surrender themseleves to the language of the conquerors'.[80] The expansion of the language, to 'augment our tongue' as Sir Thomas Smith wrote in 1572 as he sought to attract other Englishmen to settle in the Ards, was regarded as the best policy against linguistic degeneration and reverse translation, that great fear that lurks beneath texts like Rich's, Spenser's *View* and also *Stukeley*.[81] Rich's suggestion of native surrendering to English implies the need for enforcement: as Eudoxus observes in *A View* upon hearing that the old English readily took to Irish, 'it hath ever beene the use of the conqueror, to despise the language of the conquered, and to force him by all means to learn his'.[82] A significant number of new English colonists, Spenser included, were of the view that the 'civilizing power of English' alone was not sufficient. For such men, William Gerrard's question – 'can the sword teache theim to speake Englishe?' – could only be answered in the affirmative.[83] Moreover, in a period when concepts of political reform were inseparable from questions of faith, it was recognized that force might assist the English language to have a proselytizing effect in Ireland. Archbishop Loftus remarked to Burghely that 'the sword alone without the word is not sufficient, but unless they be forced they will not come once to hear the word preached'.[84]

---

76 Quoted in Tony Crowley, *The politics of language in Ireland, 1366–1922: a sourcebook* (London, 2000), p. 21. 77 Stanyhurst, 'Historie of Ireland', p. 16; p. 14. 78 Palmer, *Language and conquest*, p. 137. 79 Quoted in Crowley, *The politics of language in Ireland*, p. 38. 80 Rich, *New description of Ireland*, p. 10. 81 Smith quoted in Palmer, *Language and conquest*, p. 113. 82 Spenser, *A view*, p. 70. For the argument that the old English community was bilingual, see Vincent Carey, '"Neither good English nor good Irish": bi-lingualism and identity formation in sixteenth century Ireland' in Morgan (ed.), *Political ideology in Ireland, 1534–1641*, pp 45–61. 83 Cited in Palmer, *Language and conquest*, p. 122. 84 Crowley, *Wars of words*, p. 9.

That the Irish rebels in *Stukeley* communicate by combining fragments of Gaelic with the language of the settler indicates a form of bilingualism that at best signifies an incomplete conquest, at worst an unsettling hybridity. As I have suggested, however, this is a play that advocates force – any sense of a threatening and contaminating Irish difference is dissipated at the moment when Shane's head is shown. His last words are in English just as the last word, although spoken by a Scot, speaks of and to English power. Nonetheless, the very presence of Irish language phrases, in the play as in the period, is of itself significant. With the Irish rebels' broken English and Irish, it is as if the Irish language has been broken up and all that is left are shards. The rebels' Irish words, however fragmentary, suggest that for all the play's ideological work – the dramatic incarnation of Shane who first feigns submission and then becomes signifier of the Irish tamed – *Stukeley* reveals the traces of its efforts to re-map the contact zone of Elizabethan Ireland as a stable binary of English/Irish. While it exerts spatial control over Ireland by bringing it on stage and linguistic control over the native Irish by representing Gaelic, the play is also a reminder that even the most ideologically static of texts on the Elizabethan problem of Ireland contains faultlines.

CHAPTER FOUR

1599

Drama, nation and the burden of war

> MacMorris, gallivanting
> round the Globe, whinged
> to courtier and groundling
> who had heard tell of us
>
> as going very bare
> of learning, as wild hares,
> as anatomies of death:
> 'What ish my nation?'
>
> And sensibly, though so much
> later, the wandering Bloom
> replied, 'Ireland', said Bloom,
> 'I was born here. Ireland'.
>
> Seamus Heaney, 'Traditions'.[1]

'It is easier to talk at home of Irish wars than to be in them', or so remarked Sir Henry Wallop of his military service in Ireland.[2] To talk of Irish wars in this period, however, was to engage with the broad subject of Ireland and the range of issues that it encompassed, from sovereignty, colonization and identity formation to alterity and degeneration. The Elizabethan stage provided a key space where this multivalent subject was talked about; representations in the drama reveal how Ireland entered the Elizabethan conscious and unconscious. But Wallop's observation, which implies that the full impact of war, or a similar trauma, is rarely conveyed through its contemporaneous representation, prompts us to think about the function, implications and indeed limitations of figurations of Ireland in the drama. To what extent, for instance, can a play bear the burden of its present? Does the discourse of war affect the very act of representation and the forms it takes? In order to explore such questions, I want to focus on a pivotal moment in the Elizabethan staging of Ireland, 1599, when the drama and the Irish wars intersected in strikingly close ways.

1 Seamus Heaney, *Wintering out* (London, 1972), p. 32.   2 Quoted in Falls, *Elizabeth's Irish wars*, p. 130; *DNB*.

While the crisis in Ireland had a long genealogy – as one contemporary observed 'it is no sudden fallen matter: it hath been years brewing' – the year 1599 arguably marked its apotheosis.[3] The Elizabethan government appeared to have come to the realization that, unlike the numerous rebellions that had occurred throughout the reign, O'Neill's rebellion was a nationwide war. The defeat of the crown forces under Henry Bagenal at the battle of the Yellow Ford a year earlier indicated to the state that it was dealing with a formidable enemy.[4] In the aftermath of this setback, a new English tract, 'The Supplication of the blood of the English most lamentably murdered in Ireland', warned its dedicatee Elizabeth of the consequences that would follow unless immediate and decisive action was taken:

> Your crowne of Ireland shall never stand steedye upon yore head: nor England shall never stand assured to have Ireland a faithfull neighbour [...] There will never be an ende of yore charge: you shalbe constrayned yearely to bestowe the revenewes of England, for the mayneuence of the crowne of Ireland: You shall never live out of doubte, out of the fear of the treachery of that cuntry.[5]

As the image of the unsteady crown indicates, anxieties surrounding the war in Ireland exceeded concern about merely curbing rebellion there: at stake now was not just the maintenance of Elizabethan sovereignty in Ireland but also at home.[6] Alarmist in tone, the text implies a criticism of the queen as it implores her to take action. With the queen's reputation for procrastination and fiscal conservatism, as well as rumours of Spanish assistance for O'Neill, realized with the landing of the Armada at Kinsale in 1601, such urgency was well placed. In 1599, the prospect of Spain's involvement meant that the nation-wide rebellion in Ireland risked becoming a struggle between England and its old enemy. Moreover, the increasing importance of Catholicism to the confederate cause, presented as a crusade with the tacit support of the papacy, broadened the war to a contest between Protestant England and Catholic Europe.

With the situation in Ireland looking increasingly precarious, there were calls for the state to adopt a more proactive policy. As Sir John Chamberlain observed: 'Matters in Ireland are farther out of square than ever, so that there

---

3 'The Supplication of the blood of the English most lamentably murdered in Ireland [1598]', ed. Willy Maley, *Analecta Hibernia*, 36 (1995), 3–77 at 17.   4 See T.W. Moody et al. (eds), *A new history of Ireland*, iii, pp 124–6. The defeat at the Yellow Ford was the largest single defeat suffered by the crown's forces in Tudor Ireland. 5 'The Supplication', p. 71.   6 See McGurk, *Elizabethan conquest of Ireland*, pp 11–12.

is no other way but to provide the sharper sword'.[7] The 'sword' came in the form of the queen's favourite, Robert Devereux, second earl of Essex, who in January 1599 secured the post of lord lieutenant of Ireland after months of lobbying at court. 'I have beaten Knollys and Mountjoy in the council', he boasted, 'and by God I will beat Tyr-Owen in the field.'[8] Despite Elizabeth's concerns about the cost of the wars, Essex was granted an army of over 16,000 men; the massive mobilization reflected the magnitude of the crisis facing the state. A royal proclamation anticipated that the army would 'be just terror to the wicked in making them see before their eyes the short and desperate end of these their barbarous and unnatural courses'.[9] The departure for war in March 1599 was commemorated in churches across the kingdom by the reading of a prayer 'for the good success of Her Majesties forces in Ireland'.[10] It enlisted God 'to strengthen and protect the forces of thine anoynted our queen and sovereigne, sent out to suppresse these wicked and unnaturall rebels.' Considering Essex's past military successes, it was widely anticipated that, as the prayer requested, God would grant the English a 'victorie against all such as rise up to withstand them'.[11] The appeals for divine sanction were apparently echoed by shouts of support for Essex from the populace as he travelled to the point of embarkation.[12]

Less than two months into the campaign, however, with reports circulating that 'Tyrone's party has prevailed the most', as well as signs of tension between Essex and London, it was clear that such a victory would not be readily achievable.[13] Gradually, disillusionment and anxiety eclipsed the aura of expectation and excitement that had surrounded Essex's appointment. Whereas news of his departure for Ireland was heavily publicized, the state appears to have attempted to control the flow of information about the progress of the campaign. Writing in June 1599, George Fenner noted that 'it is forbidden on pain of death to write or speak of Irish affairs; what is brought by post is known only to the council.'[14] One month later, Francis Cordale wrote: 'I can send no news of the Irish wars, all advertisements thence being prohibited, and such news as comes to council carefully concealed.'[15]

Despite these reports of an official clampdown, the topical and controversial subject of 'Irish affairs' was being broached in London's public theatres. Between the spring and summer of 1599, Shakespeare's *Henry V* intersected with

7 Norman McClure (ed.), *The Chamberlain letters: a selection of letters of John Chamberlain concerning life in England from 1597 to 1626* (London, 1965), p. 5.   8 Quoted in Bagwell, *Ireland under the Tudors*, iii, p. 315.   9 'Declaring reason for sending army into Ireland' (31 March 1599) in Paul L. Hughes and James F. Larkin (eds), *Tudor royal proclamations*, 2 vols (New Haven, 1969), ii, p. 202.   10 Bagwell, *Ireland under the Tudors*, iii, p. 319.   11 *A prayer for the good successe of Her Majesties forces in Ireland* (London, 1599).   12 Bagwell, *Ireland under the Tudors*, p. 319. 13 *Calendar of state papers, domestic, 1598–1601*, ed. Mary Anne Everett Green (London, 1869), p. 225.   14 Ibid., p. 225.   15 Ibid., p. 251.

contemporary matters, as evidenced in particular by the Irish character Mackmorrice and the chorus's direct reference to rebellion in Ireland. And, in the winter of that year, there was a similar contiguity with this context in *Sir John Oldcastle*, in which an Irish servant 'Mack Chane of Ulster' appears.[16] Whereas Shakespeare's play has been analyzed in terms of events in Ireland, *Oldcastle* has not been brought into a satisfying conjunction with this context. Part of my objective here, then, is to redress this imbalance and, in the process, further contextualize *Henry V*. It is worth noting that both plays are not only shaped by the Irish wars but also coincide with them. In exploring this shaping co-incidence, the focus is on the Irish references in *Henry V* and *Oldcastle* and those contemporary materials on the wars that moulded both the plays themselves and also audience response to the plays. I interpret the play's Irish references as examples of contextual mnemonics, whereby the text reveals in conscious form the unconscious influence of its contemporary moment. As this chapter will argue, the mnemonics of context suggests that the Irish wars influenced meaning in the plays, producing moments of wish fulfilment but also ideological indeterminacy.

'WHAT ISH MY NATION?': QUESTIONS OF IRISH DIFFERENCE ON THE ELIZABETHAN STAGE

There is a sense in which *Henry V* is virtually synonymous with Elizabethan or early modern Ireland. Indeed, it has almost come to be regarded as 'Shakespeare's Irish history'.[17] The direct allusion in the fifth chorus to the queen's lord deputy coming from Ireland with 'rebellion broached on his sword' (V.o.33) alerts us to similar moments of text-context simultaneity elsewhere in the play. There is, most notably, the Irish character Mackmorrice (III.iii.66–142) but also other elements, from the Dauphin's reference to the kern of Ireland and 'foul bogs' (III.vii.51–5), Pistol's Irish refrain (IV.iv.4), the textual error 'brother Ireland' (V.ii.12) and Henry's promise to Catherine (V.ii.230), leading Gary Taylor to write of 'the playwright's preoccupation with Irish affairs'.[18] Relative to a play like *Stukeley*, with six scenes set in Ireland, Taylor's judgement of *Henry V* is of course exaggerated; yet it is one justified because the Irish wars are the most pressing context for Shakespeare's play. The

---

16 I am following the spelling in the 1600 quarto, *Sir John Oldcastle*, ed. W.W. Greg (Oxford, 1908), line 2516. This is the only time 'Irishman' is named in the play. The name is silently emended to 'MacShane' in *A critical edition of Sir John Oldcastle*, ed. Jonathan Rittenhouse (New York, 1984). All subsequent quotations are from this edition. 17 The phrase is Andrew Murphy's, though it does not refer specifically to *Henry V*. See his 'Shakespeare's Irish history', 38–59. 18 Shakespeare, *Henry V*, ed. Gary Taylor (Oxford, 1982), p. 7.

Arden edition of the play gives a similar impression, although on Shakespeare's own investment in contemporary Irish matters, the editor, T.W. Craik, is less direct than Taylor. Craik begins his introduction by quoting the fifth chorus and dating the play to between March and September 1599 or Essex's departure and return from Ireland.[19] As if suggesting a further homology between the play and Ireland, the edition includes a woodcut from Derricke's *Image of Irelande* detailing 'an English army on the march in Ireland'.[20] Certainly, critics have long noted how the play is bound up with contemporary events in Ireland. Recent readings have recast the by-now-familiar suggestion of a general analogy between the Irish wars and the play's representation of the Anglo-French war as a form of cultural work, with the play participating in the ideological struggle surrounding the Irish wars.[21] Broadly speaking, new historicist readings argue that the play stages an idealized version of imperialist incorporation and provides an imaginary resolution of the seemingly intractable Irish problem.[22] Those readings inflected by cultural materialism maintain that although the text might re-present war in Ireland, it ultimately destabilizes any sense of unity or resolution and registers doubts about English expansionism.[23] Whereas the first implies that the play is capable of organizing and resolving the ambiguities and uncertainties generated by the Irish problem, the second suggests that these cannot be contained and are, in fact, registered in the fissures in the text.

Not everyone, however, is persuaded by contextual readings of the play that relate it so closely to 1599 Ireland. Commenting on the fetishizing of *Henry V* among literary critics of early modern Ireland, Maley claims that 'conventional criticism on the topic' has produced a static politics for the play.[24] On its Irish allusions, critics are found guilty of the same methodological and interpretative blindspots: expecting to find colonial discourse, they read from and through its terms, 'projecting it into the text'. Thus, in

19 See Shakespeare, *King Henry V*, ed. T.W. Craik (London, 1995), pp 1–5. All quotations are from this edition. See also Keith Brown, 'Historical context and *Henry V*', *Cahiers Elisabethains*, 29 (1986), 77–81. Brown argues for August as date of composition and early September as date of production, thus making it a Globe play (p. 78). By this stage, however, the tone of anticipation in the fifth chorus would have been inappropriate; consequently, the general consensus is for June as the most likely date.   20 Craik (ed.), *King Henry V*, p. 4.   21 For a brief summation of approaches to the Irish material in *Henry V*, see Andrew Murphy's '"Tish ill done": *Henry the Fift* and the politics of editing' in Burnett and Wray (eds), *Shakespeare and Ireland*, pp 213–34. A brief survey is also offered in Maryclaire Moroney, 'Recent studies in Tudor and Jacobean literature about Ireland', *ELR*, 31 (2001), 131–67 at 156–8.   22 See, for example, David Cairns and Shaun Richards, *Writing Ireland: colonialism, nationalism and culture* (Manchester, 1988), pp 9–12; and Jonathan Baldo, 'Wars of memory in *Henry V*', *Shakespeare Quarterly*, 47 (1996), 131–59.   23 See Dollimore and Sinfield, 'History and ideology: the instance of *Henry V*' in Drakakis (ed.), *Alternative Shakespeares*, i, pp 206–27; Highley, *Shakespeare, Spenser*, pp 134–63.   24 Maley, 'The Irish text and subtext of Shakespeare's English histories', p. 94.

Mackmorrice, 'Shakespeare creates an Irish captain praised by an English duke and an English colleague. The critics conjure up a barbarous stereotype'.[25] Maley is right to take to task a critical practice that prejudges a text in the ways he alleges but his qualification raises larger problems besides its tendency to generalize about what are diverse and heterogeneous interpretations of Ireland in *Henry V*. The argument for critical projection or over-reading has the effect of deflecting attention from the text itself and, most fundamentally, de-politicizing it. It is necessary to recognize that though the play does not represent Mackmorrice simply as a 'barbarous stereotype', neither is his characterization a critical fabrication; it stems from an established dramatic type that, like other Renaissance dramatists, Shakespeare was drawing upon. My point here is not to return to a 'blame-game' as initiated by John Arden, who infamously held Shakespeare and other English dramatists like Bale responsible for the perpetuation of anti-Irish prejudices.[26] Instead, it is to argue for the need to attend closely to the politics of its representations of Ireland and explore the extent to which these representations are shaped by the contemporaneous wars there.

The starting point for such an analysis of *Henry V* must be a consideration of the textual variants and their provenance. There are substantial differences between the 1623 folio text and the 1600 quarto, *The Cronicle History of Henry the Fift*.[27] The quarto not only lacks all of the choruses and the four captains scene but also those key textual residues of the Irish wars mentioned above.[28] Comparing the texts, one can conclude 'that the quarto is not an accurate record of a systematically cut version of the play, and therefore that it can give no firm grounds for deciding what cuts, if any, were made for the London performances'.[29] However, textual matters can also be contextual matters. In relation to the Irish wars, the quarto suggests the systematic excision of those aspects of the play with an overtly topical valence or 'a stripping of the play of its most significant personal and political references'.[30] The inclusion of the Irish captain and, more particularly, the reference to rebellion in Ireland in the fifth chorus, with its potential figuring of Essex and the Irish wars, may well have attracted the notice of the censor. The play may have been licensed on

25 Maley, 'The Irish text and subtext of Shakespeare's English histories', p. 111. 26 See Arden, 'Rug-headed Irish kerns and British poets', 56–7. 27 For an overview of the relationship between the two texts, see Craik (ed.), *Henry V*, pp 19–31; and Annabel Patterson, *Shakespeare and the popular voice*, pp 76–7. On the quarto as an abridged version of the play for touring, see Stanley Wells et al. (eds), *William Shakespeare: a textual companion* (Oxford, 1987), p. xiv. The argument that the quarto text represents a memorial reconstruction of the play is rejected in Maguire, *Shakespearean suspect texts*, pp 257–8. 28 The other notable omissions from the quarto text include the opening scene where the clergy cynically outline the advantages of foreign war (I.i), Henry's speech, 'Once more onto the breach' (III.i.1–34) and scenes involving the French before the battle (III.vii and IV.ii). 29 Craik (ed.), *Henry V*, p. 28. 30 Evelyn May Albright, 'The folio version of *Henry V* in relation to Shakespeare's times', *PMLA*, 43 (1928), 722–56 at 756.

78   *The Life of Henry the Fift.*

Pist. And I: If wishes would preuayle with me, my
purpose should not fayle with me; but thither would I
high.

Boy. As duly, but not as truly, as Bird doth sing on
bough.

Enter Fluellen.

Flu. Vp to the breach, you Dogges; auaunt you
Cullions.

Pist. Be mercifull great Duke to men of Mould: a-
bate thy Rage, abate thy manly Rage; abate thy Rage,
great Duke. Good Bawcock bate thy Rage: vse lenitie
sweet Chuck.

Nim. These be good humors: your Honor wins bad
humors.   *Exit.*

Boy. As young as I am, I haue obseru'd these three
Swashers: I am Boy to them all three, but all they three,
though they would serue me, could not be Man to me;
for indeed three such Antiques doe not amount to a man:
for *Bardolph*, hee is white-liuer'd, and red-fac'd; by the
meanes whereof, a faces it out, but fights not: for *Pistol*,
hee hath a killing Tongue, and a quiet Sword; by the
meanes whereof, a breakes Words, and keepes whole
Weapons: for *Nim*, hee hath heard, that men of few
Words are the best men, and therefore hee scornes to say
his Prayers, lest a should be thought a Coward: but his
few bad Words are matcht with as few good Deeds; for
a neuer broke any mans Head but his owne, and that was
against a Post, when he was drunke. They will steale any
thing, and call it Purchase. *Bardolph* stole a Lute-case,
bore it twelue Leagues, and sold it for three halfepence.
Nim and *Bardolph* are sworne Brothers in filching: and
in Callice they stole a fire-shouell. I knew by that peece
of Seruice, the men would carry Coales. They would
haue me as familiar with mens Pockets, as their Gloues
or their Hand-kerchers: which makes much against my
Manhood, if I should take from anothers Pocket, to put
into mine; for it is plaine pocketting vp of Wrongs.
I must leaue them, and seeke some better Seruice: their
Villany goes against my weake stomacke, and therefore
I must cast it vp.   *Exit.*

Enter Gower.

Gower. Captaine *Fluellen*, you must come presently to
the Mynes; the Duke of Gloucester would speake with
you.

Flu. To the Mynes? Tell you the Duke, it is not so
good to come to the Mynes: for looke you, the Mynes
is not according to the disciplines of the Warre; the con-
cauities of it is not sufficient: for looke you, th'athuer-
sarie, you may discusse vnto the Duke, looke you, is digt
himselfe foure yard vnder the Countermines: by *Chesu*,
I thinke a will plowe vp all, if there is not better directions.

Gower. The Duke of Gloucester, to whom the Order
of the Siege is giuen, is altogether directed by an Irish
man, a very valiant Gentleman yfaith.

Welch. It is Captaine *Mackmorrice*, is it not?

Gower. I thinke it be.

Welch. By *Chesu* he is an Asse, as in the World, I will
verifie as much in his Beard: he ha's no more directions
in the true disciplines of the Warres, looke you, of the
Roman disciplines, then is a Puppy-dog.

Enter Mackmorrice, and Captaine Iamy.

Gower. Here a comes, and the Scots Captaine, Captaine
Iamy, with him.

Welch. Captaine *Iamy* is a maruellous falorous Gentleman, that is certain, and of great expedition and know-

ledge in th'aunchiant Warres, vpon my particular knowledge of his direction: by *Chesu* he will maintaine his
Argument as well as any Militarie man in the World, in
the disciplines of the Pristine Warres of the Romans.

Scot. I say gudday, Captaine *Fluellen*.

Welch. Godden to your Worship, good Captaine
Iames.

Gower. How now Captaine *Mackmorrice*, haue you
quit the Mynes? haue the Pioners giuen o're?

Irish. By Chrish Law tish ill done: the Worke ish
giue ouer, the Trompet sound the Retreat. By my Hand
I sweare, and my fathers Soule, the Worke ish ill done:
it ish giue ouer: I would haue blowed vp the Towne,
so Chrish saue me law, in an houre. O tish ill done, tish ill
done: by my Hand tish ill done.

Welch. Captaine *Mackmorrice*, I beseech you now,
will you voutsafe me, looke you, a few disputations with
you, as partly touching or concerning the disciplines of
the Warre, the Roman Warres, in the way of Argument,
looke you, and friendly communication: partly to satisfie
my Opinion, and partly for the satisfaction, looke you, of
my Mind; as touching the direction of the Militarie discipline, that is the Poynt.

Scot. It sall be vary gud, gud feith, gud Captens bath:
and I sall quit you with gud leue, as I may pick occasion:
that sall I mary.

Irish. It is no time to discourse, so Chrish saue me:
the day is hot, and the Weather, and the Warres, and the
King, and the Dukes: it is no time to discourse, the Town
is beseech'd: and the Trumpet call vs to the breech, and
we talke, and be Chish do nothing, 'tis shame for vs all:
so God sa'me 'tis shame to stand still, it is shame by my
hand: and there is Throats to be cut, and Workes to be
done, and there ish nothing done, so Chrish sa'me law.

Scot. By the Mes, ere theise eyes of mine take themselues to slomber, ayle de gud seruice, or Ile ligge i'th'
grund for it: ay, or goe to death: and Ile pay't as valo-
rously as I may, that sall I surely do, that is the breff and
the long: mary, I wad full faine heard some question
tween you tway.

Welch. Captaine *Mackmorrice*, I thinke, looke you,
vnder your correction, there is not many of your Nation.

Irish. Of my Nation? What ish my Nation? Ish a
Villaine, and a Basterd, and a Knaue, and a Rascall? What
ish my Nation? Who talkes of my Nation?

Welch. Looke you, if you take the matter otherwise
then is meant, Captaine *Mackmorrice*, peraduenture I
shall thinke you doe not vse me with that affabilitie, as in
discretion you ought to vse me, looke you, being as good
a man as your selfe, both in the disciplines of Warre, and
in the deriuation of my Birth, and in other particularities.

Irish. I doe not know you so good a man as my selfe:
so Chrish saue me, I will cut off your Head.

Gower. Gentlemen both, you will mistake each other.

Scot. A, that's a foule fault.   *A Parley.*

Gower. The Towne sounds a Parley.

Welch. Captaine *Mackmorrice*, when there is more
better opportunitie to be required, looke you, I will be
so bold as to tell you, I know the disciplines of Warre:
and there is an end.   *Exit.*

Enter the King and all his Traine before the Gates.

King. How yet resolues the Gouernour of the Towne?
This is the latest Parle we will admit:

There-

2 *The Life of Henry the Fift*, in *Mr William Shakespeares Comedies, Histories, and Tragedies* (1623).
Reproduced with the permission of the Folger Shakespeare Library, Washington DC

the basis that these and other topically allusive lines were omitted in performance.[31] There is certainly a case to be made for the censorship of the play, one
supported by circumstantial evidence, from the bishops' ban on the publication of English histories in June 1599 to the sensitivity of Irish matters
mentioned in the correspondence of Fenner and Cordale. More significantly,
perhaps, there is the official touchiness about the public discussion of Essex
which, following his premature and unsanctioned return from Ireland, was
especially acute. The problem, however, is twofold. Firstly, the assumption that
censorship extended to performance; and secondly, the assumption that the
quarto text bears the closest resemblance to what was performed on the
London stages between the spring and summer of 1599. Evelyn Albright offers
a way around this latter problem, arguing that, owing to the precarious political atmosphere in 1600, Shakespeare withheld the fuller version of the play
from publication.[32] The folio text, she argues, reflects the play as performed in
1599.

Underpinning these interpretations is the assumption that because one
aspect of the play aroused concern, it inevitably rendered the entire play
controversial and censorable. There are grounds, then, to question the argument for its wholesale or systematic censorship. Neither of the above
hypotheses concerning dramatic or print censorship explains the absence in
the quarto of those scenes which do not appear to have even a general resonance with contemporary issues, nor do they consider why Gower's mention
of 'a beard of the General's cut' (III.vi.75–6), widely accepted as a reference to
Essex's characteristic Cadiz beard, should remain in the quarto, if it was the
association with him that generated suspicion. Furthermore, while the fifth
chorus allusion to the 'general' in Ireland might have promoted an analogy
with Essex that, by September, had become inappropriate, there is no reason
why the remainder of the fifth chorus and all of the other choruses would have
to be excised as well. Indeed, T.W. Craik demonstrates that the choruses were
included in the London performances.[33]

As even a brief discussion of these issues suggests, there is a discrepancy
between the play as performed and the printed text that we work from, a
difference that illustrates the difficulty of recovering a text's local meaning.
Locating the debate about the two texts against the fiasco surrounding Essex,
Annabel Patterson argues for the need to think in terms of different versions

31 Clare, *"Art made tongue-tied by authority"*, pp 92–4.   32 Albright, 'The folio version of *Henry V* ', p. 726.
33 Craik (ed.), *Henry V*, p. 25. Craik bases this argument on some textual detective work. He points toward the
inclusion in the quarto text of the verse line 'Sir Thomas Grey, Knight, of Northumberland' (II.0.25) in its
version of the folio's II.2.66–68 and also the quarto's incorrect immediate re-entry for Fluellen at the start of
V.1.

of the play rather than textual variants. The quarto, Patterson observes, is a 'more crudely patriotic' play that lacks what she sees as the folio's troubling indeterminacy on topical matters and Essex.[34] While Patterson's distinctions might be overdetemined – the differences in tone could be said to stem from the cuts to the quarto – her suggestion of 'versions' may throw further light on *Henry V* and the Irish wars. For the texts can be regarded as products of the ideological struggle surrounding the Irish crisis, with the quarto reflecting a version of the play without overt references to Ireland but nonetheless sharing with the folio text a resonance, albeit less direct, with contemporary events there. The idea of versions of the play encourages a consideration of the quarto in relation to and marked by an Irish context.

Mackmorrice, or 'Irish' (as in the speech prefixes in the folio), or Macmorris (as his name is generally spelt in modern editions of the play) is referred to before he is seen or heard in the so-called four captains scene of *Henry V*. The English captain Gower describes him as 'a very valiant gentleman, i'faith' (III.ii.67). What follows is well known, with Fluellen's judgement 'he's an ass' (III.ii.70), paving the way for a quarrelsome exchange between the two over the disciplines of war that itself provokes more contentious issues. Mackmorrice's words are ones of complaint about military inaction – 'By Chrish, la,'tish ill done; the work ish ill done' (III.ii.89) – that become a refrain within his speech: 'I would have blowed up the town' (III.ii.92); 'It is no time to discourse' (III.ii.106); "tis shame to stand still, it is shame, by my hand; and there is throats to be cut, and works to be done' (III.ii.112–4). Although presented as pugnacious and irksome, attributes associated with the stage Irishman, Mackmorrice is keen to direct his energies toward the campaign against the French. So when Fluellen asks him, 'Captain Macmorris, I think, look you, under correction, there is not many of your nation' (III.ii.121–3), there is a sense in which he does not have time to talk of, or about, it. Of course, precisely how 'it' is to be understood has become the crux of this scene. Critics have poured over Mackmorrice's questions 'Of my nation? What ish my nation?' (III.ii.124), according him an importance in excess of his minor character status in the play. Such privileging of Mackmorrice has much to do with Shakespeare's centrality to the canon: stage Irish characters in other plays from the period have not been analyzed to the same extent. Yet, it would be misguided to see the debate about Mackmorrice as a reflex of Shakespeare's canonicity, for his questions are arguably at the heart of this play about war, conquest, cultural difference and national identity. Indeed, for a play increasingly understood as an ambivalent, if not sceptical, take on war and patriotism,

its title could well have been *Henry V, or What ish my nation?* The suggestion that
the play might be read through Mackmorrice's question, so that his character
is regarded as emblematic of its concerns and politics more generally, raises
questions about his place in the play and his relation to the Irish crisis. What
I want to argue here is that it is in this scene, structured around the related
issues of language, assimilation and hybridity, that the play not only reveals the
shaping influence of the wars in Ireland but comes closest to addressing their
cultural impact.

Mackmorrice has been understood as an instance of the ubiquitous stage
Irishman, a largely comic figure that realizes on stage the political fantasy of
Irish assimilation.[35] This interpretation stems from a specific view of the four
captains scene, one which holds that in bringing clearly marked representatives
of England, Scotland, Ireland and Wales together on soon to be conquered
French soil, the scene effects a British geography and unity. As early as 1874,
Richard Simpson suggested that Shakespeare included the four captains 'as if
to symbolize the union of the four nations under one crown, and their co-
operation in enterprises of honour, no longer hindered by the touchiness of a
separatist nationalism'.[36] The 'ideal of intra-British co-operation under a
beloved monarch' is read simultaneously as a paean to Elizabeth's capacity to
unite the different nations of her kingdom and also an anticipation of King
James' idea of Great Britain.[37] Recent debates about the British question, which
have placed emphasis on union as construct and process, have partially unsettled such assumptions about the scene.[38] However, it is worth stating
unequivocally that the scene does not naturalize 'island unity'.[39] As David
Baker notes, those who 'insist in regarding the "incorporation" of its Irish,
Welsh, and Scottish characters into British identity as entirely successful [...]
are implicitly endorsing a particular version of the history of the British Isles',

---

35 On Mackmorrice as one of the earliest examples of the stage Irishman, see Bartley, *Teague, Shenkin and Sawney*,
pp 16–17; Annelise Truninger, *Paddy and the Paycock: a study of the stage Irishman from Shakespeare to O'Casey* (Biel, 1976),
pp 26–7; Leerssen, *Mere Irish and Fior-Ghael*, pp 84–6. See also Declan Kiberd, 'The fall of the stage Irishman' in
R. Schleifer (ed.), *The genres of the Irish literary revival* (Norman, OK, 1980), where Mackmorrice is said to be the
first example of the phenomenon.   36 Cited in Philip Edwards, *Threshold of the nation: a study in English and Irish
drama* (Liverpool, 1979), p. 74. For a similar view, see Barton, *Links between Ireland and Shakespeare*. Barton quotes
approvingly Georg Brandes' assertion that 'Shakespeare evidently dreamed of a greater England' (p. 118).
37 Leerssen, *Mere Irish and Fior-Ghael*, p. 86. For the view that, along with Jamy, Mackmorrice is a later interpo-
lation into the text as a concession to King James, see Bartley, *Teague, Shenkin and Sawney*, p. 16.   38 See Willy
Maley, '"This sceptred isle": Shakespeare and the British problem' in John J. Joughin (ed.), *Shakespeare and national
culture* (Manchester, 1997), pp 83–108; Andrew Hadfield, '"Hitherto she ne're could fancy him": Shakespeare's
"British" plays and the exclusion of Ireland' in Burnett and Wray (eds), *Shakespeare and Ireland*, pp 47–63.
39 Edwards, *Threshold of the nation*, p. 74. One of the earliest critics to comment on the irony of the supposed
British union scene was David Comyn; see *Irish illustrations to Shakespeare, being notes on his references to Ireland* (Dublin,
1894), p. 11; see also Highley, *Shakespeare, Spenser*, pp 145–7.

that is England's domination of non-English identities.[40] Instead, Mackmorrice, Fluellen and Jamy should be interpreted as traces of the differences that union tries to erase. Yet, despite Baker's efforts to deconstruct Anglocentric readings of the play, his concern with 'imagining Britain' imposes limits on his interpretation: Mackmorrice and Fluellen are described as 'British characters'.[41]

Reading Shakespeare's Irish character as a stage Irishman can involve assumptions about the politics of the scene and the play. It is therefore necessary to extend understandings of the stage Irishman beyond seeing it as merely a reflex of colonial power or as a series of static colonialist stereotypes that elicit a laughter of superiority in an audience. An ideologically indeterminate play like *Henry V* offers more than one type of interpretative response: the four captains scene enables the theatre audience to do more than simply laugh at, or even with, Mackmorrice. It is equally necessary to think of the stage Irishman not just as a political category, the site where an ideology of English hegemony and nationality is produced and, frequently questioned, but also as a dramatic category that, contrary to critical opinion, was not a Shakespearean invention. In dramaturgical terms, the stage Irishman 'does not stand in need of much elaboration' yet his inclusion in the play is determined by 'the highly stratified expectations of the audience'; accordingly, 'he can only with great difficulty be characterized in terms other that the current stereotype'.[42] Of relevance here is Homi K. Bhabha's formulation of the colonial stereotype 'as a form of knowledge and identification that vacillates between what is always "in place", already known, and something that must be anxiously repeated'.[43] But in a highly competitive dramatic and theatrical environment, it seems probable that there would have been a strong imperative to extend the possibilities of a stock character like the stage Irishman. While Mackmorrice in *Henry V* denotes recognizable Irish stereotypes and is an instance of their repetition, his questions are also in excess of the requirements and expectations of his character. They lend him a self-reflexive quality that is found in later stage Irish characters from Mack Chane in *Oldcastle* to Dekker's *Old Fortunatus* (1599) where, shedding his disguise as an Irish costermonger, Shaddowe asks 'Did I not clap a good false Irish face?'[44] A similar moment occurs in Beaumont and Fletcher's *The Coxcomb* (1609): disguised as an Irish footman, Antonio says, 'I hope I am wild enough to be known.'[45] When it came to Irish characters,

---

40 David Baker, *Between nations: Shakespeare, Spenser, Marvell and the question of Britain* (Stanford, 1997), p. 22.   41 Baker, *Between nations*, p. 22.   42 Leerssen, *Mere Irish and Fíor-Ghael*, p. 78.   43 Homi K. Bhabha, *The location of culture* (London, 1994), p. 66.   44 *Dramatic works of Thomas Dekker*, i, p. 179, IV.ii.98.   45 *Dramatic works in the Beaumont and Fletcher canon*, ed. Fredson Bowers (Cambridge, 1966), i, p. 297, II.iii.1.

dramatic imitation could be active and dynamic; indirectly, it could effect an unsettling of the very stereotypes that were being invoked. The space of the stage enabled ironic explorations of national identities.

The dramatic and theatrical dimension of the stage Irishman, though significant, can only partly explain Mackmorrice's presence and the force of his questions. In exploring who or what Mackmorrice is, we invariably return to the demands of the contemporary moment and the context of the Irish wars. Any discussion of the kind of responses that Mackmorrice elicited from contemporary audiences must begin with his name.[46] Plunket Barton makes the salient, yet frequently overlooked point, that Shakespeare obviously regarded the name as typically Irish: 'his captains were national types and he chose names to fit them'.[47] To Elizabethans, 'Mac' could, like other names, serve as a metonym for the Irish. 'Mac, fitz and O "in action" are we say | when bare tayld rogues in woodes the rebells play', writes Parr Lane in 'News from the Holy Ile' (1621), recalling the description of the Irish chieftains by Lord Mountjoy, Essex's successor as lord deputy in Ireland.[48] As Barton explains, Mackmorrice's name incorporates an Irish prefix and Norman termination, thus marking him out as old English.[49] It may be the Irish form of Fitzmaurice; the Fitzmaurices of Kerry being a branch of the Geraldines.[50] This suggests that Shakespeare's Irishman should be thought of as an old Englishman and that 'the origins of his identity crisis, the apparently modern questioning of cultural identity, lie in the twelfth century'.[51] While the genealogy might be medieval, the resonance of Mackmorrice's name is early modern. From an Elizabethan perspective, the name would have brought to mind those descendants of the twelfth century Anglo-Norman settlers, whose mingling with the native Irish had, the new English believed, initiated a process of cultural and social degeneration. Hybrid surnames such as Mackmorrice's were testimony to this process, and were targeted in plans for the reformation of Ireland. In Spenser's *View*, Irenius states, 'I wish all the O's and Mac's [...] to bee utterly forbidden and extinguished.'[52] The 'Supplication', that later and arguably more radical new English text, similarly addresses the degeneracy of the old English, blaming their 'matches', or intermarriages with the Gaelic Irish, for the inversion of the social order:

46 For a fascinating analysis of the variant spellings of the name in editions of the play since the folio, see Murphy, '"Tish ill done": *Henry the Fift* and the politics of editing', pp 221–7. 47 Barton, *Links between Shakespeare and Ireland*, p. 119. 48 Quoted in Carpenter (ed.), *Verse in English from Tudor and Stuart Ireland*, p. 142, n.35. 49 Barton, *Links between Shakespeare and Ireland*, p. 119. 50 See Edward MacLysaght, *The surnames of Ireland* (6th ed. Dublin, 1991), p. 222. 51 Willy Maley, 'Shakespeare, Holinshed and Ireland: resources and con-texts' in Burnett and Wray (eds), *Shakespeare and Ireland*, p. 34. 52 Spenser, *A view*, p. 148.

> What hath made the Geraldins, the Lacyes, the Purcells, to alter the nature of themselves from the nature of theire names, but theire former Irishe matches? what hath made the neighbourhood, the sight, nay the thought of as Englishman soe hatefull unto them, but such Irishe matches? what hath turned them from English whch they sounde in name, to Irishe wch they appear in nature? from men to monsters? but theire Irishe matches? They were in former times, as wee are now, meere Englishe in habite, in name, in nature. They now retaine nothinge of that they were but the bare name.

The narrator proceeds by juxtaposing old English names with Gaelic Irish ones in order to ask what difference there is between them. 'They are nowe all one: there is no difference,' is the conclusion arrived at.[53] Miscegenation produces a threatening alterity, which unsettles notions of linguistic purity. The problem, as identified by the narrator, is that an old English name is no longer a guarantee of Englishness: the signifier does not correspond to what it once signified. The same can be said of Mackmorrice: his name indicates an old English genealogy but to an Elizabethan audience he appears Irish in nature. In this respect, Mackmorrice is a personification of the process of degeneration, a dramatic realization of the cultural transformation that, it was believed, the old English were most susceptible to. Sir John Davies had likened the old English to 'those who had drunk of Circe's cup and were turned into very beasts, and yet took pleasure in their beastly manner of life as they would not return to their shape of men again.'[54] Among the list of these degenerates who, according to Davies, were ashamed of their English nation and names, is an example from Munster, where 'of the great families of the Geraldines, one was called Macmoris.'[55] From degenerate old Englishman, Shakespeare's 'Irish' transmogrifies into native Irishman.

To view Mackmorrice in such terms is to place him in context of Elizabethan concepts of degeneration and Irish barbarism. A potentially revealing analogue for Shakespeare's character is Patrick Macmaurice. Of old English descent, Macmaurice was a servant to the queen at court, whose perceived hybrid status is recorded into the Irish sections of Holinshed's *Chronicles*. John Hooker noted that whereas at court, Macmaurice was 'apparelled according to his degree, and dailie nurtured and brought up in all civilitie', he 'was no sooner home, but awaie with his English attrires, and on

---

53 'The Supplication', p. 33.   54 Sir John Davies, *A discovery of the true causes why Ireland was never entirely subdued, nor brought under obedience of the crown of England, until the beginning of his majesty's happy reign* in Myers (ed.), *Elizabethan Ireland*, pp 161–2.   55 Davies, *Discovery*, p. 162.

with his brogs, his shirt, and other Irish rags, being become as verie a traitor as the veriest knave of them all'.[56] Hooker's account of sartorial difference is illustrative of what Anne Jones and Peter Stallybrass describe as the 'animatedness of clothes' in the Renaissance, or their capacity to endow a person with a form, shape and identity. 'Clothes [...] inscribe themselves upon a person who comes into being through that inscription.'[57] What Hooker's account registers is typically Elizabethan anxieties about Gaelic dress as indicative of native barbarity and old English degeneration, but also the possibility that beneath English dress and civility, there might lurk an insidious difference. Hooker, in a related context, explains: 'they maie be verie well resembled to an ape, which (as the common proverb is) an ape is but an ape, albeit he be clothed in purple and velvet'.[58] Hooker's description has the hybrid Irish servant 'living a sort of "Jekyll-Hyde" existence' between London and Ireland.[59] Shakespeare's Mackmorrice is a similarly hybrid and troubling figure. His volubility, arguably the dominant impression of him, is barely contained within the scene and often threatens to break it up; it suggests more than the impatience of a soldier. It has been argued that out of Shakespeare's 'valiant gentleman' (III.ii.67) critics fabricate a barbarous stereotype but this is to ignore Elizabethan ethnographic assumptions about the Irish. In these terms, Mackmorrice embodies a potential challenge to the state whose interests that he appears to serve. His insistence that 'there is throats to be cut and works to be done' (III.iii.55–6) and threat to cut off Fluellen's head (III.iii.76) recalls those images of Irish violence in plays such as *Stukeley* and in Elizabethan culture more generally. There is a suggestion of violence in Mackmorrice that neither the common sense of Gower nor the comic presence of Fluellen and Jamy seem capable of diffusing.

Like Hooker's cross-dressing royal servant, then, Shakespeare's Mackmorrice raises issues about concepts of Irishness and the recognition of difference. In one sense, as Andrew Murphy has noted, Mackmorrice 'highlights a certain Irish proximate liminality' or the 'encountering of sameness at the heart of presumed difference'.[60] Murphy draws on Bhabha's concept of 'colonial mimicry', where the colonizer's desire for a 'recognizable Other as a subject of difference that is almost the same but not quite' produces a problematic ambivalence that disrupts the coherence of colonial power.[61] There is another sense of Irishness, however, one suggested by Hooker's simian

---

56 Hooker, 'Supplie of the Irish Chronicles', p. 417.   57 Ann Jones and Peter Stallybrass, *Renaissance clothing and the materials of memory* (Cambridge, 2000), p. 2.   58 Hooker, 'Supplie of the Irish Chronicles', p. 417. 59 Barton, *Links between Shakespeare and Ireland*, p. 126.   60 Murphy, *But the Irish sea*, p. 119; p. 13.   61 Bhabha, *The location of culture*, p. 86.

metaphor, which implies something more threatening than partial recognition or incomplete assimilation, that is an ineluctable Irish difference, even essence, lurking beneath the mask of obedience, service and civility. In other words, what is discovered behind Mackmorrice's presumed similitude is difference. But on the stage, any sense of Irish difference as something that resists assimilation into Englishness or Britishness is undermined by the very forms that enable its representation; ultimately, the audience knows that Mackmorrice or 'Irish' is a part in a play, a role to be realized by an actor. Audience awareness of the dynamic between character and actor is especially acute in *Henry V*, where the subject of mimesis is addressed in the prologue and choruses. As Robert Weimann points out, the play derives energy from 'the threshold between the imaginary, represented product (the shown play) and the material processes of bringing it about (that is, the playing of the play, the showing of the show)'.[62] The practice of doubling, which foregrounds the mechanics of playing, may have meant that the actor who played Mackmorrice would also have played the part of Exeter, a staunch supporter of the king and his war throughout.[63]

As a figure of hybridity, both in an ethnic and also a theatrical sense (considering the nature of doubling), Mackmorrice highlights a contemporary dilemma concerning the employment of the native Irish and old English in the standing army. This issue served to localize the broader cultural question of incorporation and assimilation. During the Nine Years War, the recruitment of men in Ireland was practised and encouraged. In 1600, the privy council recommended to Lord Mountjoy men of 'speciall note for theire good service who are inhabitantes of that realme of Ireland'.[64] The council outlined the reasons behind its thinking:

> when you finde any of those Irishe servitors that are of approved fidelitie and valour and are so engaged by their services paste to stande firme in their allegeance as there is no liklyhood of their revolting, wee thincke there might be speciall use of their employment with such forces as of necessitie her Majestie must maintayne, because they knowe the countrie and passages better than strangers, and especially for that they having themselves some interest in that State.[65]

The professed faith in the loyal service of the potential recruits suggests their potential incorporation into the queen's army, where their local knowledge of

---

62 Robert Weimann, *Author's pen and actor's voice: playing and writing in Shakespeare's theatre* (Cambridge, 2000), p. 70. See also Pamela Mason, '*Henry V*: "the quick forge and working house of thought"' in Michael Hattaway (ed.), *The Cambridge companion to Shakespeare's history plays* (Cambridge, 2002), pp 177–92.   63 See Thomas Berger, 'The disappearance of Macmorris in Shakespeare's *Henry V*', *Renaissance Papers* (1985), 13–26 at 20–1.   64 *Acts of the privy council, 1599–1600*, ed. John Roche Dasent (London, 1905), p. 708.   65 *Acts P.C.*, p. 709.

the topography can be harnessed by English power. But concerns about degeneracy, combined with a belief among the English that they that they themselves were especially susceptible to transformation by alien identities, gave rise to anxieties about such 'Irish servitors'.[66] As Fynes Moryson noted, 'it was obserued that generally they did no service, but lying still [in garrison], wasted the queenes treasure, and [...] did make our counsells knowne to the rebells, did underhand releiue them, and vsed all meanes to nourish and strengthen the rebellion'.[67] Moryson's report about their dubious or false loyalties provides an insight into the kind of suspicions that Mackmorrice might have provoked. He is a captain in Henry's army but he can also appear to be the enemy within. In this regard, Mackmorrice literalizes those images of 'being invaded or being breached from behind' that, Patricia Parker argues, register fears about reversed conquest.[68] There is, for instance, Henry's concern that in moving towards France, England itself will be open to attack from the Scots, as in the past when they 'came pouring like a tide into a breach' (I.ii.149) to England, that 'being empty of defence, | Hath shook at th'ill neighbourhood' (I.ii.153–4). By contrast, there is Henry's call to arms – 'Once more unto the breach, dear friends, once more' (III.i.1) – that signals an attempt to metaphorically seal those holes of the vulnerable or leaky nation. This 'rhetoric of straightforward advance' is immediately parodied by Bardolph's 'On, on, on, on, on, to the breach, to the breach' (III.ii.1–2) and later, in the same scene, appears to be denied through the collection of the four discordant captains.[69] Of the four, it is Mackmorrice who, like Bardolph, echoes Henry when he notes that 'the town is besieched, and the trumpet calls us to the breach, and we talk, and be Chrish, do nothing' (III.ii.109–10). There is an eagerness to fight here but, uttered by an Irishman, with all the connotations that suggests, there is some ambivalence about his sense of 'breach'; it is not entirely clear if he can be trusted to serve the interests of English power.

Mackmorrice is a 'a Mr Facing-both-ways' but compared to the Irish characters in *Stukeley*, his hybrid identity seems, at least initially, to be barely audible.[70] Whereas that play contains Irish language phrases, the only Irish in *Henry V* is Pistol's riposte to the bewildered French solider, 'Calin o custure me!' (IV.iv.4), apparently the phonetic version of the Irish refrain to a popular song.[71] Mackmorrice's lexicon does not contain any native words. One could

---

66 On the vulnerability of Englishness, see Mary Floyd-Wilson, *English ethnicity and race in early modern drama* (Cambridge, 2003), pp 56–60.   67 Moryson, 'Itinerary', p. 44.   68 Parker, *Shakespeare from the margins*, p. 42.   69 Ibid., pp 41; and 168–9.   70 The description of Mackmorrice is from W.F.P. Stockley, *King Henry the fifth's poet historical* (London, 1925), p. 73; Bhabha, *Location of culture*, p. 2.   71 Craik notes that 'the refrain represents the Irish words 'cailin og a' stor' or 'young maiden, my treasure'. Edmund Malone was the first Shakespearean editor to suggest a source for Pistol's remark: a song, printed in Clement Robinson's *A Handful of Pleasant Delights* (1584),

argue, then, that like Fluellen and Jamy, Mackmorrice is 'always already trans-lated'.[72] It has been argued that the scene effects political unity through linguistic equivalence if not similarity: 'the Welsh, Scots and Irish must [...] be seen to speak English as evidence of their incorporation within the greater might of England, but they must speak it with enough deviations from the standard form to make their subordinate status in the union manifestly obvious'. To include the native languages of these characters 'would be to stage the presence of the very contradictions which the play denies in its attempt to stage the ideal of a unified English nation state'.[73] Several qualifications are necessary here. In a play where the king himself shifts between verse and prose, English and French (V.ii.181–3; 214–5), any sense of a 'standard form' must remain extremely fluid. We should remember that when Shakespeare was writing, the concept of 'standard' English had yet to emerge.[74] Furthermore, while Mackmorrice speaks the same language as Henry or Gower, his enunci-ation of English does not necessarily presume a 'subordinate status' but rather a difference, which suggests that his assimilation into Henry's band of brothers is not as effortless as it might first appear. As Michael Cronin notes, the 'fiction of transparency that must shadow language unity' in the play is inad-vertently exposed by Gower who highlights the risks attached to mistranslation: 'you will mistake each other' (III.3.77).[75] But the exposure is not particular to the English captain: it is heard in Mackmorrice's reiterated 'It is no time to discourse' (III.ii. 106, 108), Fluellen's 'if you take the matter other-wise than is meant' (III.ii.127–8) and Jamy's 'that's a foul fault' (III.ii.137). While the four captains converse in English, the scene is one of mutual misun-derstandings and miscommunication.

To say that the scene produces discordant voices should not lead to a dismissal of the individual characters as comically inchoate before an audience: critics go too far when they refers to Mackmorrice's 'frenzy of incoherence' or the scene's 'distracting comedy of dialects'.[76] Fluellen, Jamy and Mackmorrice

'A sonnet of a Louer in the praise of his Lady. To Calen o Custore me: sung at euerie lines end' (Craik, p. 297). For another translation, 'cailin o cois tSiuire me' or 'I am the girl from the banks of the Suir', see Declan Kiberd's brief comment on the play in *Inventing Ireland*, p. 13. **72** Michael Cronin, 'Rug-headed kerns speaking tongues: Shakespeare, translation and the Irish language' in Burnett and Wray (eds), *Shakespeare and Ireland*, p. 198. **73** Cairns and Richards, *Writing Ireland*, p. 11. For a comparison of the Irish, Welsh and Scottish stage dialects, see Bartley, *Teague, Shenkin and Sawney*, pp 272–3; and Paula Blank, *Broken English*, pp 148–9. **74** See Maley, 'The Irish text and subtext of Shakespeare's English histories', p. 110. On contemporary debates about the language, see Emma Smith, '"Signes of a stranger": the English language and the English nation in the late sixteenth century' in Schwyzer and Mealor (eds), *Archipelagic identities*, pp 169–79. **75** Cronin, 'Rug-headed kerns speaking tongues', p. 197. **76** Michael Neill, 'Broken English and broken Irish', p. 19; Dillon, *Language and stage*, p. 178.

each have distinctive phonetic features that foreground their difference but these remain within audience comprehension. Mackmorrice's broken English, to borrow Henry's description of the language of his French bride (V.ii.243), is defined by his pronunciation of the copula; it 'becomes a sign of the ambiguity, which invades assigned identity'. Like Mackmorrice himself, it is simultaneously 'recognizable', yet 'marked with an elusive difference'.[77] Language, like clothing in the case of Hooker's Irish servant, foregrounds the issue of recognizing difference. Does Mackmorrice's broken English denote only a partial alterity? After all, while he uses 'ish' seven times, he also uses the common form 'is' six times. The dual usage is suggestive of the 'in-between' space that he occupies both in Henry's army and the play.[78] If, in these instances, Mackmorrice reveals a partial difference, his enunciation of English, like that of the Scottish and Welsh characters, nonetheless gives expression to cultural and racial difference.[79] In this sense, Mackmorrice's broken English might denote the very thing that it seems to displace, the Irish language.

In a play that foregrounds the active process of translation in the context of conquest, the traces of Mackmorrice's prior translation are visible. The four captains scene is followed by Henry's language of conquest as he threatens violence on the citizens of Harfleur, a scene that is immediately followed by a different type of language lesson as Alice teaches the monolingual Katherine how to anatomize her body in English (III.iv.1–56). We might detect in this scene and also Henry's wooing of Katherine at the end of the play, a symbolic parallel to Mackmorrice's linguistic bind. In the language lesson, English slowly supplants Katherine's French in a process that mirrors the gradual conquest of France itself. Later, in the courtship scene, where Henry invites Katherine to express her love 'brokenly with your English tongue' (V.ii.106), she moves between French and her newly acquired 'broken English'. Among the hegemonic voices of English power, and after English victory has been achieved, Katherine's native tongue can still be heard.[80] The articulation of French here and its translation in the earlier scene symbolically registers the silencing of the Irish language, a language of which echoes are heard in Mackmorrice's Hiberno-English or English as it was spoken in Ireland. Comparisons are also available with *Stukeley*, which demonstrates the fragmentation of the Irish language in the interests of English power but also foregrounds Irish linguistic and cultural difference in the same way that *Henry V* emphasizes that of the French. As with the earlier play, *Henry V* is shaped by

77 Baker, *Between nations*, p. 39.   78 Bhabha, *Location of culture*, p. 2.   79 Blank, *Broken English*, p. 130; p. 149.
80 On the ambivalence of the scene, especially in terms of the threat of reverse translation, see Parker, *Shakespeare from the margins*, pp 170–2; conversely, for the argument that Katherine is contained by English power, see Dillon, *Language and stage*, pp 179–81.

the demands of the contemporary moment: on the London stage in 1599, at the height of efforts to secure the conquest of Ireland, Mackmorrice must speak the queen's English precisely because so many of her subjects there did not. Yet, as he speaks English, Mackmorrice inflects and marks it with his difference. The consequence of this double meaning is that while, like Caliban, Mackmorrice's every utterance is a reminder of the hold of ideology on the individual, he is nonetheless able to speak in a way that troubles any cohesive vision of a British identity and language.

The question remains, however, concerning what it is that Mackmorrice's voices when he reacts so explosively to Fluellen's reference to 'nation':

> Of my nation? What ish my nation? Ish a
> villain, and a bastard, and a knave, and a rascal?
> What ish my nation? Who talks of my nation?   (III.ii.66–8)

The questions are familiar, even famous. The repetition of 'nation' four times and, significantly, in each case, as a question, captures in microcosm the four different groupings that the scene brings together in disharmony. Giving prominence to a minor character, this word in particular gives us pause. In mentioning 'nation', Mackmorrice may simply be referring to his clan in accordance with the usage by Gaelic chieftains in the period who styled themselves chief of their nation. Alternatively, the 'outburst' might be that of a mercenary soldier in the English army: 'mercenaries were though to be rascals and knaves and villains, and had no nation'.[81] However, in the context of a scene about difference and differences, in a play about conquest and nationhood performed in a year when considerable military resources were being deployed in Ireland, the use of the word 'nation' exceeds such surface significations. Mackmorrice's questions have prompted critics to paraphrase and attempt answers, most notably in Philip Edwards' extraordinary act of critical ventriloquism:

> What is this separate race you're implying by using the phrase 'your nation'? Who are you, a Welshman, to talk of the Irish as though they were a separate nation from you? I belong to this family as much as you do.

Edwards's attempt to arrive at what he called 'the essence of it' robs Mackmorrice's inquiry of all its troubled uncertainty. In this view, the questions are a 'furious repudiation of difference' but how can they be when that very

---

81 Andrew Gurr cited in Murphy, *But the Irish sea*, p. 191, n. 45.

difference is encoded in his speech, the broken English that is inseparable from, and may even partly define, this 'nation' that he talks of?[82] David Baker appears to offer a corrective in seeing Mackmorrice as among the fissures in the play that destabilise the idea of unity. Thus, Mackmorrice constitutes a 'felt presence, just beyond the reach of England's power, of an Irish alien identity so radically different that it cannot be represented in itself'. Qualifying Edwards, Baker writes that Mackmorrice is a 'threatening difference' that '*is* furiously repudiated'.[83] Yet, the circumlocutory argument that Mackmorrice's absolute alterity can only be obliquely registered fails to take into consideration those Elizabethan assumptions about the Irish, which as I suggested earlier, inform audience understandings of Mackmorrice as Other. Moreover, through his enunciation of English, Mackmorrice's difference is represented and is always in view.

What tends to get overlooked in these and other interpretations is the force of the lines, a force that stems from the words – 'villain', 'bastard', 'knave', 'rascal' – Mackmorrice uses in glossing 'nation'. They each have negative connotations; combined, they amount to a lexicon of negativity that shocks both Fluellen (III.ii.127–8), who was after all referring to the 'disciplines of war', and also Gower (III.ii.136). That lexicon can be regarded as a colonial one for the Irish, so that the Irishman's utterance is ultimately scripted by English colonial discourse. Subverting this reading, however, one can argue that Mackmorrice utters these words in order to question the English right to speak for the Irish; from this perspective, Mackmorrice is an Irish Caliban, whose profit in speaking English is to appropriate and re-signify the very terms of his negation. On the one hand, this postcolonial reading involves a desire to recuperate the seemingly Shakespearean complicit text from colonialism in particular or the hold of ideology more generally. On the other, by locating an ambivalence and pluralism in the play, the reading reminds us of the capacity of Mackmorrice to give rise to a range of meanings. This in turn raises the question that many critics have been inclined to deny in exploring Mackmorrice's questions: do they evoke precisely what they appear to disavow, an emergent Irishness?

A contextual reading provides further insight into this issue. It is difficult not to infer a connection between Mackmorrice's question and the events surrounding the Nine Years War. As Declan Kiberd argues, Mackmorrice mentions his 'nation' in order to deny that he has one 'for the good reason that Hugh O'Neill [...] had just called and led the first nationwide army of resistance against the English'.[84] Less inclined to see the questions as an instance of what Kiberd calls the 'extracted confession', Andrew Murphy describes them

---

82 Edwards, *Threshold of the nation*, p. 76.   83 Baker, *Between nations*, p. 41.   84 Kiberd, *Inventing Ireland*, p. 12.

as 'an interrogation of what constitutes the Irish nation', through which Mackmorrice 'raises the spectre of a self-defined Irish identity'.[85] Murphy concludes by generalizing, extending the questions to include English national identity and even the identity of the playwright himself. Certainly, the questions carry these and wider resonances; viewed more broadly, they can be regarded as an interrogation of what shapes an individual and collective sense of self. Moreover, by implicating the actor's voice and body, the questions can also have a metadramatic and theatrical dimension. Nonetheless, we should attend closely to the fact that it is Mackmorrice, rather than Jamy, Fluellen or Gower, who talks of nation, of 'my nation'. This in itself suggests the precise, contemporary force of his questions. The force, I would suggest, is an early modern dilemma or at least one emerging in this period. Depending on one's perspective, this is either the English process of defining and identifying the Irish, or the Irish process of ascertaining what an Irish 'nation' might mean. On the stage in 1599, what the Irishman voices can only be framed as a question or a qualified signifier – 'nation?' – precisely because it is in formation.

Parr Lane's observation that 'Irishmen in England act as it were a part in a play, they are never themselves but in their own countrie' captures the emergent identity implicit in Mackmorrice's questions.[86] While the theatrical metaphor conveys the performative nature of identity, Lane's comment does more than cast the Irish as dissemblers, for it also claims that it is in Ireland that they possess self-knowledge. What this suggests is that Irish identity is constructed at the point of difference between Irishness as understood and defined by others, constituted in England, and its corollary in Ireland, 'in their own countrie'. Mackmorrice's questions are about spatial belonging and home raised from a space that requires and produces dissembling but, crucially, it is that space that initiates questions of identity. The implication of Mackmorrice's questions is that concepts of national identity are, at the same time, inherently fluid and historically determined. In this way, they speak from the fraught process of national imagining in the early modern period but also carry within them the capacity to speak to ongoing debates about identity on the two islands.

'FROM IRELAND COMING': *HENRY V* AND THE SHAPING CO-INCIDENCE OF THE IRISH WARS

While Mackmorrice evokes the Irish wars, the fifth chorus is the most revealing contextual mnemonic in the play, inviting playgoers to draw explicit correspondences between what is represented in the theatre and events outside

85 Kiberd, *Inventing Ireland*, p 13; Murphy, *But the Irish sea*, p. 119.   86 See above pp 11–12.

it. Of course, in a play that uses its choruses to continually address theatrical illusion, the audience is prepared for this moment. The emphasis on theatrical illusion does not limit 'the freedom of reference from events on stage back to ordinary everyday reality' as Graham Holderness maintains.[87] Instead, the chorus enables audience participation, urging them to employ their powers of interpretation: 'Piece out our imperfections with your thoughts' (Prologue, 23), 'Play with your fancies' (III.0.6), 'Entertain conjecture' (IV.0.1). Through these reiterated demands, the chorus extends its self-conscious theatricality to the audience, which is made aware of both its present and presence in the theatre. The effect of this present consciousness is particularly evident in the fifth chorus as the audience is implicated in the act of representation and, by extension, the making of history. Describing the return of a triumphant Henry to a curiously idyllic London following his victories at Agincourt, the fifth chorus enlists the imaginative powers of the audience to weave together dramatic, theatrical and present time. It proceeds by searching for illustrious analogies to enhance the king's achievement, firstly by invoking a classical precedent, then, almost in parenthesis, a present exemplum, before returning to Henry himself:

> But now behold,
> In the quick forge and working-house of thought,
> How London doth pour out her citizens.
> The Mayor and all his brethren, in best sort,
> Like to the senators of th'antique Rome
> With the plebians swarming at their heels,
> Go forth and fetch their conquering Caesar in-
> As, by a lower but high-loving likelihood,
> Were now the General of our gracious Empress-
> As in good time he may – from Ireland coming,
> Bringing rebellion broached on his sword,
> How many would the peaceful city quit
> To welcome him! Much more, and much more cause,
> Did they this Harry.
>
> (V.0.22–35)

The assumption that the 'General' in question is Essex is so well established that it has been treated as empirical fact; critics find present in the text what is a potential subtext.[88] To the extent that *Henry V* is shaped by and responds to

---

87 Graham Holderness, *Shakespeare's history* (Dublin, 1984), p. 137. 88 See Maley, 'The Irish text and subtext of Shakespeare's English histories', pp 116–17.

the Irish wars, the allusion, although opaque and general, points to Essex. He was directly associated with the Elizabethan campaign in Ireland in 1599, an association that dated back to 1596 and persisted until 1601, with the investigations into his treason including his conduct in Ireland. The allusion to rebellion in Ireland initially seems to endorse those readings that find in *Henry V* a containment of the Irish problem. The comparison with the young, popular and victorious Henry appears to 'effect a direct articulation of the epic heroism of the past with the potentiality for such action in the present', anticipating military success in Ireland.[89] Plunket Barton, for instance, notes, somewhat rhapsodically, that 'our ears appear to jingle with the applause with which this topical allusion to the most interesting of current events must assuredly have been received by a popular audience at the Globe in the Spring of 1599'.[90] Certainly, the chorus captures the sense of expectation surrounding Essex's campaign but can we assume that the audience interpreted the analogy in such a celebratory manner? It is useful to consider here what Annabel Patterson has described as the chorus's 'self-imposed controls'. Patterson highlights both 'the care with which this passage establishes its own protocols as metaphor, and the posture in which the metaphor is offered'.[91] Thus, Essex is 'lower' than Henry in that he is not the triumphant monarch, merely the 'General of our gracious Empress'. As soon as a hierarchy is suggested, however, the playing field is levelled: Essex is mentioned in as 'loving' a similitude. The qualification of the analogy does not preclude an implicit parallel between Elizabeth's general and the 'conquering Caesar', a parallel that, intriguingly, operates in two directions. On the one hand, the analogy offers the reassuring image of Essex as Caesar returning to the imperial city having forcefully subjugated rebellion overseas. On the other, it points to Essex as over-mighty subject.[92] At issue, then, is the double or even multiple significations of the fifth chorus.

While the allusion to Caesar may have suggested itself as Shakespeare began work on *Julius Caesar*, for the play's first audiences it may have resonated with the Cockson engraving of Essex, which also styled him as an imperial conqueror. The engraving circulated in London both before his departure for Ireland and while he was under house arrest in 1600. It depicts Essex mounted on his horse, clasping a staff and wearing his sword. He is flanked by his past successes in the Azores and Cadiz; in the foreground is another previous location of the earl's military success, Rouen, while Ireland is positioned to the extreme left of the picture 'looming ahead on the horizon', as Richard McCoy writes, 'awaiting his triumphant arrival'.[93] Like the engraving, the chorus's

89 Holderness, *Shakespeare's history*, p. 141. 90 Barton, *Links between Shakespeare and Ireland*, p. 189. 91 Patterson, *Shakespeare and the popular voice*, p. 86; p. 85. 92 See Highley, *Shakespeare, Spenser*, p. 158. 93 Richard McCoy, *The*

words are deeply symbolic, with the general's sword denoting a specifically masculine power that acts for the 'the gracious Empress' in suppressing rebellion. More specifically, 'broached', as in spitted or pierced on a stake, implies the use of brute force. Catherine Belsey suggests that this image of the Irish rebellion symbolically impaled on Essex's sword 'might evoke innumerable medieval representations of Herod's soldiers with the innocents spitted on their broadswords, except that the connotations seem all wrong'.[94] The connotations, could be exactly right, however, for the image echoes the play's earlier reference to 'naked infants spitted upon pikes' (III.iii.38), one of a series of threats issued by Henry to the citizens of Harfleur. This speech is also extant in the quarto text. In what amounts to an inversion of the king's appropriation of Christian imagery elsewhere in the play, the king compares the rape and murder that his soldiers could unleash on the town to Herod's Slaughter of the Innocents. The crucial difference, however, is that whereas Henry offers the French the option of peaceful surrender – 'Will you yield, and this avoid?' (III.iii.125) – the chorus insinuates that this alternative is unavailable to the Irish. Emphatically positioned as rebels, the Irish are only offered military conquest. Similarly, if 'broached' is understood to mean that the rebellion is inscribed on the earl's sword like an emblem, an engraving on the shaft or blade, then the sword signifies the containment of the Irish threat by English military might.

There is a further meaning provided for, however, since 'broached' also has the sense of to 'set loose, begin, introduce, or initiate', which significantly alters the impact of the allusion to Essex.[95] Understood as 'a verb of mischievous political intention', the use of 'broached', implies that 'the rebellion that Essex is anticipated as bringing on his sword is not past but future, not behind him in Ireland but before him at home'.[96] From this perspective, the chorus's curiously indeterminate inquiry – 'How many would the peaceful city quit | To welcome Him!' – could be construed as a gesture towards Essex's popularity, which was a source of official concern, but also an-all-too accurate anticipation of actual events.[97] During Essex's trial for treason, it was alleged that he planned to use the 'army in Ireland' and 'march with his power to London'.[98] It was also said 'that he would never leave the one sword, meaning

rites of knighthood: the literature and politics of Elizabethan chivalry (Berkeley, 1989), p. 97.   **94** Catherine Belsey, 'The illusion of empire: Elizabethan expansionism and Shakespeare's second tetralogy', *Literature and History*, 1 (1990), 13–21 at 19.   **95** Albright, 'The folio version of *Henry V*', p. 733.   **96** Patterson, *Shakespeare and the popular voice*, pp 86–7. Patterson develops Albright's suggestion regarding the double meaning of 'broached'.   **97** On the state's response to Essex's popularity in London, see Patterson, *Shakespeare and the popular voice*, pp 82–3.   **98** Francis Bacon, 'A declaration touching the treasons of the late earl of Essex and his complices' in James Spedding, Robert Leslie Ellis and Douglas Denon Heath (eds), *Works of Francis Bacon*, 14 vols (London, 1857–74), ix, p. 256.

that of Ireland, till he had gotten the other in England'.[99] On this basis, Essex's dramatic counterpart is less Henry V than York in *2 Henry VI* who, 'newly come from Ireland' (IV.viii.25), threatens the capital and the court with rebellion and usurpation.

There is an ambiguity in the chorus that suggests conflicting senses of Essex's power, both in terms of his service in Ireland and also his potential ambitions beyond that. However, this should not be interpreted as evidence of 'Shakespeare's misgivings about Essex'.[1] We should be careful of reading the chorus from events in 1601; to regard it as prophetic of Essex's rebellion disassociates it from the immediate context of the Irish wars. As expressed within this context, the ambivalence of the choric allusion can be understood quite differently. While the comparison with Henry implies Essex's success in Ireland, the symbolic impact of the image of the general 'bringing rebellion broached on his sword' would have been undermined by the reality of the situation there in 1599. Essex himself was certainly aware of the difficulty of the task demanded of him. Writing to the privy council in April 1599, less than a fortnight after his arrival in Ireland, he noted 'how great and almost desperate the indisposition of Ireland is, and consequently how long and difficult the cure thereof is likely to prove'.[2] The earl had expediently resolved to march towards Ulster, where 'these monstrous treasons took their first root'; it was, he wrote, 'therefore requisite to have a main blow at this root, the sooner to shake and sway all the branches, that are grown out of it'.[3] But the Irish council advised him 'that the invasion of Ulster should be for a time respited', recommending instead marches through Leinster and Munster.[4] No significant gains were made during these progresses, which succeeded only in exhausting Essex's army. In July, an increasingly frustrated Elizabeth wrote to Essex asking him when he intended 'to proceed with the northern action'. She used the opportunity to admonish her lord deputy for his inaction and remind him of precisely what was at stake in the war:

> if you compare the time that is run on, and the excessive charges that is spent, with the effects of anything wrought by this voyage […] yet you must needs think that we, that have the eyes of foreign princes upon our actions, and have the hearts of people to comfort and cherish, who groan under the burden of continual levies and impositions, which are occasioned by these late actions, can little please ourself hitherto with anything that hath been effected. For what can

99 Bacon, 'A declaration touching the treasons of the late earl of Essex', in Spedding et al. (eds), *Works of Francis Bacon*, ix pp 256–7.   1 Highley, *Shakespeare, Spenser*, p. 135.   2 *Calendar of state papers, Ireland, 1599–1600*, ed. Ernest George Atkinson (London, 1899), p. 21.   3 Ibid., pp 16–17.   4 Ibid., p. 17.

be more true, [...] than that your two month's journey hath brought in never a capital rebel, against whom it hath been worthy to have adventured one thousand men.[5]

Undoubtedly, these official misgivings filtered through to those outside court politics in the form of rumour and anecdote. A soldier arrested for desertion, one Harry Davis, claimed that on leaving Waterford, Essex had been attacked by the 'wild Irish [...], where he lost fifty thousand men and the earl himself [...] wounded in the right arm in such sort that he was like to lose his arm'.[6] Within the context of discussion about the Irish campaign, the fifth chorus works as a timely expression of optimism. Yet, in its conditional form of utterance, it also captures the contemporary anxieties that it is often understood as dissipating. Essex may return from Ireland victorious but the possibility that he may not is also obliquely registered. The expression of hope, 'As in good time he may', also reads as an expression of doubt. That phrase might appear to indicate a probability (Essex's imminent return from Ireland) but the mention of a time frame here, as in the previous line 'were now', endows the chorus with an ambiguous topicality. Complaints about the perceived mismanagement of the campaign persisted into the late summer. In August, the council reprimanded the earl 'that there should have been a prosecution of the capital rebels in the north, whereby the war might have been shortened'; the queen, the council added, did 'mislike still of the time that hath been spent all this while in other places'.[7] By early September, frustration with the slow pace of the campaign had given way to accusations of deliberate procrastination on Essex's part. 'We require you to consider', Elizabeth wrote to him, 'whether we have not great cause to think that your purpose is not to end the war, when yourself have often told us that all the petty undertakings in Leix, Munster, and Connaught, are but loss of time?'.[8] As the fifth chorus of *Henry V* implies, Essex had not made 'good time' in Ireland.

The chorus may go further and actually confront the possibility of Essex's failure. The sword is, as I have noted, a symbol of repressed rebellion in the sense that it signifies what Essex 'may' have succeeded in broaching but it is also a symbol of transgression and resistance, evoking the wars in Ireland. It is, then, a double-edged sword. Moreover, just as rebellion must be given a presence in order that its subjugation can be recorded, so the 'General' requires the absent figure of the rebel both to justify and to affirm the power of his sword. This need to invoke the perceived enemy is also evident in official correspondence between the government and Essex, where the Irish war was

5 Ibid., p. 98. 6 Quoted in Shapiro, *1599: a year in the life of Shakespeare*, p. 292. 7 *Cal. S.P. Ire., 1599–1600*, pp 117 and 118. 8 Ibid., p. 152.

frequently personified as a clash between the two figures of 'our Generall' (Essex) and 'the arch-rebell' (O'Neill).[9] Essex participated in this official cate- gorization of O'Neill, employing the same synonyms as the queen in referring to him. He also contributed to the impression that O'Neill was his antagonist, boasting 'by God I will beat Tyr-Owen in the field'.[10] In a campaign character- ized by wastage, confusion and indecision, Essex failed to live up to his boast. When he did finally meet with O'Neill in the field on 7 September 1599 at Bellaclinthe on the Louth–Monaghan border, the outcome, as we shall see, was far removed from what the state had desired. During the summer, however, Essex had reiterated his boast, vowing that 'as fast as I can call these troops together I will go look upon yonder proud rebel; and if I find him on hard ground and in an open country [...], yet will I by God's grace dislodge him'. His objective was 'to pull down the pride of the arch-traitor'.[11]

This binary opposition of Essex and O'Neill is symbolically evoked in the fifth chorus. As the necessary corollary to the 'General of our gracious Empress', the chorus implies her 'capital rebel', O'Neill. It may be significant that *Henry V* does not particularize the Irish rebellion in the way that both *The Contention* and *Edward II* do. The play may not want to allude to O'Neill, given the potential for resistance that the name creates. Moreover, in its reluctance, or even refusal, to name O'Neill, the chorus hints at what contemporaries regarded as his elusive- ness or, as the privy council described it, his capacity to appear 'as a person that may not be touched'.[12] Others commented upon his dissembling nature, dismissing his military victories as no more 'than the robberies of thieves and vagabonds lurking in the woods and bogs and places of strength, privily watching to do their mischief'.[13] The image of the native Irish as secretive and as denizens of hidden spaces was, as noted in chapter two, almost proverbial in the period. Applied to O'Neill, it suggests that he operates by stealth, evading the watchful eye of the Elizabethan state and frustrating the queen's policies in Ireland. Hugh O'Neill is a symbolic absence in the fifth chorus. He lurks between its lines, seemingly beyond representation, just as he might be, the chorus implies, beyond the reach of the 'conquering Caesar'.

There may, however, be an indirect evocation of O'Neill earlier in the play, where in a revealing context-shaping moment, the French lords use an equine metaphor to discuss their mistresses:

9 Although O'Neill was regarded as a liminal figure in the period, this kind of synonym was used with greater frequency in official discourse at the height of the war. There are several instances of this in the state papers. I quote here from *Cal. S.P. Ire., 1599–1600*, p. 152. 10 Quoted in Bagwell, *Ireland under the Tudors*, p. 315. 11 Essex quoted in Spedding et al. (eds), *Works of Francis Bacon*, ix, p. 138; p. 139. 12 *Cal. S.P. Ire., 1599–1600*, p. 118. 13 'Ireland: A draft for an answer to Tyrone's libel, written by the honest Catholic lords of the pale' in Hiram Morgan, 'Faith and fatherland or queen and country: an unpublished exchange between O'Neill and the state at the height of the Nine Years war', *Duiche O'Neill*, 9 (1984), 9–65 at 61.

CONSTABLE [...] for methought yesterday your mistress shrewdly shook your back.

DAUPHIN So perhaps did yours.

CONSTABLE Mine was not bridled.

DAUPHIN O then belike she was old and gentle, and you rode like a kern of Ireland, your French hose off, and in your strait strossers.

CONSTABLE You have good judgement in horsemanship.

DAUPHIN Be warned by me then: they that ride so, and ride not warily, fall into foul bogs. I had rather have my horse to my mistress.

(III.vii.47–57)

The Dauphin's image of Irish kern suggests riding fiercely; the Irish, who traditionally went barelegged (hence the 'strossers', implying the skin itself) had a reputation as capable horsemen. But in this play, 'kern' can suggest the Irish captain of the earlier scene, the Irish rebels Essex had been dispatched to fight and Hugh O'Neill himself, who to contemporaries was 'an upstart kern'.[14] Complaining to Essex about the lack of progress against O'Neill, Elizabeth wrote that 'it must be the queen of England's fortune [...] to make a base bush kern to be accounted so famous a rebel'.[15] The allusion to bogs is equally suggestive. Used here in both the literal sense and the figurative sense of filthy or diseased female bodies, the image intensifies the innuendo that pervades the scene. As with kern, bogs would have had a particular connotation for Elizabethans, invoking those hidden spaces in Ireland that gave the natives a tactical advantage over the English. Given these associations, the Dauphin's phrase discloses the difficulties facing English soldiers in Ireland. Indeed, in view of the anxieties surrounding the Essex campaign, both in terms of the government's frustration with his lack of progress and his own concern for his standing during a prolonged absence from court, Essex himself might be said, on a metaphoric level, to have 'fall[en] into foul bogs'. Essex's reservations about service in Ireland bear out this reading. 'Into Ireland I go', he wrote on New Year's day 1599, 'the queen hath irrevocably decreed it, the council do passionately urge it, and I am tied in my own reputation to use no tergiversation'.[16] By September of that year, shortly before his abrupt depar-

14 'Ireland: A Draft for an answer to Tyrone's libel', p. 56. 15 *Cal. S.P. Ire., 1599–1600*, p. 99. 16 Quoted in Bagwell, *Ireland under the Tudors*, p. 318.

ture from his post, this despondent tone had given way to bitterness; he advised Elizabeth not to expect much from one whose actions in the past had been rewarded by 'banishment and proscription into the most cursed of all countries'.[17] The potential for missed opportunity and loss that Ireland could occasion is, I would argue, captured in the ambivalence of the choric allusion. There is a similar ambivalence encoded in the Cockson engraving of Essex, for although Ireland is on the horizon, ripe for conquest and the next theatre for the earl's military exploits, it is also tantalizingly distant and, like the shadowy figure of O'Neill in the chorus, appears beyond Essex's grasp. Thus, from the vision of a prospective victory in Ireland that *Henry V* initially appears to offer emerges the nightmare of possible defeat.

To view the chorus in these terms has wider implications for the play's relation to the Irish wars. It is, after all, the choric allusion that prompts inter-pretations of the text as an extended analogy for the wars, an explicit disclosure of a parallel that elsewhere in the play is only implied. Thus, while noting that the play registers the 'the human costs of imperial ambition', Jonathan Dollimore and Alan Sinfield ultimately see it as 'a displaced imagi-nary resolution of one of the state's most intractable problems'.[18] Christopher Highley finds the play sceptical about English expansionism, yet his subse-quent argument that it 'tests the limits of its own wish-fulfilments' assumes the prior existence of some degree of ideological containment.[19] Rather than seeing *Henry V* as merely reacting to the Irish wars, I have been emphasizing its shaping co-incidence with this context. What I now want to briefly consider is to what extent the ambivalence at the root of the play's representation of war is informed by this context. At issue here are the play's formal contradic-tions, or what Norman Rabkin describes as 'an eloquent discrepancy between the glamour of the play's rhetoric and the reality of its action'. Rabkin's argu-ment is that the play 'points in two opposite directions' that cannot be viewed simultaneously.[20] In this play, then, the Shakespearean 'recognition of the duality of things' leads to a crisis of meaning about perceptions of reality. Borrowing terminology from Gestalt psychology, Rabkin explains: 'some members of the audience knew that they had seen a rabbit, others a duck. Still others [...] Shakespeare's best audiences, knew terrifyingly that they did not know what to think'.[21] The doubleness and ambiguity of the play can be understood as an effect of its simultaneity with the Irish wars, a point Joel Altman touches on when he notes how the 'contrariety we have come to admire

17 Bagwell, *Ireland under the Tudors*, p. 342.   18 Dollimore and Sinfield, 'History and ideology' in Drakakis (ed.), *Alternative Shakespeares*, p. 225.   19 Highley, *Shakespeare, Spenser*, pp 135–6; p. 143.   20 Norman Rabkin, 'Rabbits, ducks and *Henry V*', *Shakespeare Quarterly*, 28 (1979), 279–96 at 285; 279.   21 Rabkin, 'Rabbits, ducks and *Henry V*', p. 296; p. 285.

in *Henry V* is closely related to the complexity of response that the Irish struggle was evoking in Shakespeare's audience'.[22] Qualifying Rabkin, however, I do not think the play forces its audience to embrace one position but manages to keep its dual perspectives or modes of representation simultaneously in view.

The play contains what might be described as the Henrician ideal, evidenced in the language of common purpose and remembrance that extends from the chorus through to the king. At the same time, however, it also provides a more grounded sense of war that is articulated in Williams' questioning of Henry and given a felt presence through images of blood and violence. The first of these dialectical representations of war comes into view through the chorus, which through its panoramic, celebratory narrative, vicariously involves the audience in the allure and excitement of war. 'Now all the youth of England are on fire', the chorus declaims, quickly passing over the material costs – 'They sell the pasture now to buy the horse' (II.o.4) – to mention how Englishmen eagerly follow Henry, that exemplar of 'all Christian kings' (II.o.6). Enabling the audience to imagine itself accompanying Henry's army, leaving England behind 'guarded with grandsires, babies, and old women' (III.o.20), the chorus asks: 'For who is he, whose chin is but enriched | With one appearing hair, that will not follow | These culled and choice-drawn cavaliers to France?' (III.o.22–4). The allusion to stay-at-homes, one of several in the play, produces a consonance between spectator, solider and king: as the chorus draws upon the audience's imaginative powers – 'work, work your thoughts' (III.o.25) – the business of playing works in tandem with the martial powers of the king's men. Later, it is the king himself who supplements the role of the chorus, facilitating participation and unity:

> For he today that sheds his blood with me
> Shall be my brother; be he ne'er so vile,
> This day shall gentle his condition.
> And gentlemen in England now abed
> Shall think themselves accursed they were not here,
> And hold their manhoods cheap whiles any speaks
> That fought with us upon Saint Crispin's day.
>
> (IV.iii.61–7)

Henry has the effect here that the chorus anticipated he would have, so that 'every wretch, pining and pale before, | Beholding him, plucks comfort from

22 Joel B. Altman, '"Vile participation": the amplification of violence in the theatre of *Henry V*', *Shakespeare Quarterly*, 42 (1991), 1–32 at 8.

his looks' (IV.o.41–2). The speech, which is also in the quarto, is a careful manipulation of collective experience as the imminent battle is cast as remembrance.[23] In a self-empowering moment, the king instils a sense of common purpose, pride, and confidence in his men previously described by himself as sick (III.iii.55) and weak (III.vii.144; 154), and by the French as 'island carrions' (IV.ii.38). In view of these images, Henry's address is a necessary call to arms that can be seen to extend beyond the theatre to answer the harsh realities of war in Ireland, where desertion and privation were among the recurrent logistical and practical problems for the authorities.

Sir John Chamberlain described how the levying of troops for Ireland, which placed considerable demands on shires throughout England and Wales, involved 'taking, and as it were, sweeping and carrying them violently to the ships'. This action was, he felt, both 'a general grievance and scandal at home and a great dishonour to be heard of abroad'.[24] Desertion, both at the point of departure and from the war itself, was also a continual problem.[25] Such was the reluctance to serve, Lord Burghley reported, that 'better be hanged at home than die like dogs in Ireland' was a proverbial saying in the town of Chester.[26] In 1599, the privy council ordered that all healthy soldiers returning home without permission were to be imprisoned until such time as they could be sent back to Ireland, because many of them 'do give forth very slanderous speeches to discourage others'.[27] Presumably, included among these 'speeches' were the frequent reports and complaints about the state of the queen's forces in Ireland. Fynes Moryson, for instance, reported that Essex's soldiers were 'weary, sick, and incredibly diminished in number' following their expedition through Leinster in July 1599.[28] A report from a commander in Munster in 1599 presented an equally grim picture. 'Most part of the army', he noted, 'seem beggarly ghosts, fitter for their graves than to fight a prince's battle'.[29] Indeed, the campaign in Ireland had such a physical impact on English soldiers that Hugh O'Neill apparently included among his allies 'Captains Hunger, Toil, Cold, and Sickness'.[30] These are among the physical hardships from which Henry deftly deflects attention as he fashions his code of fellowship. Continuing the language of the Crispian speech, Henry seizes upon the poor state of his men and inverts it, translating the appearance of his men as a 'beggared host' from a sign of weakness into a sign of strength. 'We are but warriors for the working day' (IV.iii.109), he boasts. Through this appropria-

2 3 See Jonathan Baldo, 'Wars of memory in *Henry V*, 131–59.   2 4 Quoted in McGurk, *Elizabethan conquest*, p. 97. 2 5 See *Acts P.C.*, p. 153; on the punishment of deserters, see p. 246; p. 570; p. 760.   2 6 Quoted in McGurk, *Elizabethan conquest*, p. 194.   2 7 McGurk, *Elizabethan conquest*, p. 169.   2 8 Fynes Moryson quoted in Spedding et al. (eds), *Works of Francis Bacon*, ix, p. 138.   2 9 'Sir John Dowdall to Secretary Cecil', quoted in Maxwell (ed.), *Irish history from contemporary sources*, p. 213.   3 0 Cited in McGurk, *Elizabethan conquest*, p. 241.

tion of impoverishment as a normative aspect of combat and sign of English resilience, the king 'nourishes' his men metaphorically.[31]

To see *Henry V* as marching in step with the queen's army in Ireland, however, is to obscure the knowledge that the play always holds in view; that is, the knowledge that Henry's words are forms of sublimation, where a distinctly masculine ideology of fellowship and bravery reifies suffering, violence and death. The play represents the realities that the king's rhetorical manipulations overshadow; his language, for all its buoyant, infectious confidence, is shown to be the language of war. The exposure occurs in that other version or representation of war that the audience experiences, most notably in Williams' pointed exchange with the disguised king, where Henry's claim about the legitimacy of war is met with doubt: 'That's more than we know' (IV.i.129). But it is also apparent in the emphasis on blood and violence included in Exeter's initial promise to the French of 'bloody constraint' (II.iv.97) and 'hungry war (II.iv.104); Henry's own proleptic threats to the citizens of Harfleur of 'liberty of blood' (III.iii.112); Burgundy's reference to soldiers 'That nothing do but meditate on blood' (V.ii.60) in his speech about post-conquest France; and the epilogue's characterization of Henry VI as one who 'made his England bleed' (Epilogue, 12). It is apparent too in Bardolph's comic echoing of Henry's rhetoric (III.ii.1–2) and with the equally comic Pistol. His departing promise that 'To England will I steal, and there I'll steal' (V.i.88) to feign the wounds of battle for material gain, speaks of an aspect of war that the play refuses to overlook.

It is in the final scene that the audience can perceive the two different perspectives together. The climax of the scene is the reification of Henry and Kate into 'a vision of international concord after conquest', a symbolic foreshadowing of the conquest of Ireland.[32] Henry's united kingdom of England, France and also Ireland (which Henry includes among the lands that he and Katherine will now share sovereignty over) is presented as the outcome of marriage rather than of conquest and war. In the ceding of political power and sovereignty to Henry by the French king, Katherine is also past on, figuratively translated into a symbol of union:

> Take her, fair son, and from her blood raise up
> Issue to me, that the contending kingdoms
> Of France and England, whose very shores look pale
> With envy of each other's happiness,
> May cease their hatred, and this dear conjunction

31 See Highley, *Shakespeare, Spenser*, pp 141–3.   32 Edwards, *Threshold of the nation*, p. 82.

> Plant neighbourhood and Christian-like accord
> In their sweet bosoms, that never war advance
> His bleeding sword 'twixt England and fair France.
>
> (V.ii.342–9)

But this is preceded by Katherine's pertinent question, 'Is it possible dat I should love de *ennemi* of France?' (V.ii.169), which, like the translation of her language more generally, exposes what is really at stake in Henry's courtly wooing. Moreover, there is Burgundy's lengthy preamble to union, which in its personification of peace as 'naked, poor, and mangled' that 'hath from France too long been chased' (V.ii.34; 38) uncovers the devastating effects of conquest. Just as the day of combat and wounds of war are celebrated and memorialized in the Crispian speech, so Burgundy's extended encomium to peace records into memory the scars that war leaves on the landscape. In such moments, the play's ambiguous take on war is apparent but it is through its formal contradictions that it is asserted. For, in this play, despite the recourse to the conventions of comedy that the closure in marriage signals, the imperatives of history (in terms of source text) and art (in terms of Shakespeare's earlier dramatization of history in the Henry VI plays) win out:

> Thus far, with rough and all-unable pen,
> Our bending author hath pursued the story,
> In little room confining mighty men,
> Mangling by starts the full course of their glory.
> Small time, but in that small most greatly lived
> This star of England. Fortune made his sword,
> By which the world's best garden he achieved,
> And of it left his son imperial lord.
> Henry the Sixth, in infant bands crowned King
> Of France and England, did this king succeed,
> Whose state so many had the managing
> That they lost France and made his England bleed,
> Which oft our stage hath shown —and, for their sake
> In your fair minds let this acceptance take.
>
> (Epilogue, 1–14)

It is possible to hear in these final words the crowning of Henry's reign as a rarefied moment in English history. Ultimately, the effect is to leave the audience in their present, with memories of dissolution and reversal. In this play about the conquest of France performed as efforts were underway to effect the conquest of Ireland, the coda foregrounds the doubts implied in the fifth chorus about success there. Fixing on history and its making, the epilogue recognizes the limitations of idealizing war and acknowledges the arbitrariness of the play's own resolution. Thus, in its self-reflexive closure, *Henry V* moves away from the Henrician ideal to bring into sharp focus the unpredictable contours of the present.

The ambiguity within *Henry V*, those moments of equivocation that I have traced, facilitates a range of potential meanings and interpretations that are testimony to the dynamic relationship between the play and its Irish context. The play addresses the allure of national unity at a moment of crisis but also the excesses such a moment can produce, uncovering the assimilationist rhetoric and brutal violence that lurks beneath Henry's language of national unity. Such functional simultaneity is exhibited throughout, as the play represents and questions Henry's expansionist project. 'We'll not offend one stomach with our play' (II.o.40) might suggest the intersection of the play's politics and aesthetics. Included among the range of interpretative possibilities the play provides for is the questioning of the Elizabethan colonial project in Ireland.[33] Within the range of meanings, one can go further to see the play as a pointed critique of the English colonial project. For, as I noted earlier, the fifth chorus implies that Essex does not measure up to the analogy with Henry, the inference being that the qualities celebrated in the play as central to Henry's political and martial success are missing in Elizabethan England. Essex was made a scapegoat for the failure of the state to conclude the Irish war but criticism of his lieutenancy was matched by dissatisfaction with what was perceived as the indecision and leniency of the ageing queen when it came to Irish affairs. Among the most worrying manifestations of this discontent were reports that 'some traitorous monsters have railed against her by railing speeches and slanderous libels' while 'others scatter libels about London and the court itself taxing the queen with not providing for the troubled state of Ireland'.[34] Elizabeth did, however, take responsibility for the state of the campaign. Writing to Essex after his departure from Ireland, she observed: 'whosoever shall write the story of this year's action, must say that we were at too great charge to hazard our kingdom, and you have taken great pains to prepare for many purposes, which perish without undertaking'.[35] A queen reluctant to take risks, a deputy whose plans were never executed: such was the 'story' of the Irish wars. *Henry V* can be included among the seditious materials about the Irish campaign, for in its dramatization of the conquest of France it highlights the lacunae with the Elizabethan conquest of Ireland. This

33 See David Baker, '"Wildehirissheman": colonialist representation in Shakespeare's *Henry V*', *ELR*, 22 (1992), 37–61 at 54; and Highley, *Shakespeare, Spenser*, pp 149–56.   34 *Cal. S.P. domestic*, p. 347.   35 Ibid., p. 153.

may well explain why the 'story' of the French conquest is, as the epilogue acknowledges, only taken 'thus far'. To have proceeded any further would mean giving expression to an Elizabethan reality that should be acknowledged only by the queen herself.

'THAT MONSTER OF INGRATITUDE': IRISH SERVANT AND ENGLISH MASTER IN *SIR JOHN OLDCASTLE*

Less than five months passed between the first performances of *Henry V* and *Sir John Oldcastle*, a play also informed by the synchronous 'story' of the Irish wars. For the play was performed within the context of frustrations surrounding Essex's missed opportunity in Ireland, frustrations exacerbated by prior expectations of his success there. The lord deputy's encounter with O'Neill in September 1599, rather than ending the war, resulted in a truce that effectively signalled Essex's surrender. Essex's subsequent abandonment of his Irish post and return to England in disgrace initiated investigations into his conduct in Ireland and also controversy about the state's campaign there. It is through its Irish character, Mack Chane, that the play discloses the impact and, crucially, the pressure of this context. Of course, the appearance of an Irish character has obvious echoes of Mackmorrice and, although this can be understood as an instance of the intertextuality of the stage Irishman, we may be dealing here with direct theatrical borrowing from and allusion to *Henry V*. This is supported by the play's reactive relationship with Shakespearean drama and theatre. Writing for the Admiral's Men, the *Oldcastle* collaborators Michael Drayton, Anthony Munday, Robert Wilson and Richard Hathaway, exploited the rivalry with the Chamberlain's Men and their recent play, Shakespeare's *Henry V*.[36] But in dramatizing the life of Oldcastle – the Lollard leader executed in 1417 following his religious rebellion against Henry V – they were also concerned with redressing the comic portrayal of Oldcastle as Falstaff in Shakespeare's *Henry IV* plays.[37] Thus, where the name was by 'forg'de invention [in] former time defac'te' (Prologue, 14), the playwrights claim to present the true history of the martyr. There is a strong imperative in the play to rescue Oldcastle's reputation, with the leader of the proto-Protestant movement depicted as an essentially loyal subject whose name is misappropriated by opponents of the king for their own ends.

My focus is on the Irish character in *Oldcastle* who, like Mackmorrice, fore-

---

36 On date and authorship, see Rittenhouse (ed.), *Sir John Oldcastle*, pp 43–65.   37 For the theatrical and political background to the play, as well as its relationship with Shakespeare's tetralogy, see Peter Corbin and Douglas Sedge (eds), *The Oldcastle controversy* (Manchester, 1991), pp 9–19.

grounds the interconnectedness of text and Irish context. Intriguingly, one of the collaborators, Anthony Munday had addressed Irish matters previously in a pamphlet ostensibly justifying lord deputy Grey's massacre of foreign forces at Smerwick, Co. Kerry, in 1580.[38] The pamphlet may be considered among the range of materials informing the play's representation of Mack Chane. What is revealing here is the play's overt racial stereotyping, which brings it ideologically closer to a play like *Stukeley* than *Henry V* but also its anxiety about the recognition and classification of 'Others'. These issues are refracted through the Irishman's relationship to English authority figures, a relationship that was a social reality in the period and one that could express figuratively political relations between the queen and her Irish subjects.

Where the character of the Irish servant is found in Renaissance drama, it usually constitutes the symbolic realization of a political fantasy: the domestication of the wild Irish. This is especially evident in the entertainment for Elizabeth performed at the Norris estate, Rycote in 1591, where 'an Irish lacquey' bears a letter with the motto, 'I flye onely for my soveraigne'.[39] Similarly, in Heywood's *Four Prentices of London* (1594), an Irish servant unequivocally professes his duty to his master: 'Maister, so Crist me saue, I shal waite on thee, wake thee when thou sleepest, runne for thee when thou biddest, and flye a thy errands, like an arrow from a bow.'[40] The deployment of the servant to stage the fantasy of the Irish tamed anticipates Jonson's *Irish Masque* (1613), where four footmen, each representing a province of Ireland, profess the loyalty of James' Irish subjects, who will 'run t'rough fire and water' and even 'over te bog' for their king.[41] To a certain extent, these representations constitute perceptions of the social reality of Irish immigrants and, more specifically, domestic servants, in London. However, in the context of implicit assumptions about the Irish in the period, the domestic servant could be viewed as masking a threatening difference. In *Oldcastle*, the Irish servant is presented as a thief and murderer. First seen on stage leaning over the body of his master, the Irishman finds himself outwitted by the parson of Wrotham, who has earlier referred to himself as 'A priest in show, but in plain terms, a thief' (II.157) and his accomplice, Doll. The parson remarks 'Some Irish villain methinks that has slain his master' (XVII.20). Mack Chane himself is first heard admitting to his crime: 'Alas po'mester, Sir Richard Lee, be Saint Patrick, I's rob and cut thy t'roat, for [...] dy money, and dee gold ring. Be me truly, I's

38 On Munday's Smerwick pamphlet, *The true reporte of the prosperous successe which God gave unto our English souldiours against the forraine bands of our Romanie enemies, lately arrived in Ireland* (1581), see Donna B. Hamilton, *Anthony Munday and the Catholics,1560–1633* (Aldershot, 2005), pp 22–3.   39 John Lyly, *Works*, 3 vols (Oxford, 1902), i, p. 486.
40 *Dramatic works of Thomas Heywood*, 3 vols (New York, 1964), ii, p. 186.   41 *Ben Jonson* ed., C.H. Hereford and Evelyn Simpson, 11 vols (Oxford, 1927), vii, pp 181–3.

love thee well, but now dow be kill' (XVII.23–5). Mention of throat cutting here connects the play to that putative inventory of native Irish violence that *Stukeley* and *Henry V* also draw on. His broken English is interrupted by the parson who, intent on robbing him, threatens: 'Sblood, you rogue, deliver, or I'll not leave you so much as an Irish hair above your shoulders, you whoreson Irish dog' (XVII.30–2). From the outset, then, the Irishman is figured as a threat in that he is a further addition to a criminal underworld already populated by Catholic priests and prostitutes.

If, through the portrayal of the parson as a scheming, comic villain, anti-Catholic stereotypes are played on, then, equally the scene signals Irish difference as an equally refractory entity. The implicit reference to the Irish glib or long fringe – those ubiquitous signifiers of Irish barbarity in the period – suggests racial stereotyping, which is further insinuated through the bestial image. 'Dog' and 'Irish' appear to be used as interchangeable terms here, with the former functioning synecdochically for the latter. This recalls Hooker's proverbial characterization of the Irish as like 'the dog to his vomit' because they always 'returne to their old and former insolencie, rebellion, and disobedience' or, as noted earlier, his insistence that, though the Irish may be clothed in velvet, underneath they are simians.[42] *Oldcastle* is continuous with this new English discourse on the Irish, for there is, at this point in the play, a presumption of an inalterable Irish difference in the depiction of the Irish servant as murderer. Thus, where Mackmorrice suggests the sceptre of difference lurking beneath the clothes of civility, Mack Chane's act of murder marks him out as an immediately identifiable Other.

In broad terms, the wars in Ireland account for and also compound the force of the parson's anti-Irish feelings. What is interesting to consider is whether or not these views are fully endorsed in the play. The parson has already been shown as a morally dubious character, whose judgements are, unwittingly, self-revealing. In the following scene, we see Mack Chane, deprived of the profits of his crime by the parson, pleading with an innkeeper for lodging: 'I's poor Irishman, I's want ludging, I's have no money, I's starve and cold. Good mester, give her some meate, I's famise and tie' (XVIII.1–3). What the audience is confronted with here is, on the one hand, the criminal deservedly reaping the effects of his crime and, on the other, the masterless servant, who evokes the social problem of vagrancy. There is a foreshadowing of this issue in an earlier scene in which a group of beggars, among them soldiers returned from Henry's French wars, queue for alms outside Sir John Oldcastle's house. While the good nature of Oldcastle is illuminated, the

42 Hooker, 'Supplie of the Irish chronicles', p. 369.

plight of the king's soldiers is also stressed. As one soldier remarks, 'There's law for punishing, | But there's no law for our necessity! | There be more stocks to set poor soliders in | Than there be houses to relieve them at' (III.1–2). Complaints of this nature were frequently aired in the period but in the context of the Irish wars, and those reports of disease and desertion noted earlier, they lend the play a notable degree of social realism and a topically charged social commentary. *Oldcastle* thus bears comparison with Shakespeare's *Henry V* where, as we have seen, the French wars also figure the Elizabethan Irish wars. In *Oldcastle*, the explicit criticism of what is presented as an oppressive state is modified only slightly by another soldier's assertion that 'lame as I am, I'll with the King into France [...] I had rather be slain in France than starve in England' (III.17–9). As in Shakespeare's play, the rhetoric of national purpose that accompanies war is critically examined. A potential effect of this focus on the condition of the soldiers is to make Mack Chane's crime seem less like an act of random violence that is symptomatic of Irish barbarity, than one motivated by hunger and necessity. Clearly, however, the play implies that, of those who have been reduced to vagrancy, the soldiers are more deserving of alms than the 'poor Irishman' (XVIII.11), in the host's description, is. As with Cade in *2 Henry VI*, then, Mack Chane becomes a cipher through which disparate social and cultural anxieties, including those arising from what Thomas Dekker later called 'more beggars than ever dropping out of Ireland', are confronted.[43]

In these scenes, *Oldcastle* certainly reveals a conspicuous topicality that, as the play proceeds, appears to indicate the emergence of an ideological position in the text. This is especially evident as the father of Mack Chane's master discovers his son's body 'mangled cruelly with many wounds' (XXV.75). Sir Richard Lee is unaware who has committed the crime but as he apostrophizes the body, it comes to signify the savagery of the absent Irishman:

> Alack it is my son; my son and heir,
> Whom two years since, I sent to Ireland,
> To practice there the discipline of war.
> And coming home (for so he wrote to me),
> Some savage hart, some bloody devilish hand,
> Either in hate, or thirsting for his coin,
> Hath here sluiced out his blood. Unhappy hour,
> Accursed place, but most inconstant fate,

43 Thomas Dekker, *Lanthorne and Candlelight* (1608), quoted in A.V. Judges (ed.), *Elizabethan underworld: a collection of Tudor and early Stuart tracts*, p. 368. On the Irish in London, see D.B. Quinn, *The Elizabethans and the Irish*, pp 147–51.

> That hadst reserved him from the bullets fire,
> And suffered him to escape the wood-kern's fury,
> Didst here ordain the treasure of his life,
> (Even here within the arms of tender peace,
> And where security gat greatest hope)
> To be consumed by treason's wasteful hand?   (XXV.77–90)

With the reference to service in Ireland bringing current events there to the fore, it is possible that the Lee name is topically allusive, resonating with that of Thomas Lee, a captain in Ireland who was a supporter of Essex and had acted as intermediary between him and Hugh O'Neill.[44] Underlying Lee's belief that fate has cheated himself and his son is the fundamental assumption that Ireland is a dangerous place, as evidenced by his reference to war and the notorious kern. The words are rich in dramatic irony for, as the audience already knows, the threatening Irishness Lee thought his son had escaped has in fact taken his life within the 'tender peace' of England. What emerges from the lament is the impossibility of an Irish servant like Mack Chane being anything other than 'a wood-karne'.

Two contemporary texts provide a further sense of the broader signification attached to the play's figuration of the Irish servant. An anonymous tract, 'A Discourse of Ireland' (1599), uses the example of the loyal Irish servant in support of its radical proposal to re-settle the native Irish in England. 'The removing of the Irish maye happily alter their disposition when they Shall be planted in another Soyle', it argues:

> For doubtless in England wee find the Irish servant very faithfull and Louing, and generally the people kinde the rather when here there malice can not profit them anye waye. Withall they be heere industrious, and commonly our best Gardiners, fruiterers, and keepers of horses, refusing no labour besides: So that throughout England there will be use of them as servants, to a very great number.[45]

The rationale behind this proposal is that the indigenous Irish will have an economic value in England. However, the text does not consider the potential drawbacks of assimilating the native Irish into English society because it is operating on the prior assumption that environment determines the behaviour of the Irish; exposure to English society, it is assumed, will have a civilizing

---

44 See above, p. 75.   45 D.B. Quinn, '"A discourse of Ireland": a sidelight on English colonial policy', p. 165.

effect. In suggesting that the Gaelic Irish can be redeemed, the 'Discourse' represents one side of the contemporary reform debate. However, in texts like Derricke's *Image of Irelande* and Spenser's *View* it was also argued that the Irish were incontrovertibly barbarous and, consequently, beyond reform.[46] This radical position finds full expression in the 'Supplication' written following the defeat of crown forces at the battle of the Yellow Ford in 1598. Employing the example of the Irish servant, this text urges the queen, the implied reader, and by extension her subjects

> for the preservation and safetie of her majesty geve over this credulitie; geve over to trust them no longer; remove yore Irish servants from yore elboes; prefer yore poore Countrimen that are farre honester then they; have many better parts in them than they: that wilbe secret to the state, sure to yore selves, when others will betraye both the state and yore selves.[47]

The juxtaposition of English and Irish servants implies a series of rigid binary oppositions (civility/ wildness; loyalty/ rebelliousness) and serves to reinforce social and racial hierarchies. Even though the Irish servants are figured in a symbolically submissive role, at the elbows of the master, they are perceived as a threat to master and state. The concern about the Irish servant registered in the text masks a deeper fear of Irish alterity. In dramatizing the murder of an English master by his Irish servant, *Oldcastle* adopts a similar position to the 'Supplication', confirming the unease about Irishness, the fear of the cultural Other, that the tract displays.

The play's insistence that Mack Chane's behaviour is not environmentally conditioned but racially determined is reinforced in the penultimate scene, where following a series of misplaced judgements in which Oldcastle and his wife are charged with the murder, the Irishman is brought before a judge. A constable refers to 'this savage villain, this rude Irish slave' whose 'tongue hath already confessed the fact' (XXVII.95–6). This stereotyping is continued as the grieving, irate father confronts the captured and condemned servant:

> Is this the wolf whose thirsty throat did drink
> My dear son's blood? Art thou the snake
> He cherished, yet with envious piercing sting,

46 On the correspondence between the ethnographic and theological assumptions in the two texts, see Maryclaire Moroney, 'Apocalypse, ethnography and empire in John Derricke's *Image of Irelande* (1581) and Spenser's *View of the present state of Ireland* (1596)', *ELR*, 29 (1999), 355–74. Conversely, Andrew Hadfield emphasises the difference between the two texts; see *Edmund Spenser's Irish experience: wilde fruit and savage soyl* (Oxford, 1997).   47 'The Supplication', p. 5.

> Assaild'st him mortally? Foul stigmatic
> Thou venom of the country where thou lived'st
> And pestilence of this! Were it not that law
> Stands ready to revenge thy cruelty,
> Traitor to God, thy master, and to me,
> These hands should be thy executioner.   (XXVII.108–16)

The configuration of Mack Chane as bestial, wild and a menace to England is evident in Lee's hyperbolic tirade. With the suggestion of cannibalism implicit in Lee's question, the demonization of the Irish servant is intensified. The allegation of cannibalism was a crucial tool in the 'de-humanization of the outsider' and was common to European descriptions of the indigenous peoples of the new world. But it could also be deployed to delineate difference within Europe itself: St Jerome had levelled the same accusation at the ancient Irish and Scots.[48] The association of cannibalism with the Irish had a currency in the Elizabethan period. In Holinshed's *Chronicles*, for instance, John Hooker describes the impact of the wars in Munster on the indigenous population: 'for they were not onelie driven to eat horses, dogs and dead carions; but also did devoure the carcases of dead men.'[49] As in Hooker's description, the implication of cannibalism in *Oldcastle* positions the Irish as absolute rather than proximate Others; the distinction is an important one.[50] On an implicit level, then, the play is continuous with texts like Derricke's *Image of Irelande* and Spenser's *View*, which signalled a new ethnography of the Gaelic Irish and old English based on a racialist discourse of barbarism.[51] Subjected to the gaze of a distressed father and to the watchful eye of a judge whose very presence obviates Lee's desire for revenge, Mack Chane becomes a negative cynosure, or centre of repulsion. The judge urges Lee to be patient, assuring him justice through the punishment of the Irishman: 'And being hanged until the wretch be dead, | His body after shall be hanged in chains, | Near to the place where he did act the murder' (XXVII.120–2). Such bodily punishment, the play intimates, is entirely fitting for a monstrous figure like Mack Chane and the inalterable Irish difference he signifies.

In detailing the punishment of Mack Chane, the *Oldcastle* playwrights may have been influenced by the scene in *Stukeley* where the decapitated head of the

---

48 Anthony Pagden, *The fall of natural man* (Cambridge, 1982), p. 81. See also Andrew Hadfield, *Spenser's Irish experience*, pp. 101–8.   49 Hooker, 'Supplie of the Irish chronicles', p. 459.   50 For the argument that the native Irish represented a 'proximate' or imperfect alterity to the English, see Murphy, *But the Irish sea*, pp. 1–32.   51 See Carroll, *Circe's cup*, pp. 11–27.

rebel Shane O'Neill is held aloft to the pronouncement 'And may all Irish that with treason deale, | Come to like end or worse then Shane Oneale' (ll. 1369–70). But the playwrights may also have been recalling an extra-dramatic instance of 'punishment-as-spectacle': the 1597 trial for treason of the Irish chieftain, Brian O'Rourke, as described in Stow's *Annales*.[52] O'Rourke had been accused of plotting with the Spanish and of being responsible for the defamation of the royal image in Ireland.[53] It was ordered that O'Rourke be hanged at Tyburn, 'untill he were halfe dead, then to bee let downe, and his members and bowels to bee taken out, and burnt in the fire, his head to bee striken off, and his body to be quartered.'[54] The protocol and pageantry of state punishment outlined in Stow's narrative is invoked in the play, albeit indirectly. Although Mack Chane's punishment occurs offstage, the judge's instructions suggest the systematic marking his body. As Foucault notes, the punishment of the body functions as 'a ceremonial by which a momentarily injured sovereignty is reconstituted'.[55] By referring both to Mack Chane's execution and to the exhibition of manacled body, *Oldcastle* not only registers Elizabeth's authority over treasonous subjects but, like *Stukeley*, also underwrites her ability to eradicate Irish recalcitrance. Perhaps what we are noting in the play here are residual traces of the ideological conformity that has been identified in Munday's Smerwick pamphlet of 1581. However, I would argue that it was circumstances in Ireland in 1599 that occasioned and necessitated such faith in the power of the state.

On the stage in 1599, the character of Mack Chane undoubtedly brought the figure of the Irish rebel to mind, an association that the explicit reference to patrimony and place, 'Me be Mack Chane of Ulster', can only have furthered. The name suggests that he is a member of the MacShanes (Mac Seain), a branch of the O'Neills of Tyrone, and the descendants of Shane O'Neill.[56] In this sense, Mack Chane's name can read as 'Mac Shane' (literally, 'son of Shane/Seán'); to a London audience unfamiliar with the genealogy of the O'Neills, this could potentially point to Hugh O'Neill himself, who was Shane's nephew. But the spelling of the character's name may have an alternative derivation, linking to the Mac Kanes (Mac Cathain), or the O'Kanes (O'Cathain) of Ulster, who were vassals to the O'Neills. The last chief of the O'Cathain clan was inaugurated in 1598 and fought with Hugh O'Neill in the

52 Michel Foucault, *Discipline and punish*, p. 9. 53 On this episode, see Christopher Highley, 'The royal image in Elizabethan Ireland' in J.M. Walker (ed.), *Dissing Elizabeth: negative representations of Gloriana* (Durham, 1998), pp 60–71. 54 Quoted from Stow's *Annales* in Patricia Palmer, *Language and conquest*, p. 213. 55 Foucault, *Discipline and punishment*, p. 48. 56 Edward MacLysaght, *The surnames of Ireland* (6th ed. Dublin, 1991), p. 268. Corbin and Sedge (*Oldcastle controversy*) follow Rittenhouse in suggesting that the name would 'bring to mind the Irish rebel Shane O'Neill' (p. 137).

Nine Years War.[57] It is possible, then, that *Oldcastle* invites its audience to infer a connection between its Irish character and O'Neill, a connection that could have been easily foregrounded in performance through the substitution of the name Mack Chane for O'Neill.

Indeed, there is a suggestive similitude between the perception of Mack Chane's relationship with his English masters and that of the earl of Tyrone's relationship with the queen. For the latter was frequently represented in contemporary discourse as a relationship of Irish servant and English master. An example of this is provided by the proclamation of O'Neill as a rebel, issued in 1595 as a prelude to the march of the queen's army into Ulster. It observed that 'whereas the queen advanced' O'Neill 'to the noble dignity of an earl' and 'endowed him with larger territories than any other earl in Ireland', he had 'fallen from allegiance'.[58] This referred to the late 1580s when the crown granted O'Neill extensive powers in Ulster in the hope of gaining control of local politics there. What is interesting about the proclamation is that it creates the impression that O'Neill's power stemmed largely from royal munificence. This was an impression Elizabeth herself gave, variously referring to O'Neill 'as a creature of her own' or one 'whom she had raised from a blacksmith's son to an earldom'.[59] With the relationship between queen and earl-turned-rebel personalized in this way, O'Neill's rebellion could be figured as the treachery of an ungrateful servant towards a benevolent and generous master. Thus, at the end of the poem 'England's Hope against Irish Hate', O'Neill is apostrophized: 'Thou base abuser of sunshyning favours' (line 219).[60] However, such figurations could also reverberate negatively on the monarch, as in the 'Supplication' where, addressing the queen, the narrator inquires:

> How longe had that monster of ingratitude the traytor of {Tirone}, pay out of yore coffers to traine up soldiers, whom nowe he useth against you and yores? how many yeares was he held up by you, who now seeketh all that in him lieth to put you downe? But this is past not to be recalled.[61]

The finality of the closing phrase, which hints at the sensitivity of the subject only to deny its topicality, belies the fact that the rhetorical questions speak to and of present concerns. Tyrone might be a 'monster of ingratitude' but the barely disguised implication is that royal largess and leniency has nourished such monstrosity. Playing on the image of the Irish as bestial, the text de-

57 MacLysaght, *Surnames*, pp 190–2; Robert Bell, *The book of Ulster surnames* (Belfast, 1988), p. 107. 58 Quoted in *Irish history from contemporary sources*, p. 99. 59 Quoted in Morgan, *Tyrone's rebellion*, p. 85; *Cal. S.P. domestic*, p. 350. 60 Carpenter (ed.), *Verse in English*, p. 106. 61 'The Supplication', p. 36.

humanizes Elizabeth's lapsed Irish subject in a similar way to the play's de-humanization of Mack Chane.

If, in its representation of the Irish servant, *Oldcastle* mirrors the trajectory of Hugh O'Neill's career from royal dependent to rebel, then it also endeav-ours to assuage English fears about the Gaelic leader's rebellion. Through the capture and subsequent trial of the Irish servant – which promises, but crucially does not deliver, the 'spectacle of the scaffold' – the play enacts a powerful form of ideological containment. The Irishman is presented before the audience in order to affirm English mastery and control native intractability. This strategy of containment would appear, however, to have a more specific objective in the context of Essex's abrupt departure from his post as lord deputy and the resultant crisis in the state's Irish policy. The purpose of Essex's expedition was, as Sir Robert Cecil noted, to 'set upon the chief rebel Tyrone'; his meeting with O'Neill on 7 September 1599 on the Louth–Monaghan border should have been the culmination of efforts to bring the wars to what Elizabeth called a 'happy conclusion'.[62] When Essex did meet O'Neill, however, it was not to fight but to negotiate a truce that effec-tively signalled his surrender. Frustration with the turn of events is registered in 'England's Hope against Irish Hate': listing the enemies of the Elizabethan state that had fallen and been defeated, it asks 'And they suppress: then why not now *TERONE?*' (line 63).[63] Performed just one month after these dramatic events in Ireland, *Oldcastle* attempts to effect the kind of closure that, in the autumn of 1599, had eluded the state. With Mack Chane functioning as a filter through which the audience can imagine O'Neill, the play, by contrast, delivers precisely what Essex could not: the captured and defeated Irish rebel. On a symbolic level, then, the control of the Irishman on the Elizabethan stage compensates for Essex's failure against the Irish in the battlefield.

While the play endorses the state's ability to reverse the situation in Ireland, I would argue that there are traces of equivocation, which disrupt its strategy of containment in subtle, though significant, ways. Donna Hamilton rightly suggests that the dramatists 'leave no doubt that the play takes a strong position on behalf of loyalty to the state' but simplifies matters when she says Mack Chane is 'represented unambiguously'.[64] The text may offer the image of the punished Irish body but the broken English of the condemned man inter-rupts the symbolism of that image. Mack Chane neither expresses remorse nor pleads to the judge for mercy. Instead, in a moment that affords the Irishman dignity, he asks to be hanged in his native dress: 'Prethee Lord Judge let me

---

62 *Cal. S.P. domestic, 1598–1601*, p. 350. Cecil was one of the commissioners appointed to investigate Essex's misconduct. See *DNB*.   63 Carpenter (ed.), *Verse in English*, p. 100.   64 Hamilton, *Anthony Munday*, p. 144.

have mine own clothes, my strouces there, and let me be hanged in a with after my cuntry, the Irish, fashion' (XXVII.123–5). Mack Chane's final request to be hung in a 'with', a band consisting of tough, flexible twigs twisted together, may not appear to have much significance beyond indicating that the condemned man is resigned to his fate. His choice, however, is in accordance with native Irish custom, as mentioned in Francis Bacon's essay, 'Of custom and education'. Bacon recalls how 'an Irish rebel condemned, put up a petition to the deputy that he might be hanged in a with, and not in a halter; because it had been so used with former rebels.'[65] Sir Walter Ralegh had directly experienced this native custom after capturing kern in possession of withy halters, the aim being 'to hang up English churls'; the Irishman finds himself quite literally outwitted by Ralegh, who says 'they shall now serve for an Irish kerne'.[66] In *Oldcastle*, however, the Irishman chooses his own rope, retaining a degree of control over his body. Hanged in 'the Irish fashion', Mack Chane insists upon his Irishness and makes an act of resistance, albeit already contained, at the very point of execution. It seems the state cannot exert complete control over the spectacle of the punished body.

Oldcastle gestures toward the arbitrary nature of state surveillance in its comic portrayal of the process that leads to the capture of the Irishman. In an earlier scene, Mack Chane steals clothes belonging to Harpool, Oldcastle's servant, leaving Harpool with, as he says, 'nothing but a lousy mantle, and a pair of brogues' (XXII.7–8). The significance of clothes in constituting identity has already been noted; and, in an Irish context, native clothes such as the mantle were regarded as contaminating articles from which settlers had to be protected. In 1598, for instance, a proposal that the queen's army in Ireland use the notorious Irish mantle was met with disapproval from Sir Robert Cecil. 'Our difficulty in this', he wrote, 'is, that by this means our English shall become in apparell barbarous, which hath hitherto been avoided'.[67] In the play, the consequences of sartorial exchange are fully apparent as the Constable, who has been searching for Mack Chane, discovers the Irishman and thinks he is Harpool in an Irish disguise:

CONSTABLE   Come, you villainous heretic, confess where your master is!

IRISH MAN   Vat mester?

MAYOR   'Vat mester?' You counterfeit rebel, this shall not serve your turn.

---

65 Bacon, *The essays*, ed. John Pitcher (London, 1987), p. 180. 66 Hooker, 'Supplie of the Irish chronicles', p. 437. 67 Quoted in McGurk, *Elizabethan conquest*, p. 213.

IRISH MAN	Be sent Patrick, I ha' no mester!
CONSTABLE	Where is the Lord Cobham, Sir John Oldcastle, that lately is escaped out of the Tower?
IRISH MAN	Vat Lort Cobham?
MAYOR	You counterfeit, this shall not serve you. We'll torture you, we'll make you confess where that arch-heretic Lord Cobham is.
IRISH MAN	Ahone, ahone, ahone, a cree!
CONSTABLE	Ahone, you crafty rascal? (XXI.23–35)

The scene evinces the *Oldcastle* playwrights' awareness of the theatrical potential of the Irish stage character and the Irish stage dialect, already explored in *Henry V* and *Stukeley*. In the moment of confusion, the laughter comes largely at the expense of the Irishman: juxtaposed with English, his fractured Irish speech is heard mainly as an inchoate utterance ('ahone, a cree').[68] However, the laughter can also reverberate on those in positions of authority. For instance, when the Constable apprehends Harpool, assuming from his Irish attire that he is the wanted Irishman, the law begins to look ridiculous. As he is arrested, Harpool says: 'Sblood, Constable, art thou mad? am I an Irishman?' (XXIII.8). In a response indicating that the play's scene of mistaken identities exceeds the purely comic, the Mayor says 'Sirra, we'll find you an Irish man before we part' (XXIII.9). The authorities will produce the required Irish villain; yet, it seems it is the very presence of Mack Chane, the "real" Irishman, which creates disorder.

Ultimately, as we have seen, the correct Irishman is apprehended and faith in the law restored. Yet, while the breakdown in authority was only ever temporary, the comic tone of the scene of mistaken identities belies a deeper anxiety about alterity and, by extension, English identity. Marcus Gheerhaerts' portrait of a sartorially hybrid Thomas Lee provides a pictorial analogue to this scene. In its purposeful blurring of the categories of English and Irish, Lee's staged hybridity has the capacity to unsettle its Elizabethan viewer. Implied in the picture, then, is a question explicitly addressed in *Oldcastle*: how can the Other be recognized? The unease about the instability of assigned identity is

68 This can be translated as 'Ochon, a croi', or 'alas, my heart'. Corbin and Sedge (*Oldcastle controversy*) note that 'Ahone' is an Irish and Scottish expression of lamentation (p. 128). Rittenhouse interprets this as 'O hone a rie', meaning 'alas for the prince or chief' (p. 231). While it would be appropriate for the Irishman to lament his master at this point in the play, there is no basis for this translation.

apparent in the culmination of Harpool and Mack Chane's ethnic cross-dressing. In advance of his appearance before the judge, the Irish servant appears before the bishop of Rochester, who proceeds to question him:

> What intricate confusion have we here?
> Not two hours since we apprehended one
> In habit Irish, but in speech not so.
> And now you bring another that in speech
> Is altogether Irish, but in habit
> Seems to be English. (XXV.1–6)

Confusion arises because of a disparity between the visual and aural registers, which not even the Irishman's direct assertion of identity is able to clarify. 'You cannot blind us with your broken Irish' (XXV.11) is the bishop's response, with the phrasing conveying the blurring of identities that occurs in the scene. The confusion over real and sham Irishmen demonstrates the extent to which the categorization of cultural Others is dependent upon a specific structure of signs. The representatives of authority, the bishop and the constable, look for what they previously understood to be indicators of Irishness – mantle, brogues, fractured speech – that function as vital elements within a repertoire for the cultural production of Irish alterity. Arguably, the play performs a form of cultural work here, invoking an Irish identity through Mack Chane's naming of self, only to expose the artificiality of that identity. 'Mack Chane' is exposed as character type, as 'Irishman', and the threatening difference and intractability that he represents are emptied of signification. In one sense, then, the scene undercuts the perceived threat of native Irish difference but in the process, it also questions the stability of racial identities. The bishop's inability to read the situation, to distinguish the real Englishman from the one who 'seemes' English, as he notes in a resonant phrase, evokes unease about hybrid identities.

The implication of *Oldcastle*'s scene of comic reversals is suggested by a contemporary analogue where, revealingly, a similar awareness of the mutability of national identities is evident. During the investigations into Essex's campaign, it was claimed that

> from the reports of sundry rebels in Ireland, it appears that Essex was generally esteemed by the rebels in Ireland as their special friend; that secret letters and intelligences had passed between him and Tyrone, and that they had combined together that the earl should be King of England, and Tyrone Viceroy of Ireland.[69]

69 *Cal. S.P. domestic, 1598–1601*, p. 455.

The Essex debacle, which saw royal favourite and deputy cast in the role of rebel, must have unsettled assumptions about fixed identity. Essex's solitary encounter with O'Neill and subsequent decision to desert his post meant that he was vulnerable to these accusations of treasonous conduct. As Thomas Gainsford observed, the 'private parley with Tyrone' had left the earl 'much affected by the Irish'. [70] Whether or not Essex really had been 'affected' by the Irish, the political implications of his meeting with Tyrone were unavoidable. Unsurprisingly, following Essex's failed coup, the allegations of collusion with the enemy that had been levelled against him were stepped up. It was rumoured that Essex loved the Irish 'better than his own countrymen', and that he 'would wear the Irish *truses*'.[71] Clothing the deputy in an Irishness he was meant to oppose, the canard against Essex played on English fears of degeneration. Essex found himself occupying a similar position as O'Neill in official discourse; he too was being proclaimed an 'arch-traitor'.[72] Elizabeth's former favourite had, it would seem, degenerated. The fear of cultural transformation, used by Essex's enemies to discredit him, is also exploited for comic effect in *Oldcastle*'s scene of mistaken identities. Yet, like the allegation that Essex had crossed the line to collude with O'Neill, the bishop's inability to recognize either the Irishman or Englishman demonstrates that identity is friable. In both instances, there is underlying disquiet about the stability of Englishness; the binaries of self and Other collapse.

The anxieties about cross-cultural contact and racial difference addressed in this scene reveal how the Irish wars are more than a topical occurrence in *Oldcastle*. Evident in this and other scenes, are textual traces of the play's engagement with its contemporary moment and also the influence of that moment over the production of meaning. As with *Henry V*, then, the play bears the burden of its present rather that exerting control over it. While the condemned Irishman is presented, the play also betrays unease about the categories employed to classify him as Irish, thus unsettling fixed concepts of racial difference. Mack Chane's story may amount to little more than a subplot but it does reveal how *Oldcastle* struggles to re-shape the anxieties about the contemporary Irish wars that it was largely shaped by.

The Elizabethan Irish wars formally ended in March 1603 with the submission of Hugh O'Neill, earl of Tyrone, before the lord deputy of Ireland, Lord Mountjoy, a surrender of which much was made. 'At the first entrance into the roome', wrote Thomas Gainsford describing the scene of O'Neill's submis-

70 Thomas Gainsford, *The true, exemplary, and remarkable history of the earle of Tirone* (London, 1619), p. 27.   71 *Cal. S.P. domestic, 1598–1601*, p. 570.   72 Ibid., p. 568.

THE PLOT OF THE PLAY, CALLED
ENGLANDS JOY.

To be Playd at the Swan this 6. of Nouember. 1602.

FIRST, there is induct by shew and in Action, the ciuill warres of England from *Edward* the third, to the end of Queene *Maries* raigne, with the ouerthrow of Vsurpation.

2 Secondly then the entrance of Englands Ioy by the Coronation of our Soueraigne Lady *Elizabeth*; her Throne attended with peace, Plenty, and ciuill Pollicy : A sacred Prelate standing at her right hand, betokening the Serenity of the Gospell: At her left hand Iustice : And at her feete Warre, with a Scarlet Roabe of peace vpon his Armour : A wreath of Bayes about his temples, and a braunch of Palme in his hand.

3 Thirdly is dragd in three Furies, presenting Dissention, Famine, and Bloudshed, which are throwne downe into hell.

4 Fourthly is exprest vnder the person of a Tyrant, the enuy of *Spayne*, who, to shew his cruelty causeth his Souldiers dragge in a beautifull Lady, whome they mangle and wound, tearing her garments and Iewels from off her : And so leaue her bloudy, with her hayre about her shoulders, lying vpon the ground. To her come certaine Gentlemen, who seeing her pitious dispoylment, turne to the Throne of England, from whence one descendeth, taketh vp the Lady, wipeth her eyes, bindeth vp her woundes, giueth her treasure, and bringeth forth a band of Souldiers, who attend her forth : This Lady presenteth *Belgia*.

5 Fiftly, the Tyrant more enraged, taketh counsell, sends forth letters, priuie Spies, and secret vnderminers, taking their othes, and giuing them bagges of treasure. These signifie *Lopus*, and certaine Iesuites, who afterward, when the Tyrant lookes for an answere from them, are shewed to him in a glasse with halters about their neckes, which makes him mad with fury.

6 Sixtly, the Tyrant seeing all secret meanes to fayle him, intendeth open violence and inuasion by the hand of Warre, whereupon is set forth the battle at Sea in 88. with Englands victory.

7 Seuenthly, hee complotteth with the Irish rebelles, wherein is layd open the base ingratitude of *Tyrone*, the landing there of *Don Iohn de Aguila*, and their dissipation by the wisedome and valour of the Lord *Mountioy*.

8 Eightly, a great triumph is made with fighting of twelue Gentlemen at Barriers, and sundrie rewards sent from the Throne of England, to all sortes of well deseruers.

9 Lastly, the Nine Worthyes, with seuerall Coronets, present themselues before the Throne, which are put backe by certaine in the habite of Angels, who set vpon the Ladies head, which represents her Maiestie, an Emperiall Crowne, garnished with the *Sunne*, *Moone* and *Starres*; And so with Musicke both with voyce and Instruments shee is taken vp into Heauen, when presently appeares, a Throne of blessed Soules, and beneath vnder the Stage set forth with strange fireworkes, diuers blacke and damned Soules, wonderfully discribed in their seuerall torments.

3 Richard Vennar, 'The Plot of the Play called *England's Joy*' (1602). Reproduced with the permission of Society of Antiquaries, London.

sion, 'he prostrated himselfe groveling to the earth with such a dejected coun-
tenance that the standers by were amazed'.[73] In effect, the outcome of the long
and expensive war had been determined in 1601, following the defeat of the
combined Irish and Spanish forces at the battle of Kinsale. The English
victory at Kinsale had been followed by the systematic pacification of Ireland,
which Mountjoy's hard military campaigning had realized. A post-conquest
ballad lauded his success in the battlefield as divinely sanctioned: 'Oh, give
Him thanks for that which He hath done! | In *Ireland* through Him hath
England won | A victory, which doubted was of all, | Till through God's help
they saw the rebels fall' (lines 121–4).[74] Richard Vennar's putative play *England's
Joy* (1602) evinces a similarly celebratory tone in dramatising the downfall of
the queen's Irish and Spanish enemies.[75] In the play, Spain is figured as the
tyrant who 'complotteth with the Irish rebelles, wherein is layd open the base
ingratitude of *Tyrone*, the landing there of *Don Iohn de Aguila*, and their dissipation by the wisedome and valour of the Lord *Mountjoy*' (lines 25–7). For
Elizabeth herself, the symbolic closure, the undoing of Tyrone, never actually
came. Alleging that O'Neill had made desperate appeals to Elizabeth for
clemency, Gainsford observed that she would 'rather have seen his body on the
ground headlesse, then himselfe succourlesse on his knees begging for
pardon'.[76] The queen would in fact witness neither of these symbolically
submissive scenes, for she died six days before Tyrone made his formal submission. Mountjoy deliberately concealed news of her death from the earl.

Reflecting on the death of Elizabeth and the proclamation of James as
king in 1603, Dekker observed in *The Wonderful Yeare*: 'That wonder begat more,
for in an hour, two mightie nations were made one: wilde Ireland became tame
on the sudden, and some English great ones that before seemed tame, on the
sudden turned wilde.'[77] Dekker's comment about the rapid cultural reversal
occasioned by the Jacobean succession offers the kind of wish-fulfilment that,
as we have seen, the plays that engaged with the Irish wars were not always
capable of providing. Of course, Dekker's wry reference to the pacification of
Ireland is merely the comic vehicle for his topical jibe at the social pretensions
of an English upper class threatened by the influx of Scots. Relative to the
1590s, Ireland had indeed been tamed militarily and politically; it was the

73 Gainsford, *Earle of Tirone*, p. 41.   74 'A joyfull new ballad of the late victory obtain'd by my Lord Mountjoy' in Carpenter (ed.), *Verse in English*, p. 100.   75 Richard Vennar, 'The plot of the play, called *England's Joy*', repr.
in W.W. Greg (ed.), *Dramatic documents from the Elizabethan playhouses* (Oxford, 1931), plate viii. The performance was
intended for the Swan theatre in November 1602 but was postponed. On what appears to have been an elaborate
hoax and money-making scheme, see E.K. Chambers, *Elizabethan stage*, 4 vols (Oxford, 1923), iii, pp 501–3;
and Herbert Berry, 'Richard Vennar, *England's Joy*', *ELR* 31 (2001), 240–65.   76 Gainsford, *Earle of Tirone*, p. 39.
77 Dekker, *The Wonderfull Yeare*, ed. G.B. Harrison, Elizabethan and Jacobean quartos (Edinburgh, 1966), pp 28–9.

concept of the wild Irish and their contaminating effects, which proved more
difficult to extirpate from English minds. Cecil had warned that until 'the
name of O'Neill or earl of Tyrone [be] utterly suppressed never look for a
sound peace in Ireland'.[78] With O'Neill's submission and his later exile, part
of the Flight of the Earls in 1607 that saw the exodus of the Gaelic Irish elite
who had formed the basis of the confederacy, peace had indeed been guaran-
teed. But even after O'Neill's exile in Rome there was continued disquiet, with
the Spanish ambassador in London reporting to King James of fears in the
city concerning the possibility of O'Neill's return to Ireland, with the result
that 'the whole kingdom would take up arms'. The ambassador went on to
note that in London 'they wish to kill him by poison or by any possible
means'.[79] The figure of Tyrone, crystallizing anxieties about Irish intractability,
continued to haunt the English psyche well beyond the Elizabethan period,
much as the Irish wars had entered collective memory. The political changes
wrought by the wars in Ireland were disseminated culturally, as suggested by
several plays, not least in Jacobean drama. For instance, their material impact
is registered in Dekker's *Northward Ho* (1605), where Chamberlain explains to
Luke Greenshield that he has left Dunstable: 'the towne droopt ever since the
peace in *Ireland*, your captains were wont to take their leaves of their *London*
Polecats, (their wenches I meane Sir) at *Dunstable*'.[80] Ireland is synonymous
with war in Sharpham's *Cupid's Whirligig* (1607): disguised as a 'begging soldier',
Lord Nonsuch mentions Ireland first in the list of places he claims to have
served in.[81] As in Marston's *Dutch Courtesan* (1604), where Mary Faugh includes
'swaggering Irish captains' among her clients, these casual references suggest
that the Elizabethan Irish wars had become proverbial.[82] Arguably, the stage
Irishman had also become something of a commonplace; it is a recurrent
feature in Jacobean drama – increasingly as the domesticated servant or as a
disguise to be adopted – suggesting a powerful consonance between the theatre
and contemporary ideologies of cultural assimilation.[83] Indeed, the comical
Irish characters of Jonson's *Irish Masque* (1613) and Dekker's *Honest Whore, part two*
(1605), or laughable Irish disguises in plays like *The Coxcomb* (1609) and *The Welsh
Embassador* (1623), not only explore the contradictions of constructed Irish
difference, but also attest to its continuing and crucial importance as a marker
of difference.

While continuities across representations of Ireland in Renaissance drama

78 Quoted in McGurk, *Elizabethan conquest*, p. 16. 79 Quoted in Micheline Walsh, 'The last years of Hugh
O'Neill', *Irish Sword*, 3 (1957), 234–44 at 237. 80 *Dramatic works of Thomas Dekker*, ii, I.i.20–1. 81 Petter (ed.), *A
critical old spelling edition of the works of Edward Sharpham*, III.i.21–5. 82 *The Dutch Courtesan*, ed. M.L. Wine (London,
1965), III.ii.27. 83 See Tristran Marshall, *Theatre and empire: Great Britain on the London stages under James VI and I*
(Manchester, 2000).

were explored in this book, the specificity of their meanings and resonances as contingent on the vicissitudes of the historical moment was iterated. As refracted in Elizabethan plays, Ireland and Irish alterity are a consequence of colonization, native reaction and inter-cultural contact in the period. But the Elizabethan staging of Ireland also reveals the inevitable faultlines that inhere within ideologies of racial difference and nationhood. As Mackmorrice's open-ended questions imply, drama explored and scrutinized the broader questions about identity, and it is in the drama of history that we can continue to challenge and re-imagine the stock roles of national identity, Irish and English and Other, handed down by history.

Bibliography

Adams, J.Q., 'Captain Thomas Stukeley', *JEGP*, 15 (1916), 107–29.

Albright, Evelyn May, 'Shakespeare's *Richard II* and the Essex conspiracy', *PMLA*, 42 (1927), 686–720.

——, 'The folio version of *Henry V* in relation to Shakespeare's times', *PMLA* 43 (1928), 722–56.

Altman, Joel B., '"Vile participation": the amplification of violence in the theatre of *Henry V*', *Shakespeare Quarterly*, 42 (1991), 1–32.

Arden, John, 'Rug-headed Irish kerns and British poets', *New Statesman*, July 13 (1979), 56–7.

Armstrong, William A., 'Elizabethan themes in *The Misfortunes of Arthur*', *Review of English Studies*, 27 (1956), 238–49.

Bacon, Francis, *Works of Francis Bacon*, ed. James Spedding, Robert Leslie Ellis & Douglas Denon Heath, 14 vols (London, 1857–74).

——, *The essays*, ed. John Pitcher (London, 1987).

Bagwell, Richard, *Ireland under the Tudors*, 3 vols (London, 1890).

Baker, David J., & Willy Maley (eds), *British identities and English Renaissance literature* (Cambridge, 2002).

——, *Between nations: Shakespeare, Spenser, Marvell and the question of Britain* (Stanford, 1997).

——, '"Wildehirissheman": colonialist representation in Shakespeare's *Henry V*', *ELR*, 22 (1992), 37–61.

——, 'Off the map: charting uncertainty in Renaissance Ireland' in Bradshaw, Hadfield & Maley (eds), *Representing Ireland*, pp 76–92.

Baldo, Jonathan, 'Wars of memory in *Henry V*', *Shakespeare Quarterly*, 47 (1996), 131–59.

Bartels, Emily C., *Spectacles of strangeness: imperialism, alienation and Marlowe* (Philadelphia, 1993).

Bartley, J.O., *Teague, Shenkin and Sawney: being an historical study of the earliest Irish, Welsh and Scottish characters in English plays* (Cork, 1954).

Barton, Plunket, *Links between Shakespeare and Ireland* (Dublin, 1919).

Bell, Robert, *The book of Ulster surnames* (Belfast, 1988).

Belsey, Catherine, *Shakespeare and the loss of Eden* (London, 2001).

——, 'The illusion of empire: Elizabethan expansionism and Shakespeare's second tetralogy', *Literature and History*, 1 (1990), 13–21.

Berger, Thomas, 'The disappearance of Macmorris in Shakespeare's *Henry V*', *Renaissance Papers* (1985), 13–26.

Berry, Herbert, 'Richard Vennar, *England's Joy*', *ELR*, 31 (2001), 240–65.

Bevington, David, *Tudor drama and politics: a critical approach to topical meaning* (Cambridge, MA, 1968).

Bhabha, Homi K., *The location of culture* (London, 1994).

Binchy Daniel A, 'An Irish ambassador at the Spanish Court, 1569–1574', *Studies*, 10, (1921), 353–74.

——, 'An Irish ambassador at the Spanish court, 1569–1574', *Studies*, 11 (1922), 199–214.

——, 'An Irish Ambassador at the Spanish Court, 1569–1574', *Studies*, 14 (1925), 102–19.

Blank, Paula, *Broken English: dialects and the politics of language in Renaissance writings* (London, 1996).

Bliss, Alan, 'The English language in early modern Ireland' in T.W. Moody, F.X Martin & F.J. Byrne (eds), *A new history of Ireland*, 9 vols (Oxford, 1976), iii, pp 546–60.

Blurt Master Constable, or, the Spaniards night-walke (London, 1602).

Bottigheimer, Karl, 'Kingdom and colony: Ireland in the westward enterprise, 1536–1660' in K.R Andrews, N.P. Canny & K.E.H. Hair (eds), *The westward enterprise: English activities in Ireland, the Atlantic and America, 1480–1650* (Liverpool, 1978), pp 45–64.

Bowers, Fredson (ed.), *Dramatic works in the Beaumont and Fletcher canon* (Cambridge, 1966).

Bradley, David, *From text to performance in the Elizabethan theatre: preparing the play for the stage* (Cambridge, 1992).

Bradshaw, Brendan, & Peter Roberts (eds), *British consciousness and identity: the making of Britain, 1533–1707* (Cambridge, 1998).

——, Andrew Hadfield & Willy Maley (eds), *Representing Ireland: literature and the origins of conflict, 1534–1660* (Cambridge, 1993).

Brady, Ciaran, *The chief governors: the rise and fall of reform government in Tudor Ireland, 1536–88* (Cambridge, 1994).

——, & Raymond Gillespie (eds), *Natives and newcomers: essays on the making of Irish colonial society, 1534–1641* (Dublin, 1986).

——, 'Court, castle and country: the framework of government in Tudor Ireland' in Brady & Gillespie (eds), *Natives and newcomers*, pp 22–49.

Braunmuller, A.R., *George Peele* (Boston, 1983).

Breight, Curtis, *Surveillance, militarism and drama in the Elizabethan era* (London, 1996).

Brown, Keith, 'Historical context and *Henry V*', *Cahiers Elisabethains*, 29 (1986), 77–81.

Brown, Paul, '"This thing of darkness I acknowledge mine": *The Tempest* and the discourse of colonialism' in Jonathan Dollimore & Alan Sinfield (eds), *Political Shakespeare: essays in cultural materialism* (2nd ed. Manchester, 1994), pp 48–71.

Bullough, Geoffrey (ed.), *Narrative and dramatic sources of Shakespeare* (London, 1960).

Burnett, Mark Thornton, '*Edward II* and Elizabethan politics' in Paul Whitfield White (ed.), *Marlowe, history and sexuality: new essays on Christopher Marlowe* (New York, 1998), pp 91–107.

——, & Ramona Wray (eds), *Shakespeare and Ireland* (London, 1997).

Burt, Richard & John Michael Archer (eds), *Enclosure Acts: sexuality, property and culture in early modern England* (Ithaca, 1994).

Caball Marc, 'Faith, culture and sovereignty: Irish nationality and its development, 1558–1625' in Bradshaw & Roberts (eds), *British consciousness and identity*, pp 112–39.

Cairns, David & Shaun Richards, *Writing Ireland: colonialism, nationalism and culture* (Manchester, 1988).

Callaghan, Dympna, *Shakespeare without women: representing gender and race on the Renaissance stage* (London, 2000).

——, '"Othello was a white man": properties of race on Shakespeare's stage' in Terence Hawkes (ed.), *Alternative Shakespeares*, vol. 2 (London, 1996), pp 199–215.

Cambrensis, Giraldus, *The history and topography of Ireland*, ed. John J O'Meara (London, 1982).

Candido, Joseph, 'Captain Thomas Stukeley: the man, the theatrical record and the origins of Tudor "biographical" drama', *Anglia*, 105 (1987), 50–68.

Cannadine, David, 'British history as a "new subject": politics, perspectives and prospects' in Alexander Grant & Keith Stringer (eds), *Uniting the kingdom: the making of British history* (London, 1995), pp 12–28.

Canny, Nicholas, 'Taking sides in early modern Ireland: the case of Hugh O'Neill, earl of

Tyrone' in Vincent Carey and Ute Lotz-Heumann (eds), *Taking sides? Colonial and confessional mentalities in early modern Ireland* (Dublin, 2003), pp 94–115.

——, *The Elizabethan conquest of Ireland: a pattern established, 1565–76* (Hassocks, Sussex, 1976).

——, 'The ideology of English colonization: from Ireland to America', *William and Mary Quarterly*, 30 (1973), 575–98.

Carew: *Calendar of Carew Manuscripts, 1575–1588*, eds. J.S. Brewer & W. Bullen, 2 vols (London, 1868).

Carey, Vincent, '"Neither good English nor good Irish": bi-lingualism and identity formation in sixteenth century Ireland', in Hiram Morgan (ed.), *Political ideology in Ireland, 1534–1641* (Dublin, 2000), pp 45–61.

——, 'John Derricke's *Image of Irelande*, Sir Henry Sidney and the massacre at Mullaghmast, 1578', *IHS*, 31 (1999), 305–27.

Carpenter, Andrew (ed.), *Verse in English from Tudor and Stuart Ireland* (Cork, 2003).

Carroll, Clare, *Circe's cup: cultural transformations in early modern Ireland*, Field Day Essays (Cork, 2001).

Cartelli, Thomas, 'Jack Cade in the garden: class consciousness and class conflict in *2 Henry VI* in Burt & Archer (eds), *Enclosure acts*, pp 48–67.

Chambers, E.K., *Elizabethan stage*, 4 vols (Oxford, 1923).

Chaplais, Pierre, *Piers Gaveston: Edward's adoptive brother* (Oxford, 1994).

Clare, Janet, 'Censorship and negotiation' in Andrew Hadfield (ed.), *Literature and censorship in Renaissance England* (London, 2001), pp 17–31.

——, *'Art made tongue-tied by authority': Elizabethan and Jacobean dramatic censorship* (2nd ed. Manchester, 1999).

Comyn, David, *Irish illustrations to Shakespeare, being notes on his references to Ireland* (Dublin, 1894).

Corbin, Peter & Douglas Sedge (eds), *The Oldcastle controversy* (Manchester, 1991).

Corrigan, Brian Jay (ed.), *The Misfortunes of Arthur: a critical old-spelling edition* (New York, 1992).

Cronin, Michael, 'Rug-headed kerns speaking tongues: Shakespeare, translation and the Irish language' in Burnett and Wray (eds), *Shakespeare and Ireland*, pp 192–212.

Crosbie, Christopher J., 'Sexuality, corruption and the body politic: the paradoxical tribute of *The Misfortunes of Arthur* to Elizabeth I', *Arthuriana*, 9 (1999), 68–90.

Crowley, Tony, *Wars of words: the politics of language in Ireland, 1537–2004* (Oxford, 2005).

——, *The politics of language in Ireland, 1366–1922: a sourcebook* (London, 2000).

Curtis, Liz, *Nothing but the same old story: the roots of anti-Irish racism* (Belfast, 1996).

Dean, Christopher, *Arthur of England: English attitudes to king Arthur and the knights of the round table in the middle ages and the Renaissance* (Toronto, 1987).

Dekker, Thomas, *Dramatic works of Thomas Dekker*, ed. Fredson Bowers, 6 volumes (Cambridge, 1964).

Dekker, Thomas, *Lanthorne and Candlelight* in *Elizabethan underworld: a collection of Tudor and early Stuart tracts* ed. A.V. Judges (London, 1930).

Derricke, John, *The image of Irelande, with a discourse of woodkarne*, ed. John Small (Edinburgh, 1883).

de Sousa, Geraldo U., *Shakespeare's cross-cultural encounters* (London, 1999).

Dessen, Alan C., *Recovering Shakespeare's theatrical vocabulary* (Cambridge, 1999).

Dietz, Frederick, *English public finance*, 2 vols (London, 1964).

Dillon, Janette, *Language and stage in medieval and Renaissance England* (Cambridge, 1998).

Dodsley, Robert (ed.), *A select collection of old English plays*, 12 vols (4th ed. London, 1874).

Dollimore, Jonathan & Alan Sinfield, 'History and ideology: the instance of *Henry V* in John Drakakis (ed.), *Alternative Shakespeares*, vol. 1 (London, 1985), pp 206–27.

Dollimore, Jonathan, *Radical Tragedy: religion, ideology and power in the drama of Shakespeare and his contemporaries* (Brighton, 1984).

Doob, Penelope, *The idea of the labyrinth from classical antiquity through the Middle Ages* (Ithaca, 1990).

Dowling, Harold M., 'The date and order of Peele's plays', *N&Q*, 164 (1933), 164–8.

Dubhthaigh, Padraic, *The book of Dundalk* (Dundalk, 1946).

Duggan, G.C., *The stage Irishman* (London, 1937).

Dutton, Richard, *Mastering the revels: the regulation and censorship of English Renaissance drama* (Basingstoke, 1991).

Dyce, Alexander, (ed.), *Dramatic and poetical works of Robert Greene and George Peele* (London, 1861).

Edelman, Charles, (ed.), *The Stukeley plays* (Manchester, 2005).

Edwards, David 'Ideology and experience: Spenser's *View* and martial law in Ireland' in Hiram Morgan (ed.), *Political ideology in Ireland, 1541–1641*, pp 127–57.

——, 'Beyond reform: martial law and the Tudor reconquest of Ireland', *History Ireland*, 5 (1997), 16–21.

Edwards, Philip, *Threshold of the nation: a study in English and Irish drama* (Liverpool, 1979).

Elizabeth: *Calendar of state papers, domestic, 1581–1590*, ed. Robert Lemon (London, 1865).

Elizabeth: *Calendar of state papers, domestic, 1595–1597*, ed. Mary Anne Everett Green (London, 1869).

Elizabeth: *Calendar of state papers, Rome, 1572–1578*, ed. J.M. Rigg (London, 1926).

Ellis, Steven G., *Ireland in the age of the Tudors, 1447–1603: English expansion and the end of Gaelic rule* (Harlow, 1998).

——, 'Writing Irish history: revisionism, colonialism and the British Isles', *Irish Review* 19 (1996), 1–21.

Elyot, Thomas, *The book named the Governor* (Menston, West Yorks., 1970).

Fitzpatrick, Joan, *Shakespeare, Spenser and the contours of Britain: reshaping the Atlantic archipelago* (Hatfield, Herts., 2004).

Fletcher, Alan J., *Drama, performance and polity in pre-Cromwellian Ireland* (Toronto, 2000).

Floyd-Wilson, Mary, *English ethnicity and race in early modern drama* (Cambridge, 2003).

Fogarty, Anne, 'Literature in English, 1550–1690: from the Elizabethan settlement to the battle of the Boyne' in Margaret Kelleher & Philip O'Leary (eds), *Cambridge history of Irish literature*, 2 vols (Cambridge, 2006), i, pp 140–90.

——, 'The romance of history: renegotiating the past in Thomas Kilroy's *The O'Neill* and Brian Friel's *Making History*', *IUR*, 32 (2002), 18–32.

Foster, Roy, *Modern Ireland, 1600–1972* (London, 1989).

Foucault, Michel, *Discipline and punish: the birth of the prison*, trans. Alan Sheridan (London, 1977).

Friedman, John, *The monstrous races in medieval art and thought* (Cambridge, MA, 1981).

Fumerton, Patricia, *Cultural aesthetics: Renaissance literature and the practice of social ornament* (Chicago, 1991).

Gainsford, Thomas, *The true, exemplary, and remarkable history of the earle of Tirone* (London, 1619).

Gamble, Giles Y., 'Power play: Elizabeth I and *The Misfortunes of Arthur*', *Quondum et Futurus*, 1 (1991), 59–69.

Garner, Steve, *Racism and the Irish experience* (London, 2004).

Geertz, Clifford, *The interpretation of cultures* (New York, 1973).

Geoffrey of Monmouth, *The history of the kings of Britain*, ed. Lewis Thorpe (London, 1966).

Gillespie, Raymond, *Reading Ireland: print, reading and social change in early modern Ireland* (Manchester, 2005).

Gillies, John, *Shakespeare and the geography of difference* (Cambridge, 1994).

Gillingham, John, 'The English Invasion of Ireland' in Bradshaw, Hadfield & Maley (eds), *Representing Ireland*, pp 24–42.

Glover, Laurie Carol, 'Colonial qualms/ colonial quelling: England and Ireland in the sixteenth century' (PhD, Claremont Graduate School, 1995).

Guy, John (ed.), *The reign of Elizabeth: court and culture in the last decade* (Cambridge, 1995).

Haber, Judith, 'Submitting to history: Marlowe's *Edward II*' in Burt & Archer (eds), *Enclosure acts*, pp 170–84.

Hadfield, Andrew, 'Censoring Ireland in Elizabethan England, 1580–1600' in Hadfield (ed.), *Literature and censorship in Renaissance England* (London, 2001), pp 149–64.

——, *Edmund Spenser's Irish experience: wilde fruit and savage soyl* (Oxford, 1997).

——, '"Hitherto she ne're could fancy him": Shakespeare's "British" plays and the exclusion of Ireland', Mark Burnett & Ramona Wray (eds), *Shakespeare and Ireland* (London, 1997).

——, 'Was Spenser's *View of the present state of Ireland* censored? A review of the evidence', *Notes and Queries* 41 (1994), 459–63.

——, & John McVeagh (eds), *Strangers to that land: British perceptions of Ireland from the Reformation to the Famine* (Gerrards Cross, 1994).

——, 'Briton and scythian: Tudor representations of Irish origins', *IHS*, 28 (1993), 390–408.

Hamilton, Donna B., *Anthony Munday and the Catholics, 1560–1633* (Aldershot, 2005).

Healy, Thomas, *Christopher Marlowe* (Plymouth, 1994).

Heaney, Seamus, 'Extending the alphabet: on Christopher Marlowe's "Hero and Leander"' in *The redress of poetry* (London, 1995), pp 17–37.

——, *Wintering out* (London, 1972).

Hereford, C.H. & Evelyn Simpson (eds), *Ben Jonson*, 11 vols (Oxford, 1927).

Heywood, Thomas, *Dramatic works of Thomas Heywood*, 3 vols (New York, 1964).

Highley, Christopher, 'The royal image in Elizabethan Ireland' in J.M. Walker (ed.), *Dissing Elizabeth: negative representations of Gloriana* (Durham, 1998), pp 60–71.

——, *Shakespeare, Spenser and the crisis in Ireland* (Cambridge, 1997).

Holderness, Graham, *Shakespeare's history* (Dublin, 1984).

Holinshed: *Holinshed's chronicles of England, Scotland and Ireland*, ed. Henry Ellis, 6 vols (London, 1807–8).

Holinshed: Hooker, John, 'Supplie of the Irish Chronicles extended to this present year of Our Lord 1586' in *Holinshed's chronicles of England, Scotland, and Ireland*, ed. Ellis, vi.

Holinshed: Stanyhurst, 'Historie of Ireland' in *Holinshed's Irish chronicle*, ed. Liam Miller & Eileen Power (Dublin, 1979).

Hooper, Glenn, 'Writing and landscape in early modern Ireland', *Literature and History*, 5 (1996), 1–18.

Hopkins, Lisa, *Christopher Marlowe: a literary life* (London, 2000).

Howard, Jean E. & Phyllis Rackin, *Engendering the nation: a feminist account of Shakespeare's English histories* (London, 1997).

Howard, Jean E., *The stage and social struggle in early modern England* (London, 1994).

Hughes, Paul L., & James F. Larkin (eds), *Tudor royal proclamations*, 2 vols (New Haven, 1969).

Ireland: *Calendar of state papers, Ireland, 1586–1588*, ed. Hans Claude Hamilton (London, 1877).

Ireland: *Calendar of state papers, Ireland, 1588–1592*, ed. Hans Claude Hamilton (London, 1885).

Ireland: *Calendar of state papers, Ireland, 1592–96*, ed. Hans Claude Hamilton Hamilton (London, 1890).

Ireland: *Calendar of state papers, Ireland, 1596–97*, ed. George Ernest Atkinson (London, 1893).

Jones, Ann Rosalind & Peter Stallybrass, *Renaissance clothing and the materials of memory* (Cambridge, 2000).

——, 'Dismantling Irena: the sexualizing of Ireland' in early modern England' in Andrew Parker et al., *Nationalism and sexualities* (London, 1992), pp 157–71.

Jowitt, Claire, *Voyage drama and gender politics, 1589–1642* (Manchester, 2003).

Kastan, David Scott, *Shakespeare after theory* (New York, 1999).

——, 'Proud majesty made a subject: Shakespeare and the spectacle of rule', *Shakespeare Quarterly*, 27 (1986), 459–75.

Kay, Dennis, 'Marlowe, *Edward II* and the cult of Elizabeth', *EMLS*, 3.2 (1997) www.shu.ac.uk/emls, accessed November 2005.

Kiberd, Declan, *Inventing Ireland: the literature of the modern nation* (London, 1995).

——, 'The fall of the stage Irishman', in R. Schleifer (ed.), *The genres of the Irish literary revival* (Norman, OK, 1980),

Klein, Bernhard, *Maps and the writing of space in early modern England and Ireland* (London, 2001).

Leerssen, Joep, *Mere Irish and fíor Ghael: studies in the idea of Irish nationality, its development and literary expression prior to the nineteenth century*, Field day essays and monographs (2nd ed., Cork, 1996).

Leggatt, Alexander, *Shakespeare's political drama: the history plays and the Roman plays* (London, 1988).

Lennon, Colm, *An Irish prisoner of conscience of the Tudor era: Archbishop Richard Creagh of Armagh, 1523–1586* (Dublin, 2000).

——, *Sixteenth century Ireland: the incomplete conquest* (Dublin, 1994).

Levinson, Judith C. (ed.), *The famous history of Captain Thomas Stukeley* (Oxford, 1975).

Loomba, Ania & Martin Orkin (eds), *Post-colonial Shakespeares* (London, 1998).

Loomba, Ania, 'Shakespeare and cultural difference' in Terence Hawkes (ed.), *Alternative Shakespeares*, vol. 2 (London, 1996), pp 164–91.

Lydon, J.F., 'Richard II's expeditions to Ireland', *Journal of the Royal Society of Antiquaries of Ireland*, 92 (1963), 135–49.

Lyly, John, *Works*, 3 vols (Oxford, 1902).

MacLysaght, Edward, *The surnames of Ireland* (6th ed. Dublin, 1991).

Maguire, Laurie E., *Shakespearean suspect texts: the 'bad' quartos and their contexts* (Cambridge, 1996).

Maley, Willy, 'The Irish text and subtext of Shakespeare's English histories' in Richard Dutton & Jean E. Howard (eds), *A companion to Shakespeare's works*, volume 2: *the histories* (Oxford, 2003), pp 94–124.

——, '"This sceptred isle": Shakespeare and the British problem', in John J. Joughin (ed.), *Shakespeare and national culture* (Manchester, 1997), pp 83–108.

——, 'Shakespeare, Holinshed and Ireland: resources and con-texts', in Burnett and Wray (eds), *Shakespeare and Ireland*, pp 27–46.

——, *Salvaging Spenser: colonialism, culture and identity* (London, 1997).

——, (ed.), 'The Supplication of the blood of the English most lamentably murdered in Ireland [1598]', *Analecta Hibernia*, 36 (1995), 3–77.

Maquerlot, Jean Pierre & Michele Willems (eds), *Travel and drama in Shakespeare's time* (Cambridge, 1996).

Marcus, Leah, *Puzzling Shakespeare: local reading and its discontents* (Berkeley, 1988).

Marlowe, Christopher, *Edward II*, ed. Charles Forker (Manchester, 1994).

Marston, John, *Dramatic works of John Marston*, ed. H. Harvey Wood, 3 vols (Edinburgh, 1939).

Marston, John, *The Dutch Courtesan*, ed. M.L. Wine (London, 1965).

Mason, Pamela, '*Henry V*: "the quick forge and working house of thought"' in Michael

Hattaway (ed.), *The Cambridge companion to Shakespeare's history plays* (Cambridge, 2002), pp 177–92.

Maxwell, Constantia (ed.), *Irish history from contemporary sources, 1509–1610* (London, 1923).

McCabe, Richard A., 'Making history: Holinshed's Irish *Chronicles*, 1577 and 1587' in Baker & Maley (eds), *British identities and English Renaissance literature*, pp 51–67.

McClure, Norman (ed.), *The Chamberlain letters: a selection of letters of John Chamberlain concerning life in England from 1597 to 1626* (London, 1965).

McCoy, Richard, *The rites of knighthood: the literature and politics of Elizabethan chivalry* (Berkeley, 1989).

McGurk, John, *The Elizabethan conquest of Ireland: the 1590s crisis* (Manchester, 1997).

McLeod, Bruce, *The geography of empire in English literature, 1580–1745* (Cambridge, 1999).

Mehl, Dieter, *The Elizabethan dumb show: the history of a dramatic convention* (London, 1965).

Mignolo, Walter D., *The darker side of the Renaissance: literacy, territoriality and colonization* (Ann Arbor, 1995).

Montrose, Louis A., *The purpose of playing: Shakespeare and the cultural politics of the Elizabethan theatre* (Chicago, 1996).

Morgan, Hiram, *Tyrone's rebellion: the outbreak of the Nine Years War in Tudor Ireland* (Woodbridge, 1993).

——, 'Tom Lee: the posing peacemaker' in Bradshaw, Hadfield & Maley (eds), *Representing Ireland*, pp 132–65.

——, 'Ireland: A draft for an answer to Tyrone's libel, written by the honest Catholic lords of the pale', 'Faith and fatherland or queen and country: an unpublished exchange between O'Neill and the state at the height of the Nine Years war', *Duiche O'Neill (Journal of the O'Neill Country Historical Society)*, 9 (1984), 9–65.

Moroney, Maryclaire, 'Recent studies in Tudor and Jacobean literature about Ireland', *ELR*, 31 (2001), 131–67.

——, 'Apocalypse, ethnography, and empire in John Derricke's *Image of Irelande* (1581) and Spenser's *View of the present state of Ireland* (1596)', *ELR*, 29 (1999), 355–74.

Moryson, Fynes, *The Irish sections of Fynes Moryson's unpublished 'Itinerary'*, ed. Graham Kew (Dublin, 1998).

——, 'A description of Ireland' in Henry Morley (ed.), *Ireland under Elizabeth and James I* (London, 1890).

Mullaney, Steven, *The place of the stage: license, play and power in Renaissance England* (Chicago, 1988).

Murphy, Andrew, 'Revising criticism: Ireland and the British model' in Baker & Maley (eds), *British identities and English Renaissance literature*, pp 24–33.

——, *But the Irish sea betwixt us: Ireland, colonialism and Renaissance literature* (Lexington, 1999).

——, '"Tish ill done": *Henry the Fift* and the politics of editing' in Burnett & Wray (eds), *Shakespeare and Ireland*, pp 213–34.

——, 'Shakespeare's Irish history', *Literature and History*, 5 (1996), 38–59.

Myers, James P. (ed.), *Elizabethan Ireland: a selection of writings by Elizabethan writers on Ireland* (Hamden, CT, 1983).

Neill, Michael, 'Broken English and broken Irish: nation, language and the optic of power in Shakespeare's histories', *Shakespeare Quarterly*, 45 (1994), 1–32.

Normand, Lawrence, '"What passions call you these?": *Edward II* and James VI' in Darryll Grantley & Peter Roberts (eds), *Christopher Marlowe and English Renaissance culture* (Aldershot, 1996), pp 172–97.

O'Cuiv, Brian, 'The Irish language in the early modern period' in Moody, Martin & Byrne (eds), *A new history of Ireland*, iii, pp 509–45.

Ohlmeyer, Jane, 'Literature and the new British and Irish histories' in Baker & Maley (eds), *British identities and English Renaissance literature*, pp 245–55.

Pagden, Anthony, *The fall of natural man* (Cambridge, 1982).

Palmer, Patricia, *Language and conquest in early modern Ireland: English Renaissance literature and Elizabethan imperial expansion* (Cambridge, 2001).

Palmer, William, *The problem of Ireland in Tudor foreign policy: 1485–1603* (Woodbridge, 1994).

Parker, Patricia, *Shakespeare from the margins: language, culture, context* (Chicago, 1996).

Parks, Joan, 'History, tragedy and truth in Christopher Marlowe's *Edward II*', *SEL*, 39 (1999), 275–90.

Patterson, Annabel, *Shakespeare and the popular voice* (Oxford, 1989).

——, *Censorship and interpretation: the conditions of writing and reading in early modern England* (Madison, WI, 1984).

Payne, Robert, 'A brief description of Ireland' (1590) in *Tracts relating to Ireland*, ed. Aguilia Smith, 2 vols (Dublin, 1841).

Peele, George, *The Battle of Alcazar*, ed. John Yoklavich, in *The dramatic works of George Peele*, ed. Charles Tyler Prouty, 3 vols (New Haven, 1961), ii.

Peele, George, *The Battle of Alcazar*, ed. W.W. Greg (Oxford, 1963).

Pender, Seamus, 'Shane O'Neill comes to the court of Elizabeth' in *Feilscribhinn Torna* (Cork, 1947).

Phillips, J.R.S., *The medieval expansion of Europe* (Oxford, 1988).

Pocock, J.G.A., 'A British history: a plea for a new subject', *Journal of Modern History*, 47 (1975), 601–28.

Polemon, John, *The second part of the booke of battailes, fought in our age* (London, 1587; repr. New York, 1972).

Pratt, Mary Louise, *Imperial eyes: travel writing and transculturation* (London, 1992).

Privy Council: *Acts of the privy council, 1587–1588*, ed. John Roche Dasent (London, 1897).

Quinn, D.B., *The Elizabethans and the Irish* (Ithaca, 1966).

——, 'Ireland and Sixteenth Century European expansion' in T.D. Williams (ed.), *Historical Studies* (London, 1958), pp 20–32.

—— (ed.), '"A Discourse of Ireland": a sidelight on English colonial policy', *Proceedings of the Royal Irish Academy*, 46 (1942), 151–66.

Rabkin, Norman, 'Rabbits, ducks and *Henry V*', *Shakespeare Quarterly*, 28 (1979), 279–96.

Rabl, Kathleen, 'Taming the "wild Irish" in English Renaissance drama', Wolfgang Zach & Heinz Kosok (eds), *National images and stereotypes* (Tubingen, 1987), pp 47–59.

Rackin, Phyllis, *Stages of history: Shakespeare's English chronicles* (London, 1990).

Rambo, Elizabeth, *Colonial Ireland in Medieval English literature* (London, 1994).

Reese, Gertrude, 'Political import of *The Misfortunes of Arthur*', *Review of English Studies*, 21 (1945), 81–91.

Ribner, Irving, *The English history play in the age of Shakespeare* (London, 1965).

Rice, Warner G., 'A principal source of *The Battle of Alcazar*', *MLN*, 58 (1943), 428–31.

Rittenhouse, Jonathan (ed.), *A critical edition of Sir John Oldcastle* (New York, 1984).

Rutter, Carol Chillington (ed.), *Documents of the Rose playhouse* (Manchester, 1985).

Schmidt, Alexander, *Shakespeare Lexicon*, 2 vols (London, 1968).

Schwartz, Stuart B. (ed.), *Implicit understandings: observing, reporting, and reflecting on the encounters between Europeans and other peoples in the early modern era* (Cambridge, 1994.

Shakespeare, William, *King Richard II*, ed. Peter Ure (London, 1956).

——, *King Henry V*, ed. Gary Taylor (Oxford, 1982).

——, *King Henry V*, ed. T.W. Craik (London, 1995).

——, *King Henry VI*, part two, ed. Ronald Knowles (London, 1999).

Shakespeare's plays in quarto, ed. Michael J. Allen and Kenneth Muir (Berkeley, 1981).

Shapiro, James, *1599: a year in the life of Shakespeare* (London, 2005).

Sharpham, Edward, *A critical old spelling edition of the works of Edward Sharpham* ed, Christopher Gordon Petter (New York, 1986).

Sheehan, Anthony, 'Irish towns in a period of change, 1558–1625' in Brady & Gillespie (eds), *Natives and newcomers*, pp 93–119.

Shepherd, Simon, *Marlowe and the politics of the Elizabethan theatre* (Brighton, 1986).

Smith, Emma, '"Signes of a stranger": the English language and the English nation in the late sixteenth century' in Philip Schwyzer and Simon Mealor (eds), *Archipelagic identities: literature and identity in the Atlantic archipelago, 1550–1800* (Aldershot, 2004), pp 169–79.

Smith, James, 'Effaced history: the colonial contexts of Ben Jonson's *Irish Masque at court*', *ELH*, 65 (1998), 297–321.

Smyth, Gerry, *Space and the Irish cultural imagination* (London, 2001).

Spenser, Edmund, *A View of the state of Ireland*, ed. Andrew Hadfield & Willy Maley (London, 1997).

Spevack, Martin, *Harvard concordance to Shakespeare* (Cambridge Mass., 1969).

Spradlin, Derrick, 'Imperial anxiety in Thomas Hughes's *The Misfortunes of Arthur*', *EMLS* 10.3 (2005), www.shu.ac.uk/emls, accessed January 2005.

Stockley, W.F.P., *King Henry the fifth's poet historical* (London, 1925).

Sullivan, Garret, 'Geography and identity in Marlowe' in Patrick Cheney (ed.), *Cambridge companion to Christopher Marlowe* (Cambridge, 2004), pp 231–44.

Sullivan, Garrett, *The drama of landscape: land, property and social relations on the early modern stage* (Stanford, 1998).

The Returne from Pernassus, or, The Scourge of Simony (London, 1606).

Thomas, Vivien & William Tydeman (eds), *Christopher Marlowe: the plays and their sources* (London, 1994).

Thomson, Peter, *Shakespeare's theatre* (London, 1983).

Truninger, Annelise, *Paddy and the Paycock: a study of the stage Irishman from Shakespeare to O'Casey* (Biel, 1976).

Vennar, Richard, 'The plot of the play, called *England's Joy*' in W.W. Greg (ed.), *Dramatic documents from the Elizabethan playhouses* (Oxford, 1931).

Wallace, Charles William, *The evolution of the English drama up to Shakespeare* (Berlin, 1912; repr. New York, 1968).

Waller, Evangelia H., 'A possible interpretation of *The Misfortunes of Arthur*', *JEGP*, 24 (1925), 219–45.

Walsh, Micheline, 'The last years of Hugh O'Neill', *Irish Sword*, 3 (1957), 234–44.

Webster, John, *The White Devil*, ed. Christina Luckyi (London, 1996).

Weimann, Robert, *Author's pen and actor's voice: playing and writing in Shakespeare's theatre* (Cambridge, 2000).

Wells, Stanley, Gary Taylor, John Jowett, and William Montgommery (eds), *William Shakespeare: a textual companion* (Oxford, 1987).

Wiggins, Martin, 'Things that go bump in the text: *Captain Thomas Stukeley*', *Papers of the Bibliographical Society of America*, 98 (2004), 5–20.

Yates, Frances A., *Astraea: the imperial theme* (London, 1975).

Index

Page numbers in bold indicate the main entry.